"With wisdom and lucid prose, Levy and Mellor go straight to the sad, central truth of the American judiciary. We have created a system in which nine people are presumed to be smarter than 300 million. The Dirty Dozen shows us the results of this foolish assumption—the twelve worst Supreme Court rulings. Or, that is to say, the twelve worst Supreme Court rulings so far."

—P. J. O'Rourke, author of *On the Wealth of Nations*

"Robert A. Levy and William Mellor, both constitutional lawyers, examine 12 notorious court opinions affecting everything from wartime internments and medical-school admissions to tax policy and the rights of homebuyers. It is useful, if unsettling, to be reminded of such examples of Supreme Court overreaching."

—Amity Shlaes – *Wall Street Journal*

"Levy & Mellor are the Hamilton & Madison of our age. This book has timeless value."

—Douglas W. Kmiec, Professor of Constitutional Law, Pepperdine University; Constitutional Legal Counsel to President Ronald Reagan

"An engaging and accessible primer on constitutional law ... that deserves and I hope will receive, wide public attention and readership."

—Edwin Meese, III, former Attorney General

"Levy and Mellor have chosen 12 Supreme Court cases that, in their opinion, severely limited individual rights through the expansion of government. The authors' critiques of these issues are sure to provoke debate. However, they do examine each case on the basis of legal reasoning and in each chapter lay out the flaws in the Court's thinking that make each decision in their view a "bad" one. These explanations are the strong points of the book. Although some readers will disagree with their viewpoint, Levy and Mellor have done a good job of explaining their thinking."

—Becky Kennedy, *Library Journal*

"Cato Institute scholar Levy and Institute for Justice president Mellor unabashedly assert that their interpretation of the Constitution is "committed to the values of individual liberty, private property, and free markets." The dozen cases they examine, in their view, betrayed the principles of the Founding Fathers and vastly enlarged federal power over the course of the 20th century, specifically from the New Deal onward. These sternly libertarian arguments keep the constitutional dialogue lively and accessible."

—*Kirkus Reviews*

THE DIRTY DOZEN

THE DIRTY DOZEN

*How Twelve Supreme Court Cases Radically
Expanded Government and Eroded Freedom*

ROBERT A. LEVY AND
WILLIAM MELLOR

CATO INSTITUTE
WASHINGTON, D.C.

This paperback edition published by the Cato Institute, 2009.

First published in 2008 by Sentinel,
a member of Penguin Group (USA) Inc.

LIBRARY OF CONGRESS CATALOGING-IN-PUBLICATION DATA
Levy, Robert A., 1941-
The dirty dozen : how twelve Supreme Court cases radically expanded government and eroded
freedom / Robert A. Levy & William H. Mellor.
p.   cm.
Includes bibliographical references and index.
ISBN 978-1-59523-050-8 (cloth)—ISBN 978-1-935308-27-0 (paperback)
1. United States. Supreme Court—Cases.   2. Law—United States—Cases.   I. Mellor,
William H.   II. Title.
KF8742 .L485   2008
347 .73'260264—dc22   2008005656

Cover design by Jon Meyers.
Printed in the United States of America.

Cato Institute
1000 Massachusetts Ave., N.W.
Washington, D.C. 20001
www.cato.org

CONTENTS

PREFACE

Guns, Bailouts, and Empathetic Judges

First, the good news: Less than 60 days after publication of *The Dirty Dozen*, the Supreme Court issued its opinion in *District of Columbia v. Heller*,[1] the successful Second Amendment challenge to Washington, D.C.'s handgun ban. As a result, *United States v. Miller*,[2] discussed in Chapter 6, is no longer controlling legal authority on gun owners' rights. That's a big step in the right direction for residents of the nation's capital who want to be able to defend themselves in their own homes. Equally important, the Supreme Court has signaled its willingness to bind local legislatures with the chains of the Constitution – an example of principled judicial engagement. More about *Heller* in a moment.

We can also report modest progress in another area: political speech (Chapter 5). In June 2008, Justice Samuel Alito, the most recent Supreme Court appointee, joined by his conservative allies – Chief Justice John Roberts and Justices Clarence Thomas and Antonin Scalia, along with swing vote Anthony Kennedy – held that section 319 of the Bipartisan Campaign Reform Act, popularly known as McCain-Feingold, was unconstitutional. That section – the so-called Millionaire's Amendment – provided that maximum campaign contributions to a candidate, but not to his opponent, could be tripled from $2,300 to $6,900 if the opponent spent more than $350,000 of his own money trying to get elected. In *Davis v. Federal Election Commission*,[3] the Court declared that discriminatory burdens on rich adversaries could not prevent corruption or even the appearance of corruption. Rich candidates do not corrupt themselves when they dip into their own pockets. Instead, stated the Court, the real purpose of the Millionaire's Amendment was to level the financial playing field by punishing more affluent candidates. That purpose is anathema to the First Amendment.

Regrettably, the bad news outweighs the good. President Barack Obama and his supporters in Congress, taking full advantage of the Supreme Court's misguided interpretations of the General Welfare Clause (Chapter 1) and Commerce Clause (Chapter 2), have embarked on an unprecedented expansion of federal power. "You never want a serious crisis to go to waste," said Rahm Emanuel, Obama's chief of staff, to a Washington, D.C. gathering of top executives.[4] Evidently, Emanuel's boss sensed a golden opportunity. He has seized on the current economic turmoil to justify a radical redistributionist and regulatory agenda encompassing a far-reaching array of projects having little to do with the crisis itself.

The massive $787 billion stimulus package, enacted in February 2009, and the nearly-as-massive $410 billion omnibus spending bill, signed a month later, contemplate programs ranging from local mass transit to child care, the National Endowment for the Arts, health insurance, the Smithsonian, food stamps, and, of course, public education – none of which is authorized by Article I, section 8 of the Constitution, where the powers of Congress are enumerated and thereby limited.

If that avalanche of new spending weren't bad enough, consider how the Non-Delegation Clause (Chapter 4) has been shredded by two successive administrations with help from Congress. Both George W. Bush and Barack Obama decided to provide liquidity to the financial system by bailing out institutions that bet heavily on sub-prime mortgages and lost. The salvage operations required enactment of new laws, which are supposed to emanate from Congress. Tragically, at such a crucial time, our federal legislature simply ignored the crystalline pronouncement in the first clause of Article I of the Constitution: "All legislative Powers herein granted shall be vested in a Congress."

Note the key terms "All" and "shall." They indicate that application of the clause is neither selective nor discretionary. Yet Bush and Obama relied not on the legislature but on their secretaries of the treasury, who had been granted vast lawmaking powers by a Congress oblivious to the plain command of Article I. Some calls are tough. The unconstitutionality of the bailout is not one of them. Let's take a closer look.

Unconstitutional Relief for Troubled Assets[5]

The Troubled Asset Relief Program, known as TARP, has survived numerous transformations. Originally enacted in October 2008 as a rescue program under EESA, the Emergency Economic Stabilization Act,[6] TARP authorized former Treasury Secretary Henry Paulsen to buy toxic assets from insolvent banks. That plan morphed into a scheme to inject capital directly by acquiring stock in selected financial institutions. Shortly thereafter, the plan reverted to asset purchases. Along the way, Bush raised the stakes by allotting billions to bail out the automobile industry. Then the Treasury Department floated the idea of government insurance to guarantee private debt and restore market confidence.

None of that worked, so taxpayers and investors eagerly awaited a fresh look from Obama's new Treasury Secretary, Timothy Geithner. But Geithner, like Paulsen, seemed to be improvising. He rejected nationalization, eschewed a "bad bank" for toxic assets, and downplayed government guarantees. Instead, he proposed a public-private partnership to purchase assets by means undisclosed for prices undetermined, at a total cost of roughly $1 trillion – the vast bulk of which would come from taxpayers. Many economists and investors remained skeptical.

Perhaps they realized that more government meddling in the financial sector might make a bad situation worse. After all, a succession of misguided government policies over many years helped cause the current mess. First, Congress enacted double taxation of dividends and deductibility of interest, which gave rise to more borrowing and greater leverage. Then Alan Greenspan's Federal Reserve System fueled the credit crisis with artificially low interest rates. That was compounded by political pressure for affordable housing and implicit taxpayer guarantees to Fannie Mae and Freddie Mac – all of which led to sub-prime lending and high-risk securitized mortgages. Not a bad deal for private financial institutions: Heads, the banks win; tails, the taxpayer loses.

Of course, if we don't like the outcome when federal officials call the shots, we can vote the bums out of office. Or can we? Not if the new policies are spawned by unelected bureaucrats, unaccountable to the voters. Almost no one in the media or the policy community raised this obvious question: Where was Congress during the crafting of TARP's various iterations? Each version of the bailout was engineered, announced, and implemented unilaterally by the Secretary of the Treasury.

Congressional delegation of lawmaking power is permissible, said the Supreme Court in 1928, but only if Congress legislates "an *intelligible principle* to which the person or body authorized ... is directed to conform."[7] As we observed in Chapter 4, the intelligible principle does not have to be very precise: Not a single post-New Deal statutory program has been invalidated as an unconstitutional delegation of legislative power to the executive branch. Then again, the extent of TARP's delegation was unthinkable until now. What was the intelligible principle to which Henry Paulsen and Timothy Geithner were to conform? No one knows – least of all the taxpayers, who are bearing the cost. "Make things better" is not an intelligible principle.

According to the preamble of EESA, the objective of the law was "to purchase ... troubled assets for the purposes of providing stability to and preventing disruption in the economy and financial system" – a noble ambition, but utterly inadequate as a guide for the Treasury Secretary in promulgating specific rules for the bailout. TARP's unpredictability, fits and starts, and total lack of transparency demonstrate that Paulsen and Geithner could do whatever they wanted – unimpeded by any congressional directive. Indeed, Section 101 of EESA specifies that asset purchases can be undertaken "on such terms and conditions as are determined by the Secretary."

Essentially, the bailout reallocates resources from taxpayers to those individuals and corporations who incurred excessive risks and made bad decisions; it substitutes politicians for shareholders in running financial institutions; and it prevents capitalism from performing its periodic restorative function, which is to purge inefficient businesses and inept management. Those are major defects of TARP; yet Congress has abdicated its responsibility and conferred nearly total discretion on the secretary of the treasury.

We are not suggesting that Congress must devise and structure every aspect of the bailout. That job can still be done by "experts" in the executive branch. But Congress, at a minimum, has to review the output and give its stamp of approval. Instead, Congress enacted legislation relegating itself to the role of mere observer. Paulsen, then Geithner, was given *carte blanche*. Consequently, TARP's details were opaque – not only to the public but to Congress itself. Which of 535 legislators accepted responsibility when Geithner developed his public-private partnership? How do we know that opposing views were adequately aired in the corridors of the Treasury? Where is the record of deliberations? What factors were considered? Who is accountable to the voters and taxpayers if Geithner's plan does not work? It's hard to imagine a more secretive process or a more unconstitutional delegation of legislative power.

The scale and immediacy of the financial crisis caused many in Congress and the executive branch to dismiss constitutional concerns. But a debate over unconstitutionality serves three vital purposes: It imposes a heavy burden on proponents of the bailout to explain why the Constitution can be violated with impunity. It reinforces the case for abandoning the program once any true emergency has passed. And it helps establish a presumption against adopting similar measures that might be proposed to resolve future crises.

Maybe TARP is necessary. Maybe it will even help. But necessary or not, temporarily effective or not, the bailout is unconstitutional. And constitutionality is not restored merely by an invocation of "emergency powers" by the administration and Congress. Conservatives should have learned that lesson when the Great Depression triggered the New Deal expansion of government. Liberals should have learned it more recently when civil liberties were compromised in pursuit of real and illusory terrorists. To preserve the rule of law, we must condemn legislation that offends the Constitution – no matter how unlikely the prospect that courts will invalidate the offending acts – even if, from a policy perspective, we believe that the programs are needed.

When policy is allowed to trump constitutionality, three choices are available to honest citizens. They can abandon the proposal and try to accomplish the desired ends using alternative but constitutional means. They can change the Constitution so that the proposal is no longer unlawful. Or they can acknowledge the truth – that they are violating the Constitution in pursuit of ends that could not be otherwise attained.

But the Bush and Obama administrations chose none of the above. Instead, they launched the bailout without a word about its unconstitutionality. That's a recipe for lawlessness, not to mention a precedent that will rear its ugly head every time there's trouble that the federal government thinks it can fix.

EMPATHY ON THE BENCH[8]

What about the courts? Won't they overturn an executive branch program that blatantly contravenes the text of the Constitution? Sad to say, probably not. The technical problem is finding someone who is both willing and legally qualified to sue. The larger substantive problem is that most judges no longer treat the text of the Constitution as sacrosanct, even when its meaning is unmistakably clear. That predicament is likely to get worse before it gets better. Based on his public pronouncements, Obama's judicial appointments will not be jurists who assign predominant weight to the original meaning of the constitutional text.

With 12 years under his belt as lecturer and senior lecturer at the estimable University of Chicago Law School, Obama is no stranger to the Constitution. Nonetheless, he accepts the fashionable yet flawed notion of a malleable, "living" document, which has sufficient structural flexibility to accommodate rapidly changing social, economic, and technological conditions. Obama's implementation of that theory will be to appoint judges who "stand up for social and economic justice"[9] and have "empathy ... to understand what it's like to be poor, or African-American, or gay, or disabled, or old."[10] Obviously, empathy is a virtue, and a judge who places his or her vision of social and economic justice above the rule of law may confer benefits on some litigants. The question, however, is whether empathy and social consciousness should dictate how a judge interprets the Constitution.

The editors of the *New Jersey Lawyer*, for example, want judges to issue decisions that reflect the "felt necessities of the time."[11] In a July 2008 editorial, the *NJL* criticized the *Heller* decision, not because it misinterpreted the Second Amendment but rather because "gun violence plaguing our nation's cities is, in a word, deplorable.... [G]overnmental gun control is needed now more than ever."[12] In response, one reader wondered whether the editors would endorse "conservatives who might find among the 'felt necessities of the time' a reason to restrict reproductive rights."[13] Another reader asked whether the editorial board would have judges "prohibit the free exercise of religion by Muslim citizens because of recent acts of terrorism."[14] Evidently, one person's "felt necessities" are another person's despotism.

As the confirmation hearings for Obama's judicial nominees unfold, ask yourself whether you like the notion of a living Constitution that can be construed by empathetic judges with a social consciousness, who will render subjective judgments about felt necessities. Consider as well the alternative of "originalists" who are anchored by the written text of the founding documents. The hearings should be instructive. While senators should not seek a commitment from the nominee to rule a particular way on an issue, they should insist on an explication of the candidate's judicial philosophy. A good starting point would be to ask each nominee to identify all – or even a few – provisions of the Constitution that impose meaningful constraints on federal executive or legislative authority.

Near-term, unless something unpredictable happens to Justice Kennedy or one of the four conservative justices, Obama will not have much impact on the ideological mix of the Supreme Court. Liberal justice David Souter has announced his retirement, to be effective before the start of the October 2009 term. The next two most likely retirees are also liberal: John Paul Stevens, who's 89; and Ruth Bader Ginsburg, who's not in good health. Obama will probably nominate liberals to replace liberals.

On the other hand, Justice Scalia is 73, and two Obama terms might be more than Scalia is willing to serve. Moreover, Obama will have an enormous impact on the trial and appellate courts. George W. Bush and Bill Clinton each made roughly 300 appointments over their eight-year terms. Today, waiting to be filled are 54 trial court openings and 15 vacancies on the appellate courts,[15] where thousands of cases are decided each year. Only 70 to 80 of those cases typically make it to the Supreme Court. So appellate appointments are critically important.

A Victory for Individual Rights[16]

Naturally, we would like to end this Preface on an optimistic note. And so we return to *District of Columbia v. Heller*, the blockbuster Second Amendment case that we mentioned at the outset. The Supreme Court released the *Heller* opinion on June 26, 2008 – the last day of the Court's 2007-08 term. Nearly six years earlier, the case had been filed under the name *Parker v. District of Columbia*, but Ms. Parker and four other plaintiffs were dismissed for lack of standing – a complicated legal question that we need not explore here. Fortunately, the sixth plaintiff,

Dick Heller, had standing and was able to continue the litigation under his own name.

In Chapter 6, we wrote that *Parker* (later, *Heller*) "could well be headed to the Supreme Court; and that is where it belongs. The citizens of this country deserve a foursquare pronouncement from the nation's highest court about the real meaning of the Second Amendment." We also wrote, "the Constitution is on our side." Thankfully, the Supreme Court agreed. It took years of litigation,[17] a feckless 32-year handgun ban in the nation's capital, and a 69-year-old Supreme Court case, muddled and misinterpreted by appellate courts across the country. When it was over, the Supreme Court, by a razor thin 5-4 vote, proclaimed unequivocally that the Second Amendment secured an individual right to keep and bear arms in the home for self-defense. That was the happy ending in *Heller*, the most important Second Amendment case in U.S. history.

Essentially, Justice Scalia reinvigorated the Second Amendment. Joined by Roberts, Alito, Kennedy, and Thomas, Scalia held that the militia clause ("A well regulated Militia, being necessary to the security of a free State") announces one purpose of the Second Amendment but does not limit the right expressly stated in the operative clause ("the right of the people to keep and bear Arms, shall not be infringed"). Nor did the Court's prior precedent, *United States v. Miller*, say otherwise. It established simply that some weapons — e.g., sawed-off shotguns — are not protected unless they can be shown to have military utility and be in common use. Moreover, declared Scalia, the District of Columbia may not categorically ban "an entire class of 'arms'" that Americans overwhelmingly choose for the lawful purpose of self-defense.[18]

In his dissenting opinion, Stevens — joined by Justices Stephen Breyer, Ginsburg, and Souter — not only quarreled with Scalia's interpretation of historical events but also implied that Scalia had abandoned true judicial conservatism by dragging the Court into the "political thicket" of gun control. "Judicial restraint would be far wiser," wrote Stevens, than mediating a political process that is "working exactly as it should."[19] That's quite an astonishing statement coming from Stevens – the same justice who had no such reservations just one day earlier when he voted to invalidate Louisiana's death penalty for child rape and substitute an outright ban on capital punishment for any crime that isn't fatal to its victim.[20]

Breyer, who filed a separate dissent in *Heller*, proffered this extraordinary statement: "The decision threatens to throw into doubt the constitutionality of gun laws throughout the United States."[21] Not so. Forty-four states have constitutional provisions protecting an individual right to keep and bear arms. Legislatures in all 50 states have rejected bans on private handgun ownership. Concealed carry is permitted, with varying degrees of administrative discretion, in all states except Wisconsin and Illinois. Any of the "gun laws throughout the United States" that are now unconstitutional pursuant to *Heller* would already have been overturned under the robust pro-gun-rights legal framework existing in most states. Thus, the major impact of the *Heller* opinion will be felt not "throughout the United States" but in a few cities and other political subdivisions that were authorized by their states to enact gun control laws different from those prevailing elsewhere in the state.

In any event, *Heller* is merely the opening salvo in a series of cases that will ultimately resolve what weapons and persons can be regulated and what restrictions are permissible. The Court will also have to decide whether Second Amendment rights can be enforced against state and local governments outside of Washington, D.C., a federal enclave that is controlled by Congress.[22] Despite those remaining hurdles, it's fair to say that the Court's landmark decision in *Heller* makes the prospects for reviving the original meaning of the Second Amendment substantially brighter. Not even seven decades of uncertain precedent under *United States v. Miller* kept the Court from expanding individual liberty. For readers of *The Dirty Dozen*, that's one case down, 11 to go.

NOTES

1   *District of Columbia v. Heller*, 554 U.S. ___; 128 S. Ct. 2783 (2008).

2   *United States v. Miller*, 307 U.S. 174 (1939).

3   *Davis v. Federal Election Commission*, 554 U.S. ___; 128 S. Ct. 2759 (2008).

4   Rahm Emanuel, addressing the *Wall Street Journal* CEO Council, Washington, DC, November 18, 2008.   See http://www.youtube.com/watch?v=_mzcbXi1Tkk.

5   This section is extracted, in part, from three articles by Robert A. Levy: "Is the Bailout Constitutional?" *Legal Times*, October 20, 2008; "Constitutionally Troubled: 'TARP' and Its Delegation of Legislative Power," *Legal Opinion Letter*, Vol. 19, No. 4, Washington Legal Foundation, February 27, 2009; "Constitutional Basics for President Obama," *Cato Policy Report,* March–April, 2009.

6   Public Law 110-343.

7   *J.W. Hampton Jr. Co. v. United States*, 276 U.S. 394, 409 (1928) (emphasis added).

8   See Robert A. Levy, "Judicial Appointments: What's on Tap from Obama or McCain?" *FindLaw Writ Legal News & Commentary*, October 2, 2008, http://writ.news.findlaw.com/commentary/20081002_levy.html; Robert A. Levy, "Constitutional Basics for President Obama," *Cato Policy Report,* March–April, 2009.

9   Quoted in Juliet Eilperin, "McCain Says He Would Put Conservatives on Supreme Court," *Washington Post*, May 7, 2008.

10 Quoted in Jonah Goldberg, "Courting Disaster," *National Review Online*, April 18, 2008.

11 Editorial, "Original Intent and Right to Bear Arms," *New Jersey Lawyer*, July 21, 2008.

12 Ibid.

13 Letter to the Editor, "A Hint of Orwell," *New Jersey Lawyer*, August 4, 2008.

14 Letter to the Editor, "'Felt Necessities': The Wrong Reason," *New Jersey Lawyer*, August 4, 2008.

15 "Vacancies in the Federal Judiciary – 111th Congress," May 3, 2009, http://www.uscourts.gov/cfapps/webnovada/CF_FB_301/index.cfm?fuseaction=Reports.ViewVacancies.

16 This section is drawn from Robert A. Levy: "Second Amendment Aftermath," *Washington Times*, July 3, 2008.

17 One of the authors, Robert A. Levy, served as co-counsel to Mr. Heller.

18 *Heller*, 128 S. Ct. at 2817.

19 *Heller*, 128 S. Ct. at 2846 (Stevens, J., dissenting).

20 *Kennedy v. Louisiana*, 554 U.S. ___; 128 S. Ct. 2641 (2008).

21 *Heller*, 128 S. Ct. at 2870 (Breyer, J., dissenting).

22 Most rights in the Bill of Rights, but not yet the Second Amendment, have been enforced against state and local governments using the Due Process Clause of the 14th Amendment. The legal doctrine is known as "incorporation." A majority of legal scholars expect the Supreme Court to incorporate the Second Amendment as well. When the Court takes up that issue, it will have an opportunity to reconsider whether a different provision of the 14th Amendment – the Privileges or Immunities Clause – is a more appropriate basis for incorporation than the Due Process Clause. As we noted in Chapter 11, one principal purpose of the Privileges or Immunities Clause was to ensure that newly freed slaves would enjoy economic liberty, including the right to contract and own property. Regrettably, a mere five years after the 14th Amendment's ratification, the Privileges or Immunities Clause was stripped of its intended meaning in the *Slaughter-House Cases*, 83 U.S. 36 (1873) – an egregious example of judicial activism that ushered in Jim Crow laws and state-enforced violations of economic liberty. One hopes the Court will revisit *Slaughter-House*, the pernicious effects of which continue to this day.

FOREWORD

Many of the most harmful decisions of the U.S. Supreme Court have been subject to sustained attack in separate places. But I am not aware of any volume whose major function is to identify, gather, and systematically critique the worst of those decisions in one place. Such an effort is especially valuable because Supreme Court cases often involve complicated facts or obscure constitutional provisions but have sweeping national impact. Regrettably, the Court has too often taken the plain wording of the Constitution and interpreted it to mean exactly the opposite of what the Founding Fathers intended. By that process the Court profoundly altered the American legal, political, and economic landscape.

Into this void step two fearless writers, Bob Levy and Chip Mellor, who through their work at, respectively, the Cato Institute and the Institute for Justice, have been deeply involved in shaping our legal and political culture. Commendably, they act with one consistent objective: to increase the protection of individual rights by limiting the size and functions of government. That singular and admirable vision exerts a profound influence on their selection of cases for inclusion in *The Dirty Dozen*—the most damaging decisions of the Supreme Court since the New Deal. For many readers, lawyers and nonlawyers alike, this will be their first critical exposure to these cases.

Levy and Mellor apply two standards to select cases for inclusion in *The Dirty Dozen*. First, the constitutional foundations for the decision must be weak—measured, of course, against the theory of limited government that they and I defend. Second, the social consequences of the decision must be negative. While I am in complete agreement with the authors on the virtues of limited government, my agreement on cases worthy of inclusion is very high but not perfect. That is one reason why this book is so important. Its value lies in its ability to provoke debate and prompt the reader to check his or her assumptions about liberty and the rule of law. Whether in the context of legislation, political reform, or selection of judges, such debate will be very healthy for the future of our nation.

Let me briefly discuss each of the cases, and explain in a sentence or two my position on their inclusion.

The first case, *Helvering v. Davis* (1937), which upheld the Social Security system as a public expenditure for the general welfare, clearly meets the authors' two-part test. By endorsing Social Security as a supposed means to counter massive unemployment, the Court essentially transformed the Constitution's General Welfare Clause from a limitation on government power to a source of added power. Moreover, by taking a highly deferential view toward the constitutionality of congressional enactments—basically giving Congress carte blanche to legislate without rigorous judicial review—*Helvering* frustrated the development of comprehensive private pension systems, imposed tax barriers to new job creation, and created intergenerational inequities under a scheme that has proved virtually impossible to change now that it is embedded in the social fabric.

Unquestioned kudos also go to the authors' second selection, *Wickard v. Filburn* (1942), for its extravagant reading of the Commerce Clause. By extending federal regulatory authority to nearly every productive economic activity, *Wickard* eviscerated the principle that the federal government has only those powers expressly granted to it in the Constitution. And for this reason: to sustain an ill-conceived cartel whose chief purpose was to keep the domestic price of wheat close to three times the world price. Thereafter, federal authority spread like wildfire into countless areas of economic and personal activity.

The third case, *Home Building & Loan Association v. Blaisdell* (1934), also has a secure place on the list of ill fame. Until that decision, contracts between private parties were protected from state government interference by express constitutional provision. The Court, by holding that the Constitution allowed states to excuse defaults on home mortgages, made banks and their depositors bear the brunt of unwise federal monetary policies that were the source of deflation during the Hoover and Roosevelt administrations. And going forward, *Blaisdell* ushered in widespread state intervention regarding contracts that had no pretense of dealing with a system-wide economic breakdown.

Next, the authors critique the concentration of legislative, executive, and judicial powers in the hands of unelected administrative agencies. That development has vastly increased the size, ambition, and unaccountability of the federal bureaucracy in ways that would have been incomprehensible to the Founders. Levy and Mellor explain how *Whitman v. American Trucking Associations, Inc.* (2001) exacerbated this fundamentally antidemocratic growth of government. Still, the more significant case on administrative lawmaking, in my view, is *Chevron U.S.A., Inc. v. Natural Resources Defense Council* (1984). It was *Chevron* that inaugurated the principle of high judicial deference to administrative agencies on practically all questions of law. Those agencies—which are nowhere to be found in the original assignment of powers to the legislative, executive, or judicial branches—were allowed to push the law to its limits and beyond.

McConnell v. Federal Election Commission (2003) also holds a secure place on the roll call of most dubious Supreme Court decisions. In the name of campaign finance reform, basic principles of the First Amendment were sacrificed. It is quite simply perverse to think that political speech should be more vulnerable to government regulation than obscenity. And it is naïve at best to think that any legislative reform could somehow keep money out of politics. There is only one way to move in that direction: reduce the significance of politics by reining in the power of the federal government. Lacking the courage to do that, the Supreme Court has endorsed legislation that protects incumbents, blocks organized dissent, undermines political parties, and in general invites the massive degradation of the political process.

United States v. Miller (1939), with its cavalier dismissal of the right to bear arms, is surely an example of poor Supreme Court reasoning, but it would not make my personal list of *The Dirty Dozen* decisions. Even if we assume, as modern scholarship suggests, that the right to bear arms was held by all individual members of the unorganized militia, gun ownership—with the obvious risks that weapons pose to innocent persons—cannot escape regulation altogether. State police power clearly extends to the protection of health and safety, which may entail some firearms restrictions. Exactly where the lines should be drawn is a hard question that needs intensive reexamination. Inevitably, the Supreme Court will have to clarify its position, and this chapter does an excellent job of explaining why.

Levy and Mellor are emphatically right, however, to condemn *Korematsu v. United States* (1944). To this day it never ceases to amaze that wartime hysteria and political opportunism could allow this nation to intern 120,000 loyal citizens of Japanese descent without a shred of evidence of individual wrongdoing. It is equally incomprehensible that the Court, in slavish deference to the political branches, stood idly by. There is one silver lining: Whatever the wrongs—and there are many—of the current national policy toward enemy combatants, no future Supreme Court is likely to repeat the wholesale shame of *Korematsu*. But that case nonetheless provides a strong object lesson in what can happen when the rule of law breaks down.

Bennis v. Michigan (1996), dealing with matters of asset forfeiture, also merits inclusion in a compendium of most-dubious decisions. Why the Supreme Court should yield to the use of arbitrary police power that takes the property of innocent persons without a hearing is a mystery. One can imagine many subtleties in trying to figure out when the government denies people their property without due process of law. But denying innocent people their property without *any* process of law is not one of them.

No catalog of Supreme Court outrages would be complete without *Kelo v. City of New London* (2005), which left private property owners without meaningful constitutional protection to resist the use of eminent domain in the name of economic development. The Court again displayed a supine deference to legislative bodies by allowing local planners to run roughshod over isolated and vulnerable members of society. Eminent domain used for economic development imposes an enormous drain on taxpayer dollars for no discernible benefit. Yes, there is room at the margin for reasonable people to disagree about the purposes for which governments should exercise their eminent domain powers, but the transfer of one person's property to another private party, merely for an illusory promise of more jobs and a higher tax base, lies beyond the pale.

Hats off again to our authors for putting *Penn Central Transport Co. v. New York* (1978) on their list. *Penn Central* sustained the power of the state to designate historical landmarks without paying just compensation. But it did far more than that. The decision authorized government to regulate the use of property in myriad ways, from confiscatory environmental restrictions to zoning laws that favor those with political connections. Under the standards established in *Penn Central*, owners often receive no compensation for devastating reductions in their property's value caused by state restrictions on its use.

United States v. Carolene Products (1938) also fits on any register of infamous decisions because of a single footnote in a ten-page opinion. The decision is wholly indefensible for the proposition that no infringement of economic liberties, however egregious, is subject to meaningful constitutional review. The offending footnote literally invites countless opportunities for mischievous government intervention. But in this context *Nebbia v. New York* (1934) deserves more than dishonorable mention. Prior to *Nebbia* the power to regulate activities "affected with the public interest" had been limited to state control of monopolies. *Nebbia* reversed course by allowing states to set minimum prices, thereby *creating* monopolies, not eliminating them—a shabby performance indeed.

Coming to the last case, I must voice a dissent, for I do not think that *Grutter v. Bollinger* (2003) is, ultimately, a misguided decision. The use of racial preferences is fraught with sensitivities for historic and moral reasons. Levy and Mellor make a strong case, but I would not criticize the Court for upholding the use of preferences in university admissions. I would argue a different point—namely, that the Court should *not* diligently scrutinize affirmative action programs when the state is engaged in running businesses such as universities. The right measuring stick for evaluating the conduct of a public university, in my opinion, is the unregulated behavior of the private institutions with which they compete. Nearly all private universities have implemented some measure of voluntary affirmative action. Such measures are not required, but neither are they forbidden. That should be the standard.

The overall pattern is clear. A free society requires judges to enforce, and political actors to respect, the principles of limited government. That vital objective can only be achieved if courts understand that government regulation should be examined, in most constitutional contexts, under a presumption that the regulation is impermissible. Instead, the Supreme Court has changed the rules to rubber-stamp legislative and executive actions that expand the power of government. The result: open season for political bodies to trample the personal liberties and property rights that good government should be sworn to protect. Liberty cannot endure under such a regime.

The key, as Levy and Mellor pointedly note in their afterword, is responsible judicial engagement. For the dire consequences of disregarding that commandment, the reader need only inquire within.

Richard A. Epstein
James Parker Hall Distinguished Service Professor of Law
University of Chicago
May 2008

INTRODUCTION

Too often Americans take for granted that they are free.

But if America truly is the land of the free, should we have to ask for government permission to participate in an election? Or pursue an honest occupation? And should our government be empowered to take someone's home only to turn the property over to others for their private use?

Of course not.

So why are we less free now, in many respects, than we were two hundred years ago? How did we get from our Founders' Constitution, which established a strictly limited government, to today's Constitution, which has expanded government and curtailed individual rights? That's the story of *The Dirty Dozen*.

This book is about twelve Supreme Court cases that changed the course of American history—away from constitutional government. Surprisingly, few of these cases are widely known despite their enormous impact. Maybe *McConnell v. Federal Election Commission* (2003), because of its recent vintage, is recognized as the case that gave political speech less First Amendment protection than flag burning or Internet pornography. But how many of us recall that *Wickard v. Filburn* (1942) paved the way for the noxious notion that Congress, under the guise of regulating interstate commerce, can criminalize the use by critically ill patients of medical marijuana, grown and distributed in a single state, free of charge, under a doctor's prescription, in accordance with state law? And how many of us have heard of *United States v. Carolene Products* (1938), in which an obscure footnote virtually eliminated judicial review—that is, the power of the courts to examine, modify, and even overturn acts of the executive and legislative branches—when government restricts key liberties such as the right to earn an honest living?

Whether it is political speech, economic liberties, property rights, welfare, racial preferences, gun owners' rights, or imprisonment without charge, the U.S. Supreme Court has behaved in a manner that would have stunned, mystified, and outraged our Founding Fathers. Alexander Hamilton labeled the judiciary "the weakest of the three departments." If only he had been correct when he wrote in *Federalist No. 78* that "the judiciary, from the nature of its functions, will always be the least dangerous to the political rights of the Constitution."

Nor could James Madison have envisioned that the Court would be complicit in the exponential growth of the federal government. "The powers delegated by the proposed Constitution to the Federal Government," said Madison in *Federalist No. 45*, "are few and defined. Those which are to remain in the State Governments are numerous and indefinite." Would that it were so. Over the twelve-month period ending March 31, 2006, the federal government published more than seventy-seven thousand pages of new rules that had been proposed or implemented by various regulatory agencies.[1] That is not the way America was meant to operate. From our founding we were supposed to have a government of limited power and maximum freedom for the individual. Instead, we have been afflicted by a vast enlargement of federal power, condoned by a Supreme Court that has selectively protected some—but not all—of our constitutionally guaranteed rights.

Expanding government and eroding freedom: Here's the sad tale.

HOW THE SUPREME COURT HAS AMENDED THE CONSTITUTION

On September 17, 1787, a convention of representatives from twelve states—all except Rhode Island—completed four months of work drafting the U.S. Constitution and then submitted it to delegates in the individual states for ratification. Less than two years later, after approval by eleven states—two more than required at the time—the Constitution was formally adopted. Some of the states that ratified the Constitution insisted that further "declaratory and restrictive clauses" be added. Accordingly, on September 25, 1789, Congress transmitted to the state legislatures twelve proposed amendments. Two of those—having to do with congressional representation and congressional pay—were not adopted.[2] The remaining ten amendments were ratified effective December 15, 1791, and became known as the Bill of Rights.

Since the Bill of Rights was adopted in 1791, the Constitution has been amended *only seventeen times*. Yet the framers could never have imagined what our twenty-first-century world would resemble. How, then, did they manage to devise a document that would be changed on so few occasions over such a dynamic and tumultuous two centuries? Three explanations come to mind—two good and one bad.

The first good explanation for the stability of the Constitution is that it is an incredibly well crafted document comprising broad principles written by brilliant legal minds who had a vision of liberty that is every bit as relevant today as it was in 1791. The second good explanation is that the framers established an amendment process in Article V of the Constitution that was designed to discourage frequent revisions. Essentially, amendments are proposed by two-thirds of both the House and the Senate, after which they have to be ratified by three-fourths of the states.[3] Not surprisingly, those demanding requirements have not been satisfied very often. The result: a stable constitutional framework that has endured hot and cold wars, recessions and depressions, and scandals the likes of which have destroyed many foreign governments.

The third reason we have not seen very many amendments is more disturbing. Basically, the Supreme Court has imposed through the back door what the Congress and the states could not accomplish through the amendment process. By misinterpreting cases that have raised key constitutional questions, the Court has expanded government and curbed individual rights in a manner never intended by the framers, with profound implications for all Americans. Seldom has the ratchet of the Court's decisions turned toward greater individual liberty. To the contrary, the Court has further and further restricted the freedoms that Americans should enjoy as a birthright.

Perhaps some of the "amendments" engineered by the Supreme Court would have been ratified if constitutionally prescribed procedures had been followed. Perhaps not. We will never know. What we do know is that the framers intended for the elected representatives of the people, not the Supreme Court, to change the Constitution if and when it needed to be changed. Instead, a Court consisting of unelected justices with lifetime appointments has rewritten the Constitution without input from, or accountability to, the people of the United States.

Georgetown University law professor Randy E. Barnett graphically illustrates that point by recounting the story of Laszlo Toth, who in 1972 dashed past the guards in Saint Peter's Basilica and attacked Michelangelo's *Pietà* with a sledgehammer. With fifteen blows the madman removed the Virgin's arm at the elbow, knocked off a chunk of her nose, and chipped one of her eyelids. But suppose, asks Professor Barnett, Toth had evaded security in the National Archives and attacked the Constitution on display there. What if, using a razor, he managed to cut out key parts of the original document—such as the Ninth and Tenth Amendments, which we will soon discuss. The nation would surely be horrified, and yet, concludes Professor Barnett, "the Supreme Court has done what someone like Laszlo Toth could never do: take a razor to the text of the Constitution to *remake it from the thing it was to something quite different*. . . . At the Court's hands, what was once a system of islands of power in a sea of individual liberty . . . has become islands of rights in a sea of state and federal power."[4]

Some of the damage occurred long ago. For example, in *Dred Scott v. Sandford* (1857)—probably the Court's most infamous decision—Chief Justice Roger B. Taney held, among other things, that black slaves were property, not citizens of the United States. And in *Plessy v. Ferguson* (1890), the Court upheld a Louisiana statute requiring railroads to provide equal but separate accommodations for the "white and colored races." As repugnant as those cases were, they are no longer the law of the land. *Scott* was superseded by the Fourteenth Amendment (1868), and *Plessy* was overruled by a series of cases beginning with *Brown v. Board of Education* (1954).

Much of the Court's real mischief arose later, during the New Deal, and continues today. That period—from 1934 until today—is the focus of *The Dirty Dozen*. In the next twelve chapters we identify and dissect the worst of the Court's post-1933 decisions. The goal is to untangle those complex legal opinions and explain how they affect each and every one of us. We gear our discussion primarily to nonlawyers, with the hope they will gain a greater appreciation for the crucial role of the Supreme Court in securing liberty.

Friends of the Constitution who cherish personal freedom and limited government have good reason for concern about the modern Court. *The Dirty Dozen* is a litany of concerns—using twelve cases to demonstrate how the Court has too often abandoned the principles that were painstakingly and ingeniously shaped by our Founding Fathers. But before getting to the meat of the matter, here is a quick review of how we selected the cases, how the book is organized, and how we personally interpret the Constitution.

How We Selected the Cases

So many bad cases; so little space to examine them. That was the dilemma we faced in picking the dozen worst Supreme Court cases of the modern era. We sought help from our colleagues—specifically, seventy-four like-minded legal scholars whom we surveyed informally by email. We promised anonymity and asked them to name the post-1933 cases that had the most destructive effect on law and public policy, either by expanding government powers beyond those that are constitutionally authorized or by imperiling individual liberties that are constitutionally protected. We also requested that our survey recipients choose only those cases that have ongoing impact—that is, cases not already overturned by a subsequent Supreme Court opinion or constitutional amendment.

Further, we stipulated that the "worst" cases should be defined in terms of their outcomes, not merely bad legal reasoning. For example, many of our lawyer friends believe that the Court's school desegregation decision, *Brown v. Board of Education* (1954), was poorly reasoned. Chief Justice Earl Warren limited his opinion to public schools rather than apply the Fourteenth Amendment's Equal Protection Clause more broadly to all laws that mandated segregation; he relied on dubious psychological studies purporting to show that black students learn more efficiently in an integrated environment. That said, none of the legal scholars we surveyed believes that public schools should have remained segregated. Thus, in terms of its outcome, *Brown* was pro-liberty even if its legal rationale might have been suspect.

The scholars responding to our survey identified many awful cases, but just twenty of those were clear consensus picks, of which nine were obvious favorites. From among the leading vote-getters, we selected the cases that we thought were most egregious. Most of them are probably unfamiliar to nonlawyers by name. Still, they have vital real-life consequences consistent with the dual themes of this book: Our liberties have gradually eroded while government has expanded its control over our day-to-day lives.

In making our final selections, we were guided but not bound by the results of our survey. All of our selections received multiple votes except for *Kelo v. City of New London* (2005), which was decided after the survey was finalized. *Kelo* addresses government's authority to seize a person's land, home, or business—known as the power of eminent domain. The case stands for the shocking proposition that private property can be taken from its existing owners for transfer to new owners as part of an economic development project. Yes, the government has to pay "just compensation" when property is condemned under eminent domain, but when all is said and done, if the owner doesn't like the compensation, he'll be forced to sell anyway.

Of the top nine picks in the survey, we include all but one—*Roe v. Wade* (1973)—in *The Dirty Dozen*. Because *Roe* received considerable survey support, it deserves special comment. We discuss *Roe* in Postscript #1 at the end of the book. Also at the end of the book, in Postscript #2, we discuss *Bush v. Gore* (2000). Like *Roe*, *Bush* is excluded from *The Dirty Dozen*. Unlike *Roe*, *Bush* did not receive a single vote in our survey. Yet its importance and the popular misconception that the Court had no business involving itself in the 2000 election compel us to offer our own brief analysis.

How the Book Is Organized

Once we had identified *The Dirty Dozen* cases, our next task was to determine the sequence in which they should be discussed. We decided on a thematic approach, using the cases as a springboard to discuss various provisions of the Constitution—beginning with four chapters under the caption "Expanding Government" and then eight chapters under the caption "Eroding Freedom." Each chapter is linked to one of the twelve cases.

Here is the layout of the chapters together with their associated cases, constitutional provisions, and a preview of what is at stake just.

Part One: Expanding Government

1. Promoting the General Welfare—*Helvering v. Davis*
   Article I, sec. 8 (General Welfare Clause): Congress can tax and spend to promote the general welfare, said the Court. That opened the floodgates, through which the redistributive state was ready to pour—taking money from some, giving it to others, without any meaningful constitutional constraints.

2. Regulating Interstate Commerce—*Wickard v. Filburn*
   Article I, sec. 8 (Commerce Clause): Can Congress's power to regulate interstate commerce be extended to activities that are not interstate, not commerce, and not even regulated but prohibited? Apparently so.

3. Rescinding Private Contracts—*Home Building & Loan Association v. Blaisdell*
   Article I, sec. 10 (Contracts Clause): "No State shall . . . pass any . . . Law impairing the Obligation of Contracts," says the

Constitution. Clear enough? Not for the Supreme Court, which upheld a Minnesota statute postponing mortgage payments for financially troubled homeowners. Never mind the contract between the lender and the customer.

4. Lawmaking by Administrative Agencies—*Whitman v. American Trucking Associations, Inc.*

   Article I, sec. 1 (Non-Delegation Doctrine): If Congress passes an oppressive law, the voters can respond by throwing the bums out. But if the law is murky, and Congress lets an unelected regulatory agency fill in the oppressive details, the courts won't do much about it, and the voters can't.

Part Two: Eroding Freedom

5. Campaign Finance Reform and Free Speech—*McConnell v. Federal Election Commission*

   First Amendment (Free Speech): In pursuit of the quixotic idea that money and elections should not mix, the Court has curtailed our most basic expressive right: to support or criticize political candidates.

6. Gun Owners' Rights—*United States v. Miller*

   Second Amendment (Keep and Bear Arms): Almost seven decades ago the Supreme Court established a legal regime that has been interpreted by appellate courts across the country to mean that individuals do not have an individual right to possess firearms.

7. Civil Liberties Versus National Security—*Korematsu v. United States*

   Fifth Amendment (Due Process Clause): Guarantees of liberty, fair treatment, and equal protection of the laws may be waived during wartime—even if American citizens are arrested and imprisoned without charge indefinitely.

8. Asset Forfeiture Without Due Process—*Bennis v. Michigan*

   Fifth and Fourteenth Amendments (Due Process Clauses): It is not bad enough that your husband engages in a sexual act with a prostitute in the front seat of your car. The Court says that the criminal offense extends to the car itself, which the government can seize, and you cannot recover either the car or its value.

9. Eminent Domain for Private Use—*Kelo v. City of New London*
Fifth Amendment (Public Use Doctrine): Suppose you have a cherished home in which you've lived for many years. Along comes a private developer who promises the government more jobs and higher taxes if your home is turned over to him. Do you think your property is safe from the bulldozer? Think again.

10. Taking Property by Regulation—*Penn Central Transport Co. v. New York*
Fifth Amendment (Takings Clause): When the value of your property plummets due to government regulations, you won't be compensated unless the regulations go "too far." How far is too far? Evidently, Penn Central's $150 million loss wasn't far enough.

11. Earning an Honest Living—*United States v. Carolene Products*
Ninth Amendment (Unenumerated Rights): Do your economic liberties include a right to form your own business without unwarranted government restrictions? Not if the legislature decides to protect your rivals; then the courts pitch in and rubber-stamp the anticompetitive regulations.

12. Equal Protection and Racial Preferences—*Grutter v. Bollinger*
Fourteenth Amendment (Equal Protection Clause): No racial discrimination. That is the rule—unless, of course, a state university uses race as a mere "plus factor," part of a "holistic" approach to attain diversity. Then somehow racial preferences are not discriminatory.

Those are the cases—appalling examples of Supreme Court gaffes. To treat the cases systematically and uniformly, in each chapter, we have followed a structured format with four subheadings: (1) What Is the Constitutional Issue? (2) What Were the Facts? (3) Where Did the Court Go Wrong? (4) What Are the Implications?

The fourth subsection is especially important. Many of the cases deal with novel and narrow facts, yet the Court's holdings have repercussions that extend far beyond any one case. To illustrate: *Bennis v.*

Michigan, described briefly above, entailed the forfeiture of a car in which an illegal sex act had occurred. But the Court's opinion established a more sweeping proposition: States may seize any asset involved in criminal activity without compensation to the owner even if the owner had no knowledge of the activity. Imagine how far that pernicious doctrine could reach.

Naturally, in exploring some cases that we include in *The Dirty Dozen*, our analyses will touch on related cases as well. With help from the legal scholars who responded to our survey, we identified several post-1933 cases that were linked to, and nearly as bad as, the Dirty Dozen. We list them at the beginning of selected chapters as "Dishonorable Mentions" and then discuss them in more detail within the text.

Finally, in an afterword to *The Dirty Dozen*, we comment on judicial activism, too loosely defined as intervention by the courts to overturn decisions by our elected representatives. Judicial activism has become the denunciation *du jour* by both liberals and conservatives who want to influence judicial appointments—especially to the Supreme Court—that will shape the legal landscape over the coming decades. To a great extent today's appointments will determine whether tomorrow's Court enforces the Constitution that the framers designed or conjures up an unratified version of the Constitution that reflects the policy preferences of nine justices. We explain the vital difference between inappropriate judicial activism and the proper, indeed essential, practice of judicial engagement.

How We Interpret the Constitution

As a prelude to our discussion of the Dirty Dozen, we want our readers to know and understand the constitutional perspective that animates this book. Accordingly, we offer this synopsis of our views relating to the design, meaning, and purpose of the U.S. Constitution. For starters, we are committed to the values of individual liberty, private property, and free markets. Perhaps most significant from a constitutional perspective, we are advocates of strictly limited government.[5]

Consider, for example, the post-9/11 environment. The exercise by government of its national security powers will sometimes be incompatible with the exercise by individuals of their broad civil liberties. No one disputes that national security is a legitimate function of government. The state is responsible, first and foremost, for the protection of life, liberty, and property. The Constitution, as Justice Robert H. Jackson warned, is not a suicide pact. Even fervent champions of the Bill of Rights concede that it would be foolish to treat civil liberties as inviolable when the lives of innocent thousands may be at stake. So where to draw the line?

Paradoxically, in the current climate, normally limited-government conservatives tend to endorse an ever-increasing role for the federal government, while big-government liberals express their frustration over a federal government that commands too much power. What, then, are the contrasting perceptions that explain those apparent paradoxes? Is there an underlying constitutional theory that supports one view or another?

The framers designed the Constitution to achieve two basic ends. First, the national government had to be strong enough to impose civil order, protect citizens from foreign invaders, and secure individual rights. But second, the powers of government were to be strictly limited, thereby ensuring that government itself would not violate the rights of the people. To reconcile those potentially conflicting goals, the Constitution was crafted with great care. On one hand, the framers assigned far broader powers to the federal government than it had exercised under the Articles of Confederation. Yet, on the other hand, the powers were confined to those specifically listed in the Constitution and were divided among three branches of government.

Thus, the Constitution is often referred to as a document of "enumerated and separated powers," which means, first, that all powers of the federal government not enumerated are assumed not to exist; and second, that the executive, legislative, and judicial branches are each authorized to exercise designated powers and no others. In that way each branch was to act as a check and balance on the other two. Two years after ratification, to reinforce and reaffirm the Constitution's mandate for limited government, the framers added a Bill of Rights that provided affirmative safeguards against government excess.

Indeed, the essential structure of our federal system is captured by the final two provisions of the Bill of Rights: the Ninth and Tenth Amendments. The Ninth Amendment addresses individual rights. It provides that "the enumeration in the Constitution of certain rights shall not be construed to deny or disparage others retained by the people." The Tenth Amendment addresses federal powers. It tells us that the national government may exercise only those powers enumerated in the Constitution—such as the power to coin money and establish post offices. The powers not delegated and enumerated are reserved to the states or, depending on state law, to the people.

In considering federal power, conservatives generally agree on a tightly constrained central government, but with two conspicuous exceptions:

First, some conservatives are willing to federalize a significant amount of criminal law (for example, the war on drugs) and civil law (for example, much of Congress's tort reform agenda). We invoke a different principle: No matter how worthwhile a goal may be, if there is no constitutional authority to pursue it, then the federal government must step aside and leave the matter to the states or to private parties. The president and Congress can proceed only from constitutional authority, not from good intentions alone. If Congress deems it necessary to add to its enumerated powers, there is an amendment process crafted by the framers for that purpose. Too often Congress has simply disregarded the limits set by the Constitution.

Second, some conservatives are disposed toward excessive concentrations of national security power in the executive branch. Yet unchecked authority in the hands of the executive threatens the separation of powers, which has been a cornerstone of our Constitution since 1789. The administration may not by itself set the rules, prosecute infractions, determine guilt or innocence, and then review the results of its own actions. Congress, not the executive branch, is charged with legislative responsibility, and courts are charged with constitutional oversight. On that score, judges should defer to the executive branch on matters of national security, but the rights of citizens under the Constitution, including the right to judicial review, must be respected. When the executive, legislative, and judicial branches agree on the framework, the potential for abuse is not eliminated, but it is diminished. When only the executive acts, the foundation of a free society can too easily erode.

That is the powers-of-government perspective—grounded in the Tenth Amendment and the separation-of-powers doctrine. The Ninth Amendment imposes another powerful discipline on federal behavior: In exercising its legitimate powers, the federal government may not do so in a manner that violates our rights. And in determining what rights government may not violate, the Ninth Amendment instructs that we look both to those that are expressly enumerated, such as free speech, and to those that are unenumerated as well, such as the right to privacy.

Many conservatives treat the Ninth Amendment as an "inkblot," to use the memorable term coined by former judge Robert Bork in his 1987 confirmation hearings. He asserted that the amendment should be ignored because no one can determine what it means. It is as if someone had spilled ink on the portion of the amendment that would have identified our unenumerated rights. Bork is silent as to why the same treatment should not be accorded to other imprecise phrases in the Bill of Rights, such as unreasonable searches, probable cause, and due process.

We treat the Ninth Amendment as if it meant something. It refers to our natural rights—those rights that we had "by nature," before government was formed, and still retain. In short, the Ninth Amendment's unenumerated rights include all the rights associated with individual liberty, with two constraints. First, our exercise of such rights must not interfere with the exercise of those same rights by others. Second, we may not act in a manner that imposes obligations on others except their obligation not to use force or fraud against us.

The Ninth Amendment does not encompass "entitlements" or welfare rights, which require others to act for our benefit. Thus, your right to *pursue* happiness is a liberty right, because it imposes no affirmative duty on anyone else. By contrast, if you had a right to *attain* happiness, that would require others to act on your behalf—to make you happy or, at a minimum, to refrain from making you unhappy. That obligation might thereby restrict their own pursuit of happiness.

Entitlements, such as rights to a minimum wage or welfare, are integral to the modern liberal position on the proper role of government. Naturally, the enforcement of such entitlements presupposes government force—usually in the form of higher taxes or more regulations—when the persons who are supposed to bestow the benefits do not do so voluntarily. The result: overarching and coercive government that worms its way into every aspect of our daily lives.

Surprisingly, we are now hearing from today's liberals that big government cannot be trusted—at least not on civil liberties. But where does the left stand on government control over our retirement system, welfare, schools, and the private economy? Why hasn't the left's healthy distrust of government extended to support for privatized Social Security, school choice, and elimination of regulations that control everything from the size of a navel orange to the ergonomics of office furniture? Why can't liberals see past the Defense Department and the Justice Department when they bemoan excessive government?

Oddly enough, those two agencies are the very ones charged with protecting us against domestic and foreign predators—an appropriate job for government. If Congress were to delegate to the Justice Department the power to enact regulations over national security and civil liberties, with no more guidance than "keep us safe from terrorists," people on the left would be justifiably apoplectic. But when that same Congress delegates to the Environmental Protection Agency the power to enact environmental regulations with no more guidance than "keep us safe from pollutants," the left applauds enthusiastically. Could it be that pollutants are a greater risk than terrorists? Or is it more likely that the left's selective indignation reflects the inconsistency of the liberal mind-set on the proper role of government?

In resolving that foundational question—the proper role of government—the Constitution can be viewed through both a powers-of-government prism (the Tenth Amendment) and a rights-of-individuals prism (the Ninth Amendment). We view the powers of government narrowly and the rights of individuals broadly. That, we believe, was precisely the vision of the framers.

PART ONE

EXPANDING GOVERNMENT

CHAPTER 1

Promoting the General Welfare

The Dirty Dozen List: *Helvering v. Davis* (1937)
Dishonorable Mention: *United States v. Butler* (1936)

WHAT IS THE CONSTITUTIONAL ISSUE?

"The Congress shall have Power To lay and collect Taxes, . . . [to] provide for the common Defence and general welfare. . . ."—U.S. Constitution, Article I, Section 8.

If you think that Social Security, Medicare, and other welfare systems are bedrock American institutions without which the United States cannot survive in the modern world, then this will not be your favorite chapter. Indeed, we will be arguing that programs such as Social Security, which collect money from some taxpayers and redistribute the money to other taxpayers, are unconstitutional. It is possible, of course, that those programs are both desirable (a policy judgment) and unconstitutional (a legal judgment). If that's the case, then either the programs have to be amended to comply with the Constitution or the Constitution has to be amended to authorize the program. Instead, our politicians today enthusiastically redistribute our taxes without asking this crucial question: Where in the Constitution is the federal government authorized to rob Peter in order to pay Paul?

Typically, we hear three explanations for the proliferation of unconstitutional redistributive programs: First, whenever government transfers Peter's assets to Paul, it can generally count on Paul's wholehearted approval. And there are so many of those redistributive "deals" that we are all Pauls under one arrangement or another. Moreover, Paul will fight hard for his benefits under a particular scheme, while Peter won't fully appreciate the diffuse costs of multiple schemes, each of which confiscates an inconsequential portion of his total assets.

A second explanation is that a program like Social Security is promoted as a retirement plan, not a redistributive program. Never mind that the Constitution is no more permissive of federal retirement planning than it is of federal redistribution. Proponents correctly foresaw that Social Security would be easier to pitch to the American public if portrayed as personal savings for old age. Each participant, so the story goes, would pay taxes into the system during his working years and then extract the taxes, with interest, to meet post-employment living costs. If only it were true. In fact, however, the employment taxes paid into the system are used immediately to compensate current retirees and fund the federal government's perpetual deficit. In return for the dollars that the government "borrows" from workers, it issues IOUs that are held in a so-called trust fund, which supposedly will cover promised Social Security benefits when each worker retires.

Sadly, down the road when the retirement date arrives, changing demographics will have radically reduced the ratio of workers to retirees. As a result, rather than collecting more in taxes each year than is paid out in benefits, the Social Security system will run a deficit—as early as 2017. That's when we will begin drawing on the IOUs in the trust fund. But to generate the cash required to redeem those IOUs, the federal government must raise taxes, cut other spending, or float new IOUs. The only alternative is to cancel the old IOUs by cutting Social Security benefits. By the way, those are the same four options government would have if there were no trust fund. Thus, the fund itself is an illusory asset for workers.

Moreover, the IOUs in the trust fund will be exhausted by roughly 2040. Social Security will then have to rely solely on revenue from the payroll tax, which will not be sufficient to pay promised benefits. By law, once the fund is exhausted, benefits will automatically be reduced. That means no worker has a *legal right* to reclaim his Social Security contributions—much less any interest thereon—to pay for his retirement.[1] Benefits can be changed, cut, or taken away at any time. Contributions are just a tax, not a personal asset. If Social Security were a true retirement system, each participant would have an enforceable claim on his own account, control how the assets are invested, and be able to bequeath the assets to his heirs. Social Security, by contrast, is a Ponzi scheme that redistributes money from workers to retirees. Like other Ponzi schemes, it works only as long as current participants are willing to rely for their benefits on an ever-increasing flow of money from future participants.

Still, there is a third reason—most important for purposes of this book—that our politicians embrace unconstitutional wealth transfers. In a nutshell, the Supreme Court has said it's okay. That was the holding in *Helvering v. Davis*, the 1937 case that applied the General Welfare Clause to uphold the constitutionality of the Social Security Act.[2]

In *Helvering*, the Court rejected James Madison's advice. He had argued that the General Welfare Clause was not a grant of added power to Congress but simply a convenient shorthand for all the powers enumerated in Article I, section 8, of the Constitution—which were designed, individually and collectively, to "provide for the common Defence and general Welfare." In *Federalist No. 41*, Madison put it this way: "Nothing is more natural nor common than first to use a general phrase, and then to explain and qualify it by a recital of particulars. But the idea of an enumeration of particulars which neither explain nor qualify the general meaning, and can have no other effect than to confound and mislead, is an absurdity."

The Court disagreed. Justice Benjamin Cardozo, in a 7–2 opinion, adopted Alexander Hamilton's opposing view—that the General Welfare Clause was a separate source of congressional authority to "lay and collect Taxes" and then spend the proceeds for purposes including, but not limited to, effecting Congress's enumerated powers. Hence, the Court upheld the Social Security Act—a wealth transfer program nowhere authorized among those powers.

During the ratification debates there were three main perspectives on the power to provide for the general welfare. The most expansive view, which neither Madison nor Hamilton advocated, is that Congress can serve the general welfare in whatever way it pleases—even if no taxes are collected and even if the Constitution contains no other specified authority. Essentially, Congress's powers would be nearly all-inclusive.

The second view, advocated by Hamilton, is that Congress could tax and spend to execute its enumerated powers as well as other powers, provided only that the purpose of the tax is to promote the general (that is, national) welfare, not the narrower (that is, local) welfare of specially favored parties. In practice, however, the first and second views tend to merge. That is because the courts defer to Congress's determination whether a tax serves the "general" welfare and because the execution of Congress's powers will almost always require money and, therefore, taxation.

Only the third, Madisonian, view establishes any meaningful restriction on congressional enactments. Madison insisted that the General Welfare Clause did not empower Congress to do anything beyond those particular authorizations granted in the remainder of Article I, section 8. A broader interpretation, declared Madison, would make a mockery of the notion of limited federal government. If Congress had an independent power to tax for the general welfare, then the enumeration of its other powers, which also provide for the general welfare, would simply be excess verbiage. To the contrary, argued Madison, because the enumerated powers are those that serve the general welfare, the power to provide for the general welfare through taxation is synonymous with the power to tax in order to execute the enumerated powers.

We will revisit the Madison-Hamilton dispute in a moment. The key point is this: Article I, section 8 confers upon Congress certain enumerated powers and, potentially, a more sweeping authority to provide for the general welfare—a goal that is also set forth in the Preamble.[3] For proponents of limited central government, the General Welfare Clause has been a source of great mischief. Interpreted elastically by judges of the "living Constitution" persuasion (see page 217), the clause has helped serve up a gourmand's feast of government programs, regulations, and intrusions that would have been unimaginable to the framers. Regrettably, the Supreme Court has been a willing accomplice.

What Were the Facts?

Madison and Hamilton, coauthors (along with John Jay) of the *Federalist Papers*, had surprisingly divergent views regarding the proper role of the national government. In his 1791 "Report on the Subject of Manufactures," Hamilton proposed the equivalent of a national industrial policy, which would have distributed resources to benefit government-favored enterprises. Toward that end, Hamilton read Congress's general welfare power to encompass "the general interests of learning, of agriculture, of manufactures."[4] At that time each of those "interests" was considered to be outside the scope of Congress's authority to regulate interstate commerce. Three years later, speaking in opposition to an appropriation for relief of French refugees, Madison had a more parsimonious view of the general welfare. He could not "undertake to lay his finger on that article of the Federal Constitution which granted a right to Congress of expending, on objects of benevolence, the money of their [*sic*] constituents."[5]

For a long while Madison's perspective seemed to prevail. In 1796, for example, a relief bill for victims of a Savannah fire was soundly defeated. Virginia's William B. Giles stated bluntly that members of Congress "should not attend to what . . . generosity and humanity required, but what the Constitution and their duty required."[6] In 1828, South Carolina's William Drayton sharply criticized Hamilton's theory that the federal government could tax and spend for the general welfare without constraint by Congress's enumerated powers. He wrote that "if Congress can determine what constitutes the General Welfare and can appropriate money for its advancement, where is the limitation to carrying into execution whatever can be effected by money? How few objects are there which money cannot accomplish! . . . Can it be conceived that the great and wise men who devised our Constitution . . . should have failed so egregiously . . . as to grant a power which rendered restriction upon power practically unavailing?"[7]

Fast-forward six decades to 1887, the centennial of the Constitutional Convention. Texas farmers were suffering from a serious drought, and Congress had appropriated $10,000 for their relief. Not so fast, wrote President Grover Cleveland in his veto message: "I can find no warrant for such an appropriation in the Constitution."[8] And so it went through the Progressive era of the early 1900s when bigger government was the preferred means for addressing social and economic issues. Even during the early years of the New Deal, the Supreme Court held that several of President Franklin D. Roosevelt's economic recovery programs were unconstitutional because Congress had no authority to enact them.[9]

Not until Roosevelt asked Congress for six new Supreme Court positions in an effort to pack the Court with New Deal supporters did the justices adopt the Hamiltonian view of the General Welfare Clause and open the floodgates for the redistributive state. The case that laid the groundwork was *United States v. Butler,* which struck down the Agricultural Adjustment Act (AAA)—a 1933 statute that taxed food processors and then used the proceeds to pay farmers for reducing their production.[10] William H. Butler, a processor, challenged the tax. Even though the Court concluded that the act was unconstitutional (as explained below), six of the justices agreed that "the power of Congress to authorize expenditure of public moneys for public purposes is not limited by the direct grants of legislative power found in the Constitution."[11]

The question whether Congress could spend for public purposes outside the scope of its enumerated powers would not have arisen if *Butler* were decided today. Under the Court's current, far-reaching view of the Commerce Clause (see Chapter 2), the AAA would no doubt qualify as a legitimate congressional regulation of interstate commerce.

But that view had not quite congealed when the New Deal Congress began spending federal money with strings attached. If farmers wanted to receive the benefits of federal largesse under the AAA, they had to curtail production. In effect, Congress attempted to use its taxing power for the ulterior purpose of imposing economic regulations that might not have been sanctioned under the Commerce Clause.

When the Court reviewed that arrangement in *Butler*, it found no federal power to regulate agricultural production. That power was reserved to the states under the Tenth Amendment; and the AAA had "invade[d] the reserved rights of the states."[12] The Court's theory of the Commerce Clause and Tenth Amendment would soon be overruled, but *Butler* is an important case nevertheless.[13] That is because the Court decided in *Butler* that Hamilton was right: The General Welfare Clause allows Congress to tax and spend in pursuit of the general welfare even if its spending does not further an enumerated power. If, for example, the AAA had distributed tax proceeds to farmers without imposing conditions, and Congress had determined that such expenditures served the general welfare, then the AAA would have passed constitutional muster. Only because the AAA had tried to regulate through the back door did the Court find that the Tenth Amendment had been violated.

The Court's position was *not* the all-encompassing notion that Congress could do whatever it wanted in pursuit of the general welfare. Instead, the Court adopted the less far-reaching but still expansive stance that the power to tax and spend could be exercised for purposes beyond the enumerated powers of Article I, section 8, with two limitations: First, if the spending was quasi-regulatory, it would have to be authorized elsewhere in the Constitution. Second, the expenditures would have to promote the "general Welfare." As Justice Owen J. Roberts wrote: "The power to tax and spend is not without constitutional restraints. One restriction is that the purpose must be truly national. Another is that it may not be used to coerce action left to state control."[14]

Thus, *Butler* opened the door to the redistributive state. But it wasn't until the following year, in *Helvering*, that the Court allowed Congress to expropriate money from one group and spend it on another. The AAA in *Butler* was essentially a regulatory scheme; the Social Security

Act in *Helvering* was blatant redistribution. *Helvering* became the true test of the Court's suggestion in *Butler* that the AAA would have been upheld if the tax dollars had been spent simply to relieve farmers—an objective not within the enumerated powers of Congress—without imposing conditions on receipt of the money.

Butler's adoption of the Hamiltonian position on the General Welfare Clause was what lawyers call *dictum*—a statement, remark, or observation that is gratuitous, not essential to support the court's holding, and consequently nonbinding when the same issue arises in a later case. Recall that *Butler* overturned the AAA on Tenth Amendment grounds. Justice Roberts would have reached the same conclusion—that Congress had no power to regulate agriculture—whether he had endorsed Hamilton's or Madison's interpretation of the General Welfare Clause. Because Roberts's pronouncement on that clause was therefore *dictum*, it did not establish binding Supreme Court precedent. *Helvering* did. Not only did *Helvering* adopt the Hamiltonian view as the official rationale for upholding the Social Security Act, but it also affirmed that the Court would defer to Congress in determining what legislative acts served the general welfare. Congress itself would be the monitor of what Congress could do.

The specific question in *Helvering* was whether Titles VIII and II of the Social Security Act violated the Tenth Amendment. Title VIII imposed wage-based taxes on both employers and employees at the same rate. Title II provided for the payment of Old Age Benefits, presumably funded by the proceeds of the two taxes (although neither tax was specifically earmarked for that purpose). The suit was brought by George P. Davis, a shareholder of the Edison Electric Corporation, who asked that the corporation be enjoined from making the payments and payroll deductions required by the statute. Davis sued Guy T. Helvering, the commissioner of Internal Revenue. Writing for a 7–2 majority, Justice Benjamin Cardozo held that Congress was given the power to spend money for the public good under the General Welfare Clause. Hence, the Social Security Act did not violate the Tenth Amendment, which reserves to the states only those powers not delegated to the federal government.

Cardozo went further. First, he pointed out that the concept of the general welfare is fuzzy and not static. "Needs that were narrow or parochial a century ago may be interwoven in our day with the well-being of the Nation. What is critical or urgent changes with the times."[15] Second, Cardozo declared that the Court would allow Congress broad latitude in deciding which legislative acts were sufficiently general to be accommodated under the clause. For all intents and purposes, the Court announced that it would abandon any role in reviewing congressional enactments for compliance with a General Welfare Clause that the Court itself had characterized as imprecise and malleable: "The line must still be drawn between one welfare and another, between particular and general. Where this shall be placed cannot be known through a formula in advance of the event. There is a middle ground, or certainly a penumbra, in which discretion is at large. The discretion, however, is not confided to the courts. The discretion belongs to Congress, unless the choice is clearly wrong, a display of arbitrary power."[16]

Having demanded of Congress only that it not exercise "arbitrary power," Cardozo had no problem concluding that the Social Security Act was not irrational. Congress, he noted, had a reasonable basis for believing that security for the elderly is a national problem that the separate states cannot tackle effectively. State and local governments are lacking in resources; they don't want to place themselves at a competitive disadvantage by imposing higher taxes than their neighbors, and they are reluctant to become a magnet for the needy and dependent who might migrate to high-benefit jurisdictions.

Of course, similar arguments might be advanced for uniform sales, real estate, and state income taxes, not to mention wages, retirement benefits, and a host of other regulations. Ultimately, however, those arguments would not weigh heavily with the Court. "Whether wisdom or unwisdom resides in the scheme of benefits set forth in Title II it is not for us to say," wrote Cardozo. "The answer to such inquiries must come from Congress, not the courts. Our concern here, as often, is with power, not with wisdom."[17]

When courts declare their unwillingness to function as super-legislatures, that's welcome news. Legislating is not the role of the judiciary.

But abdication by the courts in striking down laws that offend the Constitution is quite another matter. By all means the courts should refrain from judging whether a statute is wise. Yet they should scrupulously determine whether a statute exceeds the powers of the federal government as carefully enumerated by the framers. That is not what the Supreme Court did in *Helvering*.

WHERE DID THE COURT GO WRONG?

In *Federalist No. 45*, James Madison, the father of the Constitution, reminded us that "The powers delegated by the proposed Constitution to the federal government are few and defined." Since then the Constitution has changed very little, while the powers of the federal government have exploded, as described by Roger Pilon, a legal scholar at the Cato Institute:

> [G]iven the paucity and character of the federal government's enumerated powers, it is plain that the Framers meant for most of life to be lived in the private sector—beyond the reach of politics, yet under the rule of law—with governments at all levels doing only what they have been authorized to do. Far from authorizing the ubiquitous government planning and programs we have today, the Constitution allows only limited government, dedicated primarily to securing the conditions of liberty that enable people to plan and live their own lives.[18]

What then happened to eviscerate the notion of limited federal power? Much of the harm occurred under the noses and with the encouragement of Roosevelt's New Deal administration. The president himself, in a letter promoting a 1935 bill, wrote to the chairman of the House Ways and Means Committee: "I hope your committee will not permit doubts as to constitutionality, *however reasonable*, to block the suggested legislation."[19] And Rexford Tugwell, a member of the

Roosevelt "Brains Trust," reflected in 1968 on the legislative schemes he had helped promote more than three decades earlier. He called them "tortured interpretations of a document [that is, the Constitution] intended to prevent them."[20]

Still, the politicians could not by themselves have irreparably damaged the Constitution. They needed, and they garnered, the active support of the Supreme Court. Together—the Roosevelt administration, Congress, and the Court—they turned the Constitution on its head. Instead of promoting a federal government possessing only those powers enumerated in the Constitution, the New Dealers promoted a government of nearly boundless powers, limited only by specific prohibitions in the Constitution. Nothing could have been further from the intent of the framers.

During the Roosevelt era, the Supreme Court effectively rewrote the Constitution. Many of the Court's mistakes are catalogued in other chapters of this book. If faced with identifying the worst of those mistakes, we would surely rank the Court's misreading of the General Welfare Clause high on the list. Seventy years have elapsed since *Helvering*, and not once has the Court invalidated an act of Congress because it violated the General Welfare Clause. Yet the federal government has immersed itself in matters ranging from public schools to hurricane relief, drug enforcement, welfare, retirement systems, medical care, family planning, housing, and the arts—not a single one of which can be found among Congress's enumerated powers.

The problem—in this as in many other controversial areas of the law—is that the Supreme Court has misconstrued the text of the Constitution. Nowhere in that document is there an explicit power for Congress to spend money merely to promote the general welfare. Naturally, Congress can spend money; otherwise it could not exercise its unquestioned authority to "establish Post Offices," for example, and "raise and support Armies."[21] Yet to understand the scope of the spending power, it is crucial that we correctly identify its source. Madison and Hamilton both mistakenly argued that the spending power rested within the General Welfare Clause. Yet there is no reference in that clause to spending or expenditures. Article I, section 8 confers a "Power

To lay and collect Taxes . . . [to] provide for the common Defence and general Welfare."

To be sure, the taxes collected are later spent. After all, what would be the purpose of a taxing authority unless the government could spend the proceeds? But taxes cannot be spent on anything and everything. Therein lies the difference in viewpoint between the two framers. Madison's spending power was triggered if and only if the expenditures both promoted the general welfare *and* were undertaken in furtherance of an enumerated power. Hamilton, by contrast, tied Congress's spending power to its taxing power—independent of the other enumerated powers and limited only by the requirement that the underlying taxing and spending serve general (that is, national) and not particular (that is, local) interests.

Suppose for a moment that Hamilton was right—that is, the spending power is implicit in the taxing power. If so, consider two of Congress's other powers: "To borrow Money"[22] and "to dispose of . . . Property belonging to the United States."[23] Each of those powers can result in money proceeds that Congress then spends. But if spending attaches to the taxing power, where does Congress obtain authority to spend borrowed funds or funds derived from the sale of public property? Are there really three implicit spending powers in the Constitution? If so, no one has made that argument.[24]

More important, if limited federal government is anything more than a futile aspiration, Hamilton's view of the General Welfare Clause cannot be correct. Just look at the colossal growth of the federal government since the Supreme Court blessed Hamilton's theory in 1936 and 1937. *Butler* and *Helvering* were "key to the New Deal's expansion of congressional and federal power," wrote law professor Jeffrey Renz. "The ability to effect policy by means of the purse, and to exercise powers beyond those granted to Congress in the Constitution, allowed Congress and the federal government to go where it had never gone before."[25] At least Madison's view, even though not grounded in constitutional text, would have honored the foundational principles of enumerated powers and federalism that were cornerstones of the Constitution.

Of course, that still leaves a few questions unanswered: How should the spending power and the General Welfare Clause be correctly interpreted? If Congress cannot derive its spending authority from the General Welfare Clause—whether or not linking that authority to the other enumerated powers—where does the spending authority come from? And if the purpose of the General Welfare Clause is not to authorize expenditures of tax money, then what is its purpose?

The answers are straightforward: First, the purpose of the General Welfare Clause is no more than to serve as a limitation on the taxing power. Taxes must serve the general welfare, not special interests. Hamilton agreed. His mistake, and the Court's, was to carry that proposition further and assert an independent power to tax and spend untethered to the enumerated powers.

Second, spending authority does not come from the General Welfare Clause but from the Necessary and Proper Clause, the final clause in Article I, section 8. Congress is authorized "To make all Laws which shall be necessary and proper for carrying into Execution the foregoing Powers, and all other Powers vested by this Constitution in the Government of the United States, or in any Department or Officer thereof." Spending is a "necessary and proper" means—an instrumental power—of executing government's other powers. In turn, the power to spend is limited by those other powers.

Put simply, Congress may appropriate and spend money as long as the expenditure is "necessary and proper for carrying into Execution" federal powers. Although the spending power cannot be found within the explicit text of the Constitution, it exists nonetheless. The federal government may spend in furtherance of "the Powers vested by this Constitution"—but not otherwise, even if an expenditure might promote the "general welfare of the United States."

WHAT ARE THE IMPLICATIONS?

Unfortunately, neither *Butler* nor *Helvering* even mentions the Necessary and Proper Clause. Instead, they adopt the Hamiltonian view that Congress may tax and spend for purposes outside the scope of its enumerated powers, provided only that the spending furthers the general welfare. Moreover, said the Court, Congress has nearly total authority to determine, with only minimal judicial review, whether a particular expenditure advances the general welfare. (In effect, the Court gave Congress practically carte blanche over any and all spending.)

Butler offered one saving grace, which would prove to be short-lived: If Congress tried to regulate by imposing conditions on the recipients of its spending, the General Welfare Clause, by itself, would not afford sufficient authorization. That type of quasi-regulatory spending would have to be sanctioned elsewhere in the Constitution. Revealingly, Justice Harlan Fiske Stone objected to even that modest limitation. In his *Butler* dissent, Stone declared that the "limitation is contradictory and destructive of the power to appropriate for the public welfare, and is incapable of practical application. The spending power of Congress is in addition to the legislative power, and not subordinate to it."[26]

Stone then proceeded to point out the "absurd consequences" of the majority opinion:

> The government may give seeds to farmers, but may not condition the gift upon their being planted in places where they are most needed, or even planted at all. The government may give money to the unemployed, but may not ask that those who get it shall give labor in return, or even use it to support their families. It may give money to sufferers from earthquake, fire, tornado, pestilence or flood, but may not impose conditions— health precautions designed to prevent the spread of disease, or induce the movement of population to safer or more sanitary areas. . . . It may spend its money for the suppression of the boll weevil, but may not compensate the farmers for suspending the growth of cotton in the infected areas. . . . It may support rural schools, but may not condition its grant by the requirement that certain standards be maintained.[27]

A half century later, in 1987, Stone's dissent in *Butler* would become official Supreme Court doctrine in *South Dakota v. Dole*.[28] "If the expenditure is for a national public purpose," Stone had written, "that purpose will not be thwarted because payment is on condition which will advance that purpose."[29] In *Dole* the Court agreed and proclaimed that conditional spending, designed to achieve ends admittedly not within Congress's enumerated powers, might still be constitutional. Chief Justice William H. Rehnquist, for a 7–2 majority, adopted a four-part test,[30] building on the Court's holdings in *Butler* and *Helvering*: First, the spending must serve the general welfare, although "courts should defer substantially to the judgment of Congress" in that regard. Second, any conditions imposed on the recipient of funds must be "unambiguous." Third, the conditions must be related to the particular programs being funded. Fourth, the conditions must not violate other constitutional provisions. For example, recipients of grants for public broadcasting could not be required to forgo criticism of the Iraq war.

Only the third part of the Court's test—namely, conditions must be related to the underlying program—had any prospect of restraining federal spending. But that, too, would prove to be an illusory restraint. During the twenty-year period since *Dole*, the Court has not invalidated a single expenditure on the ground that conditions were too detached from the program itself.

Indeed, the facts of *Dole* illustrate just how disconnected the conditions may be without raising constitutional concerns: To receive federal highway funds, states had to adopt a twenty-one-year-old minimum drinking age. Sound unrelated? Not according to the Court. Different drinking ages among the states supposedly created an incentive to drink and drive. Young persons would commute to border states where the drinking age was lower. Congress wanted the roads that it funded to be used safely. Drunken drivers threaten safety. Hence, Congress's goals in paying for highway construction would be compromised unless there was a uniform drinking age. Never mind that many people who drink don't drive when they drink or don't drive at all. Still others—the large majority—drink and drive safely. And, most important, highway safety depends on numerous factors that have nothing to do with the drinking age.

Justices William J. Brennan and Sandra Day O'Connor each dissented in *Dole*. Justice O'Connor's dissent was a pointed reminder of just how pernicious the precedent of *Butler* and *Helvering* had proven to be: "If the spending power is to be limited only by Congress' notion of the general welfare, the reality, given the vast financial resources of the Federal Government, is that the Spending Clause gives power to the Congress to tear down the barriers, to invade the states' jurisdiction, and to become a parliament of the whole people, subject to no restrictions save such as are self-imposed. This, of course, . . . was not the Framers' plan and it is not the meaning of the Spending Clause."[31]

The problem described by O'Connor took nearly 150 years to materialize and another 50 years before the seeds planted by the New Deal Court sprouted in *Dole*. We did not develop an overextended, unconstitutional government overnight. Nor will we be able to restore constitutional government quickly.

The nature and scope of the problem is perhaps best illustrated by our exploding federal program of farm subsidies. Although the Court held in *Butler* that there was no federal power to regulate agricultural production, that notion is now antiquated. Whether the constitutional pedigree for farm supports is the Court's unbounded view of the Commerce Clause (see Chapter 2) or the General Welfare Clause as fleshed out in *Butler*, *Helvering*, and *Dole*, there can be no question that the redistributive state is now in full bloom. Perversely, however, farm programs redistribute the meager resources of the poor to the bulging coffers of the rich.

For starters, artificial restrictions on the supply of farm products raise food prices for more than 100 million American households. That cost falls disproportionately on poor households, which spend a larger share of their income on food. Consider these disturbing facts:[32]

- Higher food prices caused by U.S. farm programs had the effect in 2004 of transferring $16.2 billion—or $146 per household—from American consumers to domestic agricultural producers.[33]

- A General Accounting Office study in 2000 reported that Americans paid more than double the world price for sugar—an extra $1.9 billion—because of U.S.-imposed import quotas.[34]
- U.S. trade policies also drive up domestic prices for milk, cheese, butter, peanuts, cotton, beef, orange juice, canned tuna, and other products.

Those consumer "taxes" are paid over and above the direct taxes that consumers shell out to farmers through the federal budget. The Office of Management and Budget estimated that taxpayers were socked with a $26 billion bill for direct agricultural subsidies in fiscal year 2005.[35] That same year the average income of farm households was $79,965, or 26 percent higher than the $63,344 average for all U.S. households.[36] Even worse, the federal largesse hasn't relieved the plight of smaller farmers. To the contrary, 72 percent of farm subsidies go to the biggest 10 percent of farm businesses—welfare for the fat cats.[37] Among the recipients are millionaire owner David Rockefeller and giant corporations such as Archer Daniels Midland, Tyson Foods, and Texaco.

Part of the problem, writes Roger Pilon, is that too many people now rely on the irresponsible promises that our politicians have made and our courts have condoned. Traditionally self-reliant farmers—to name just one group—have become dependent on government handouts. Yet the Constitution was designed to empower "government in a very limited way. It empowers people—by leaving them free—in every other way." Pilon continues: "Our forefathers gave up only certain of their powers, enumerating them in a written constitution. We have allowed those powers to expand beyond all moral and legal bounds—at the price of our liberty."[38]

Interestingly, Pilon highlights the moral as well as the legal aspect of the problem: "The most important thing to do now is to start restoring a constitutional ethos in the nation."[39] He warns that all branches of government must be involved in that process, not just the courts. But more is required: The people themselves have to be involved. Partly, that will depend on an understanding of the problem, on an awareness of the destructive implications of cases such as *Butler* and *Helvering.* And, partly, Americans will have to revive their traditional respect for liberty, which includes freedom from government in vast areas of their lives. Instead of looking to Washington, D.C., for an ever-expanding assortment of entitlements, we will have to resist the blandishments of our politicians and recognize that dependence on government saps the spirit of America.

CHAPTER 2

Regulating Interstate Commerce

The Dirty Dozen List: *Wickard v. Filburn* (1942)
Dishonorable Mention: *Gonzales v. Raich* (2005)

After reading [a modern Commerce Clause decision], you wonder why anyone would make the mistake of calling it the Commerce Clause instead of the "Hey, you-can-do-whatever-you-feel-like Clause?" —Alex Kozinski, "Introduction to Volume Nineteen," Harvard Journal of Law & Public Policy 19 (1995): 5

What Is the Constitutional Issue?

"The Congress shall have Power . . . To regulate Commerce . . . among the several states. . . ." —U.S. Constitution, Article I, Section 8, Clause 3.

As it was originally conceived, our federal government was one of limited and enumerated powers. These powers—set out in Article I, section 8 of the Constitution in eighteen separate clauses—were the subject of considerable debate among the political luminaries of the

founding generation. Among the Anti-Federalists, who initially opposed ratification of the Constitution, the power to control the militia
was viewed with suspicion, the ability to raise a standing army was
viewed as a tool of outright tyranny, and even the power to establish the
District of Columbia—over which Congress would exercise exclusive
legislative control—was seen as cause for concern. Despite the vehe-
mence of their critique, one clause avoided much of the Anti-Federalists'
wrath: the Commerce Clause.

Third among the eighteen clauses of Article I, section 8, the Commerce Clause provides in full that Congress has the power "To regulate
Commerce with foreign Nations, and among the several States, and
with the Indian tribes." But today, when the "Commerce Clause" is
used, it generally refers only to the power to regulate commerce "among
the several States," the so-called Interstate Commerce Clause.

Although its language and the lack of debate surrounding it suggest
that the Interstate Commerce Clause conveys a modest power, it was
nevertheless intended to serve a vitally important purpose. Following
the Revolution but prior to the adoption of the Constitution, a number
of states had placed restrictions or duties on goods imported from
neighboring states, which, in turn, retaliated with restrictions of their
own. To avoid this balkanization, the Constitution—via the Interstate
Commerce Clause—federalized the issue, allowing the Congress to establish uniform policies for interstate trade. At the Constitutional Convention of 1787, according to Justice William Johnson, "If there was any
one object riding over every other in the adoption of the Constitution,
it was to keep the commercial intercourse among the States free from all
invidious and partial restraints."[1]

Although it served a narrow purpose, the clause was cautiously
crafted—with two significant limitations. First, it was limited to the
regulation of "commerce," which at the time of the founding referred
to the trade of goods rather than their production or manufacture. Second, the Clause applied to commerce occurring "among the several
States"; regulation of purely *intra*state trade was left to the states themselves.

The modesty of the Interstate Commerce Clause was further

reflected in the paucity of case law construing it during the first century of its existence. Few federal laws were passed pursuant to the commerce power, and those cases that did arise concerned actions by *states* that had impermissibly frustrated interstate commerce.[2] Even in the late nineteenth and early twentieth centuries, when Congress began exercising its regulatory power more broadly, the Supreme Court maintained a fairly restrained view of the commerce power. That view prevailed until the mid-1930s when Justice Owen J. Roberts switched sides to support a more expansive view of federal authority, thereby parting company with Justices George Sutherland, Willis Van Devanter, Pierce Butler, and James Clark McReynolds.

Those more conservative justices, known as the Four Horsemen, had opposed much of President Franklin D. Roosevelt's New Deal agenda.[3] Along with Roberts they had maintained a bulwark against the expansion of the Interstate Commerce Clause. In 1937, however, Roberts became the crucial fifth vote in *National Labor Relations Board v. Jones & Laughlin Steel Corp.*, upholding the constitutionality of the National Labor Relations Act against a Commerce Clause challenge.[4]

This shift in judicial interpretation marked the beginning of a sudden rapid expansion of the Interstate Commerce Clause. No longer would the commerce power be limited to the regulation of interstate trade; it would also encompass those things having a substantial effect on trade, such as agriculture, manufacturing, and production intended for interstate sale. This expansion was so great and so rapid that when *Wickard v. Filburn* came before the Court, only five years later, the Court was willing to consider a previously unimaginable question: whether the Interstate Commerce Clause allowed regulation of purely local production of goods—even if *not* intended for interstate commerce—that in the aggregate might have a "substantial effect" on interstate trade.[5]

The constitutional issue in *Wickard* may sound arcane, but its resolution had profound consequences. The power to regulate *all* commerce is broader, of course, than the power to regulate only interstate commerce. And the power to regulate all intrastate activities *substantially affecting* interstate commerce is broader still. Perhaps most important, allowing the government to regulate *noncommercial* activity that does not itself substantially affect interstate commerce but that, taken in the aggregate with other similar activities, *may* substantially affect interstate commerce is a power so broad that it admits almost no limitations.

Once the issue is framed in that manner, it becomes difficult to overstate the constitutional stakes in *Wickard*. An essential principle of our federal system is that the federal government does *not* possess the same general police power as that enjoyed by the states. As Madison described it, "The powers delegated by the . . . Constitution to the federal government are few and defined," while "[t]hose which are to remain in the State governments are numerous and indefinite."[6] While Supreme Court decisions over the preceding five years had already tilted the balance of power away from the states and toward the federal government, *Wickard* threatened to destroy any notion of "balance" whatsoever.

Instead of serving as a shield against interference by the states, the commerce power became a sword wielded by the federal government in pursuit of a boundless array of regulations. And rather than honor the Federalist idea that the states would serve as fifty experimental laboratories, Congress shamelessly distended the Commerce Clause— unleashing it from the operative word *commerce*. The result: a federal government that now assumes dominion over all manner of human conduct. Indeed, if the Commerce Clause applies to anything that somehow affects interstate commerce, then it applies to virtually everything: divorce, child custody, driver's licenses, local zoning, public schools. That may have been the Court's view after *Wickard*, but it wasn't the framers' view.

WHAT WERE THE FACTS?

The Agricultural Adjustment Act of 1938 was one of the many pieces of New Deal legislation aimed at combating the effects of the Great Depression. Among other things, the act was designed to bolster wheat prices, which had dropped sharply as a result of a large national surplus. The act directed the secretary of agriculture to establish for wheat an annual national acreage allotment that would then be apportioned among states, counties, and, eventually, individual farmers. Those farmers who exceeded their allotment were required to pay a penalty, although the penalty could be "postponed or avoided . . . by storing the excess under regulations of the Secretary of Agriculture, or by delivering it up to the Secretary."[7] The reduced supply of wheat was expected to increase the market price, while the penalties would serve as a disincentive to "cheat" the quota system.

Roscoe Filburn operated a small farm in Ohio, producing milk, poultry, and eggs primarily. But he also grew a small amount of wheat, the bulk of which was used on his farm for feed, some of which he and his family consumed, and a small portion of which was sold within the state. The Department of Agriculture, under the direction of Secretary Claude C. Wickard, set Filburn's 1941 wheat allotment at 11.1 acres with a yield of 20.1 bushels per acre.[8] Filburn, however, planted a total of 23 acres and harvested an excess of 239 bushels.[9] At a penalty of 49 cents a bushel, the excess subjected him to a total fine of $117.11.[10]

Filburn challenged the Agricultural Adjustment Act as, among other things, an invalid regulation of interstate commerce. No portion of Filburn's crop was sold in interstate commerce, and the vast majority of it was consumed on his own farm. The act, he argued, was a direct regulation of the production and consumption of wheat and therefore not among the enumerated powers of the Congress. Under the original meaning of the Interstate Commerce Clause, which treated agriculture as distinct from commerce, there could be no question that the act was not a valid regulation of interstate commerce.[11] But the New Deal Court was now packed with seven Roosevelt appointees who had already expanded the commerce power considerably.

Only a year prior to *Wickard*, the Court had held that the Interstate Commerce Clause granted Congress the power to regulate wages and hours of workers engaged in local production if the goods were intended for interstate commerce.[12] That set the stage for the Court's transformation of the Commerce Clause into an instrument of unparalleled and unprecedented federal power.

WHERE DID THE COURT GO WRONG?

Justice Robert H. Jackson, writing for a unanimous Court, begins his analysis by dismissing the historic dichotomy between "commerce" and "production" as "attributable to a few . . . decisions of this Court which *might* be understood" to turn on such a distinction.[13] He continued: "We believe that a review of the course of decision under the Commerce Clause will make plain . . . that questions of the power of Congress are not to be decided by reference to any formula which would give controlling force to nomenclature such as 'production' . . . and foreclose consideration of the actual effects of the activity in question upon interstate commerce."[14]

Jackson's dismissive characterization of the term *production* and his insistence that its actual effects are all that matter foreshadow his willingness to abandon the text of the Constitution. He would have been more candid had he ruled that the power of Congress is not limited by the text and from here on the words written in the Constitution have no commonly understood definition but instead mean whatever we want them to mean. Such a statement would strike the reader as absurd, of course; the very "writtenness" of the Constitution suggests that "nomenclature" should be paramount in its interpretation.[15] The Founders' choice to enumerate the regulation of "commerce" as opposed to "agriculture" or "production" must carry *some* meaning. The New Deal Court, however, was not to be constrained by constitutional text.

Nor would history prove too great a stumbling block in the Court's recreation of the Interstate Commerce Clause. Jackson examined the relevant history, starting with the first Supreme Court case to interpret the clause: *Gibbons v. Ogden*.[16] "At the beginning," Jackson opined, "Chief Justice [John] Marshall described the federal commerce power with a breadth never yet exceeded."[17] A brief study of *Gibbons* reveals that Jackson's claim is a substantial exaggeration of the holding in that case.[18]

Gibbons involved a New York statute granting a steamboat monopoly within state waters. This law conflicted with a federal statute that licensed ships in the coasting trade.[19] The key question before the Court was whether navigation within individual states was interstate commerce. The Court answered that question affirmatively.

Chief Justice Marshall held that commerce "comprehends, and has been always understood to comprehend, navigation within its meaning."[20] But, he added, commerce is "something more" than just "traffic"; it describes "commercial intercourse between nations and parts of nations. . . ."[21] Notably, Marshall did not conclude that navigation was subject to regulation because of its *effect* on commerce, yet that was the extraordinary notion embraced by Justice Jackson in *Wickard*. Rather, Marshall held that navigation fell within the definition of commerce itself. "Interstate commerce" is not merely the passage of goods across state boundaries. Instead, he argued, it is an activity entailing commercial intercourse, components of which may occur within separate states. Congressional power extends to the whole of the activity, even those purely intrastate portions.

To be sure, Marshall's conception of the commerce power was expansive. "It is the power to regulate," he argued; that is, "to prescribe the rule by which commerce is to be governed. This power, like all others vested in Congress, is complete in itself, may be exercised to its utmost extent, and acknowledges no limitations, other than are prescribed in the Constitution."[22] Still, although acknowledging that the power was very broad, Marshall maintained that it was "limited to specified objects"[23] as "prescribed in the Constitution"—namely, commerce with foreign nations, among the several states, and with the Indian tribes.

What these passages reveal, in contrast to Justice Jackson's claim, is that the commerce power under *Gibbons* was constrained by the meaning of the Constitution and could not therefore extend as it did in *Wickard* to noncommerce wholly within a single state without meaningful impact on neighboring states. Jackson's overstatement was strategic; it allowed him to disguise the New Deal's constitutional revolution as a "return to the principles first enunciated by Chief Justice Marshall in *Gibbons v. Ogden*"[24] when that was surely not the case.

Disregarding textual distinctions, Jackson then purported to take an empirical approach: "[E]ven if [Filburn's] activity be local and though it may not be regarded as commerce, it may still, whatever its nature, be reached by Congress if it exerts a substantial economic effect on interstate commerce."[25]

Employing logic that can be described as "lawyerly"—in the worst sense of that term—Jackson reasoned that while Filburn did not sell his wheat in interstate commerce, he did consume wheat on his own farm. Had Filburn not grown that wheat himself, he would have had to purchase it. Even though Filburn's purchase might have an infinitesimally small effect on the interstate wheat market, there may have been many similarly situated farmers. The aggregation of all their purchases might have had a substantial effect on the price of wheat. And the price of wheat had a substantial effect on the interstate wheat trade. Therefore, the power to regulate interstate commerce includes the power to tell Roscoe Filburn how much wheat he could grow on his own farm for his own use.

Significantly, in applying its "empirical" test, the Court made no determinations concerning the number of similarly situated farmers, the estimated effect of their aggregated purchases on the price of wheat, or whether this effect would be "substantial" enough to merit federal regulation. The justices held instead: "[We have] no doubt that *Congress may properly have considered* that wheat consumed on the farm where grown, if wholly outside the scheme of regulation, would have a substantial effect in defeating and obstructing its purpose to stimulate trade therein at increased prices."[26]

In other words, Congress need not have made *actual* findings of a substantial effect on interstate commerce or even *actually* considered the issue. It is sufficient that Congress *may* have done so. Thus, the Court articulated a test that Congress could never fail, because Congress itself would determine whether the test had been satisfied. In Jackson's own words, Filburn's growing of wheat for home consumption "is within the federal power to regulate interstate commerce, if for no better reason than that the commerce clause is what Congress says it is."[27]

This result was not, as Jackson characterized it, a return to first principles. It was an abandonment of those principles. No longer was the far-reaching authority of Congress operative only within the narrow scope of "interstate commerce." Following *Wickard*, Congress wielded all-inclusive authority, period.

WHAT ARE THE IMPLICATIONS?

For more than fifty years following *Wickard*, no law was ever struck down for exceeding Congress's power under the Commerce Clause. The Interstate Commerce Clause became, and remains, the primary source of federal power. Among the many consequences of this shift has been the massive federalization of traditional state functions, particularly in the area of criminal law—absurdly characterized as regulation of interstate commerce. This trend has been so widespread that no one seems sure exactly how many federal criminal laws exist. One recent estimate suggests that there are now more than four thousand federal statutory crimes,[28] covering an unimaginable variety of activities from the most heinous crimes to the misuse of the "Smokey Bear" character or name.[29] The number of federal regulations that may be enforced criminally is even more difficult to quantify, with estimates ranging from ten thousand to three hundred thousand.[30]

This expansion of criminal law is troubling for at least two reasons. First, it risks allowing a single act to be punished twice, because it might violate both state and federal law.[31] Second, federal penalties are frequently much harsher than state law penalties for analogous crimes.[32]

The trend toward expanded federal power continued unabated until 1995 when the Court decided *United States v. Lopez*, which was hailed—and condemned by some—as a revolution in Commerce Clause jurisprudence.[33] For the first time in more than a half century the Supreme Court held that Congress had exceeded the scope of its commerce power. For a brief time it appeared that the Court might finally be willing to stand up against the federalization of traditional areas of state law and impose some limits on the Commerce Clause.

Alfonso Lopez was a twelfth-grade student in San Antonio, Texas, who in 1992 carried a concealed .38-caliber handgun and five bullets to school. After an anonymous tip led to his arrest, Lopez was charged with violating a Texas law prohibiting firearm possession on school premises. The following day, however, the state charges were dropped after federal agents charged Lopez with violating the Gun Free School Zone Act of 1990.

Chief Justice William H. Rehnquist, writing for the Court, held that gun possession on school property, a noneconomic activity, had too remote an effect on interstate commerce to fall within the scope of permissible regulation. The government had argued that gun possession increased gun violence, which in turn harmed the educational environment, which in turn produced less productive citizens, which in turn hurt the national economy. But as Rehnquist noted, "To uphold the Government's contentions here, [the Court] would have to pile inference upon inference in a manner that would bid fair to convert congressional authority under the Commerce Clause to a general police power of the sort retained by the States."[34] This, he refused to do.

Similarly, in *United States v. Morrison*, the Court—again speaking through Chief Justice Rehnquist—invalidated portions of the Violence Against Women Act, which created a federal civil cause of action for victims of gender-motivated violent crimes.[35] The laudable goals motivating the act notwithstanding, the Court reasserted the holding of *Lopez*: The Interstate Commerce Clause did not permit federal regulation of noneconomic activity having only a tenuous and remote relationship to interstate commerce.[36] Both *Lopez* and *Morrison* purported to distinguish rather than overrule *Wickard* on the grounds that *Wickard* involved "economic" activity. Before long, however, even that made-up distinction evaporated. In 2005 the Court handed down its decision in *Gonzales v. Raich*,[37] arguably obliterating what little progress *Lopez* and *Morrison* represented.

In *Raich* the Court upheld the application of the federal Controlled Substances Act (CSA) by Attorney General Alberto R. Gonzales against two women growing and using medical marijuana under a doctor's prescription pursuant to California's Compassionate Use Act. Relying heavily on *Wickard*, Justice John Paul Stevens wrote: "In *Wickard*, we had no difficulty concluding that Congress had a rational basis for believing that, when viewed in the aggregate, leaving home-consumed wheat outside the regulatory scheme would have a substantial influence on price and market conditions. Here, too, Congress had a rational basis for concluding that leaving home-consumed marijuana outside federal control would similarly affect price and market conditions."[38]

Justice Sandra Day O'Connor, dissenting vigorously, warned about the obvious consequences when the Court defers to unsubstantiated legislative assumptions. First, she recalled the role of states as experimental laboratories and then noted that the majority opinion "extinguishes that experiment, without any proof that the personal cultivation, possession, and use of marijuana for medicinal purposes, if economic activity in the first place, has a substantial effect on interstate commerce and is therefore an appropriate subject of federal regulation."[39] O'Connor's conclusion was remarkable for its starkness: "If the Court always defers to Congress as it does today, little may be left to the notion of enumerated powers."[40]

One commentator noted the inherently illogical nature of the Court's rationale. "[B]y growing and using their own marijuana they are actually advancing the federal scheme by not participating in the illegal interstate drug trade. Even if we aggregate the marijuana growing/consumption activity of all medical marijuana users, we see only a diminution of demand for the illegal interstate product."[41] Thus, in at least one respect, *Raich*'s reliance on *Wickard* was a sham. In both cases the Court claimed that home-grown products had a substantial effect on interstate commerce. Yet the effect in *Raich* is opposite what it was in *Wickard*. According to the *Wickard* Court, if intrastate home-grown wheat had been allowed, the federal regulatory scheme (price controls) would have been frustrated. But in *Raich*, if intrastate home-grown marijuana had been allowed, the federal regulatory scheme (interstate prohibition) would have been advanced.

In the aftermath of *Raich*, it is difficult to know what congressional action, if any, could ever exceed the scope of the Interstate Commerce Clause. As Justice Clarence Thomas noted in dissent: "Respondents Diane Monson and Angel Raich use marijuana that has never been bought or sold, that has never crossed state lines, and that has had no demonstrable effect on the national market for marijuana. If Congress can regulate this under the Commerce Clause, then it can regulate virtually anything—and the Federal Government is no longer one of limited and enumerated powers."[42]

"If the majority is to be taken seriously," Thomas continued, "the Federal Government may now regulate quilting bees, clothes drives, and potluck suppers throughout the 50 States."[43]

Thomas's insightful observation echoes statements he made in both *Lopez* and *Morrison*. Indeed, Justice Thomas is the only member of the Court who has consistently and persuasively argued for a reevaluation of *Wickard*. Only Thomas seems to recognize that once the scope of the Commerce Clause is extended beyond *actual* commerce, only two alternatives are possible: Either Congress possesses unlimited power to legislate in all cases or Congress is limited by a standard so rootless and malleable that the constitutionality of any given regulation becomes a matter of the arbitrary preferences of the judiciary.

One may wonder why, after all this time, it is worth overturning precedent as old as *Wickard* and restoring an "old-fashioned" view of federal power. That might be a weighty argument if Thomas's call to revisit *Wickard* were based merely on a sense of tradition or nostalgia. Of course, there is a more fundamental value to interpreting the Constitution as it was originally conceived. Its provisions were designed to safeguard against the inherent flaws in both government and men. As Madison noted:

> If men were angels, no government would be necessary. If angels were to govern men, neither external nor internal controls on government would be necessary. In framing a government which is to be administered by men over men, the great difficulty lies in this: you must first enable the government to control the governed; and in the next place oblige it to control itself. A dependence on the people is, no doubt, the primary control on the government; but experience has taught mankind the necessity of auxiliary precautions.[44]

Our federal system of limited and enumerated congressional powers was one of the "auxiliary precautions" adopted by the Founders. Another was our separation of powers scheme, which charges the judiciary with enforcing the limits of Congress's power whether Congress acts for good or for ill.

It is often protested that we live in a different world today than we did at the time of the founding. We are vastly interconnected; commerce and communication have expanded, and so, too, must the power to regulate interstate commerce. This argument is tempting. We *do* live in a world with substantially more interstate commerce than existed at the time of the founding, but no matter how interconnected our society becomes or how much more commerce we enjoy today, the essence of "commerce" itself remains unchanged. Since before the founding intrastate agriculture and manufacturing had a substantial effect on interstate commerce. The passage of time has resulted in more of those activities, but it has not converted the growing of wheat or marijuana—or anything else—into trade. Even in our modern era, "[c]ommerce succeeds to manufacture, and is not a part of it."[45] A reversal of *Wickard* is not a return to "formalism"; it is a return to constitutionalism and to proper limits on federal authority.

CHAPTER 3

Rescinding Private Contracts

The Dirty Dozen List: *Home Building & Loan Association v. Blaisdell* (1934)
Dishonorable Mention: *Gold Clause Cases* (1935)

WHAT IS THE CONSTITUTIONAL ISSUE?

"No State shall . . . pass any . . . Law impairing the Obligation of Contracts. . . ."— U.S. Constitution, Article I, Section 10.

It must have been nice to own a 143,000-square-foot office building on a prime downtown corner in a major U.S. city, fully leased long-term to a large insurance company. There was only one hitch. By law no rent increases were allowed for six decades—from 1933, shortly after the building was erected, until 1993, when the owner was finally able to obtain legislative relief. During that sixty-year period, the lessee paid a mere $23,000 in annual rent—about 20 *cents* per rentable square foot, compared to 1993 market rates of roughly $14 per square foot.

Here is how it happened: Property owner John Trostel constructed the fourteen-story building in Des Moines, Iowa, in 1931 and then leased it out for $23,000 annually plus the usual leasehold expenses.

Instead of a cost-of-living escalator, Trostel protected himself against inflation with a gold clause—a common provision at the time—that gave the lessor an option to demand payment in gold rather than dollars. Big mistake. Trostel never figured that two years later, in 1933, President Franklin D. Roosevelt and his New Deal Congress would abrogate all gold clauses, ostensibly to maintain government reserves of the metal during the economic emergency of the Great Depression.

The government might have provided that assets other than gold could be substituted as a medium of payment. Instead, the president and his fellow New Dealers wiped out existing lease provisions and gutted the rights of property owners as if they never existed. Lessors such as Trostel were not permitted to replace their gold clauses with different escalators; they were not allowed to renegotiate their leases; they received no compensation for the diminished value of their property.

Incredible? Perhaps so. But in 1935 a bitterly divided Supreme Court upheld Congress's 1933 resolution in three companion cases that became known as the *Gold Clause Cases*.[1] Chief Justice Charles Evans Hughes wrote the majority opinion in each case, over dissents by the so-called Four Horsemen: Justices George Sutherland, James Clark McReynolds, Willis Van Devanter, and Pierce Butler.

The lead case was *Norman v. Baltimore & Ohio Railroad Co.*, in which the chief justice applied his expansive vision of judicial supremacy: "We are under a Constitution, but the Constitution is what the judges say it is. . . ."[2] Hughes concluded that Congress could override private contracts to the extent necessary to regulate the value of money—a federal power expressly enumerated in the Constitution. That rationale assumes, incorrectly, that Congress's only constraint is to act within its enumerated powers. More precisely, the federal government, even when performing one of its enumerated functions, may not do so in a manner that violates rights—enumerated and unenumerated alike—secured by the Bill of Rights and other constitutional provisions.

When Congress abrogates contracts and confiscates property—even if purportedly executing an enumerated power—"this is Nero at his worst. The Constitution is gone." Those were the trenchant words spoken extemporaneously when Justice McReynolds read his dissent in the *Gold Clause Cases* from the bench. Furthermore, he wrote: "The gold clauses in no substantial way interfered with the power of coining money or regulating its value or providing an uniform currency. Their existence, as with many other circumstances, might have circumscribed the effect of the intended depreciation and disclosed the unwisdom of it. But they did not prevent the exercise of any granted power."[3]

That dissenting perspective provided little solace to John Trostel in 1935 or to his granddaughter, Anne Trostel Galbraith, who controlled the property in 1993. For six decades she and her family had leased the fourteen-floor building, receiving no more than $23,000 in rent each year. Even if the family had attempted to unload the building, prospective buyers—knowing that the rent was frozen at Depression-era levels—would never have paid what the property was worth.

Finally, in 1993, Mrs. Galbraith was able to take advantage of legislation that revived gold clauses, passed by an insightful Congress, shrewdly aware that the Great Depression had ended decades earlier. Meanwhile, the price of gold had multiplied nearly twenty times so that the lessee, an affiliate of insurance giant Conseco Inc., owed not $23,000 annually but roughly $460,000. Not to worry. In the interim, the insurance company had sublet a large part of the space. At market rates, about $12 to $16 per square foot, the building was capable of generating $1.4 to $1.8 million in annual lease fees. Even after subtracting its expenses and the $460,000 owed to Mrs. Galbraith, Conseco made a sizable profit on the deal.

Of course, there's a broader question here that transcends the financial losses of the Trostel family and the windfall to Conseco. How could Congress, without violating the Constitution, have retroactively changed the law in effect when the original building lease was negotiated?[4] According to the Contracts Clause in Article I, section 10 of the Constitution, state legislatures are not allowed to pass any law "impairing the Obligation of Contracts." The federal government is similarly constrained by other constitutional provisions.[5] Yet the New Deal Congress paid no attention to that constraint when it rescinded all gold clauses.

In the process, Congress flouted three of the central premises underlying the ban on impairment of contracts.[6]

First, the principle of private autonomy: Respect for the rights of each individual means that all persons must be at liberty to dispose of their property and their labor as they wish. By allowing people to order their affairs through contract without government intervention, the Constitution fosters individual self-determination. When government abrogates private contracts, it intrudes upon personal liberty. That is why the framers crafted the Contracts Clause: to promote personal liberty by grounding economic transactions on the right of free exchange, insulated from legislative pressures and the impulses of temporal majorities.

Second, the rule-of-law ideal: Government must announce its rules in advance, avoid applying the rules retroactively, and ensure equal treatment under the law. As a result, individuals will be able to predict with fair certainty how each rule will be implemented and plan their affairs accordingly. If existing contracts are altered by government edict, planning by private actors will be undermined. If rules are applied selectively or discriminatorily, the potential for abuse is obvious: Legislators will be tempted to use the coercive power of government to advance the interests of those with political muscle or exact retribution against unpopular groups.

Third, the separation-of-powers principle: The Contracts Clause was designed, in part, as a check against concentrated government power. Under our system of government, the legislature's task is to address broad political issues prospectively, not to examine in specific cases whether the laws have been properly applied and obeyed. The judiciary's function is to review individual cases after the fact but not to design prospective rules that address questions of policy. In that sense, the Contracts Clause prevents the legislature from assuming the institutional role of the courts—reserving to the judiciary the job of resolving individual contractual disputes.

None of those safeguards worked very well for John Trostel and his family. In 1933, President Roosevelt and the Congress ignored the Constitution. Two years later the Supreme Court—supposedly our final bulwark against the abuse of legislative and executive power—gave its stamp of approval. But the Court's 1935 decision in the *Gold Clause*

Cases wouldn't be the last time that the judiciary sanctioned the retroactive revision of private contracts. Indeed, since the New Deal, the Supreme Court has denied virtually every Contracts Clause claim presented to it.[7] For the root of the problem, however, we must go back to 1934, one year prior to the *Gold Clause Cases*. That is when the Court decided *Home Building & Loan Association v. Blaisdell*, the case that set the stage for the *Gold Clause Cases* and much of the mischief that followed.[8]

Blaisdell, like the *Gold Clause Cases*, was a 5–4 opinion authored by Chief Justice Hughes, with the Four Horsemen dissenting vigorously. The legislation at issue was the 1933 Minnesota Mortgage Moratorium Law. Mindful of the problems facing farmers during the Great Depression, the Minnesota legislature had authorized a state court to exempt property from foreclosure even though the debtor had defaulted on his contractual mortgage obligations. In *Blaisdell* the U.S. Supreme Court condoned Minnesota's misbehavior. That appalling decision was not only a harbinger of the following year's *Gold Clause Cases* but, more important, a near obliteration of the Contracts Clause.

The resultant moral and legal dilemma had been crystallized pithily by Marcus Tullius Cicero nearly two thousand years earlier. What is the meaning, Cicero had asked, of an "abolition of debts, except that you buy a farm with my money; that you have the farm, and I have not my money"?[9]

What Were the Facts?

In the aftermath of the Revolutionary War, many Americans found themselves destitute.[10] Creditors argued, however, that fairness and sound economics demanded full compliance with contractual obligations. Individual distress should be alleviated primarily by hard work and frugality, not by relaxing the law or sacrificing the rights of others. Still, there was a contrary sentiment that advocated sympathetic treatment of debtors, acknowledging their plight and relieving them of burdensome—albeit freely negotiated—contractual commitments. That more "compassionate" perspective yielded numerous state laws that suspended debt collections and delayed legal proceedings. Predictably, such laws had unintended consequences: a loss of confidence in government, diminished trust in the good faith of contracting parties, and a reluctance to extend credit.

The problems were exacerbated in 1786 and 1787 by Shays' Rebellion, an armed uprising in western Massachusetts led by Daniel Shays. The rebels, mostly small farmers, were subject to prison and property confiscation for not paying debts and taxes. In an abortive attempt to avoid mortgage foreclosures, the farmers forcibly tried to prevent local courts from sitting.

Here is how Chief Justice John Marshall characterized the situation that prevailed in 1787 under the Articles of Confederation: "The power of changing the relative situation of debtor and creditor, of interfering with contracts . . . had been used to such an excess by the State legislatures, as to break in upon the ordinary intercourse of society, and de-stroy all confidence between man and man. The mischief had become so great, so alarming, as not only to impair commercial intercourse, and threaten the existence of credit, but to sap the morals of the people, and destroy the sanctity of private faith."[11]

Debt relief laws had frustrated transactions across state borders, the states were engaged in economic warfare with one another, and the Articles of Confederation did not permit the national government to assert its authority over interstate commerce. To resolve those difficulties, the framers assembled for a Constitutional Convention in 1787. One of the urgent tasks at that convention was to craft a list of prohibitions concerning the role of the states in economic and monetary affairs. The end product was, in part, Article I, section 10 of the Constitution, which included a ban on state interference with contracts.

Rufus King of Massachusetts had proposed the ban, relying on a key provision of the recently adopted Northwest Ordinance: "[I]n the just preservation of rights and property, it is understood and declared, that no law ought ever to be made or have force in the said territory, that shall, in any manner whatever, interfere with or affect private contracts, or engagements, *bona fide,* and without fraud previously formed."

Later, during the ratification debates, James Madison stated in *Federalist No. 44* that "laws impairing the obligation of contracts are contrary to the first principles of the social compact, and to every principle of sound legislation." He noted that one such "legislative interference is but the first link of a long chain of repetitions, every subsequent interference being naturally produced by the effects of the preceding laws." For that reason, he concluded, the Contracts Clause was necessary to "banish speculations on public measures, inspire a general prudence and industry, and give a regular course to the business of society."

Once the Constitution took effect, the Supreme Court was called upon to flesh out the skeletal terms of the clause.[12] Even though the main goal of the framers had been to prohibit state impairment of *private* contracts, the text of the clause did not distinguish private from public. And the early cases to come before the Court dealt with grants and contracts made by the states themselves. The first major case was *Fletcher v. Peck*,[13] in which Chief Justice John Marshall invoked the clause to prevent Georgia from rescinding land grants. Two years later, in a 7–0 opinion, Marshall blocked New Jersey from repealing a land tax exemption.[14] Then, in the famous Dartmouth College case, the Court would not allow New Hampshire to expand Dartmouth's board of trustees.[15] The college's charter, wrote Marshall, was a contract that gave exclusive power to the trustees, not the governor or the legislature, to fill board vacancies.

In a variety of subsequent cases stretching over more than a century, the Court more fully developed its Contracts Clause jurisprudence and established a couple of key principles:

First, the clause applies to *existing* contracts and does not prevent states from barring future contracts.[16] Private parties do not therefore have an enforceable right to transact for all purposes at all times without restraint. The framers did not intend that Article I, section 10 of the Constitution would institute a general "freedom of contract."[17] Instead, they meant to ban government interference with settled contracts that conformed to laws prevailing at the time the bargain was struck.

Second, the Contracts Clause does not override "the [police] power of the state to establish all regulations that are reasonably necessary to secure the health, safety, good order, comfort, or general welfare of the community."[18] Thus, said the Court, a private company chartered by the state to operate a lottery has no redress under the Contracts Clause if the state later outlaws lotteries.[19] That notion seems straightforward, yet it presumes that the state's police power extends to regulating activities such as lotteries that are privately negotiated by consenting adults and do not visit harm on innocent bystanders.

Few would object if a state, acting under a police power exception to the Contracts Clause, annuls a contract to pollute or to bribe that might injure nonconsenting third parties. But the more complex problem, described by University of Chicago law professor Richard A. Epstein, is that "the New Deal constitutional transformation . . . greatly expanded the scope of the police power beyond these broadly libertarian objectives, so that it was no longer possible to distinguish between general welfare and special interests."[20]

Blaisdell demonstrates Professor Epstein's point. It "greatly expanded the scope of the police power" and condoned legislation designed explicitly to protect a special interest group—property owners who had defaulted on their mortgages—at the expense of creditors who had provided the capital and who were surely not to blame for the economic conditions that led to default.

Mr. and Mrs. John Blaisdell had obtained a $3,800 loan from Home Building & Loan. To secure payment they agreed to a mortgage on their land, a fourteen-room house, and garage. When the Blaisdells defaulted, Home Building put the property up for sale and then bought the property for itself at a price equal to the amount of the remaining mortgage debt—all of which was in strict compliance with the mortgage contract. Under Minnesota law in effect when the contract was negotiated and when the property was sold, Home Building would have become the owner, entitled to sole possession.

Enter the Minnesota legislature. It declared that an economic emergency existed and exempted property from foreclosure even if a debtor defaulted on his mortgage. As applied to the Blaisdells, the statute authorized a state court to delay transfer of title for two years during which the Blaisdells were to pay Home Building $40 per month (an amount later set by the court). The payment was to cover a "just and equitable" portion of the property's rental value over the grace period. Meanwhile, the Blaisdells were permitted to occupy the house and, if they paid the requisite $40 each month, resume their original mortgage at the end of the two-year period. In other words, for two years the statute wiped out the right of the creditor, Home Building, to enjoy ownership of the property and the associated right to occupy, sell, or otherwise dispose of it. Instead, Home Building remained at risk, still subject to default by the Blaisdells and exposed to declining property values as the Great Depression unfolded.

The Court had little sympathy for Home Building. As Chief Justice Hughes explained: "Official reports" showed that lenders "are predominantly corporations, such as insurance companies, banks, and investment and mortgage companies. [They] are not seeking homes or the opportunity to engage in farming. Their chief concern is the reasonable protection of their investment security."[21] There you have it, a new hierarchy of rights based on class and found nowhere in the Constitution: Corporate shareholders and employees are second-class citizens whose rights can be sacrificed to protect homeowners and farmers.

Where Did the Court Go Wrong?

In a biting dissent, Justice Sutherland minced no words and wasted no time, ripping into the majority opinion in his opening paragraph.[22] First, he affirmed the importance of the *Blaisdell* decision: "Few questions of greater moment . . . have been submitted for judicial inquiry during this generation." Next he rebuked the majority for condoning "ever-advancing encroachments upon the sanctity of private and public contracts." Then he forecast even worse repercussions: "The effect of the Minnesota legislation, though serious enough in itself, is of trivial significance compared with the far more serious and dangerous inroads upon the limitations of the Constitution which are almost certain to ensue. . . ."

After that blunt introduction, Sutherland proceeded to demolish the principal rationale—economic emergency—for the Court's novel interpretation of the Contracts Clause. Although the text of the clause, plain on its face, announced that "No State shall . . . pass any . . . Law impairing the Obligation of Contracts," Chief Justice Hughes had found that financial hardships associated with the Great Depression allowed Minnesota to do exactly what the Constitution forbids. "Emergency does not create power," Hughes conceded, but "emergency may furnish the occasion for the exercise of power. Although an emergency may not call into life a power which has never lived, nevertheless emergency may afford a reason for the exertion of a living power already enjoyed."[23] Sutherland dismissed that notion as mumbo-jumbo:

> I can only interpret what is said on that subject as meaning that, while an emergency does not diminish a restriction upon [government] power, it furnishes an occasion for diminishing it, and this, it seems to me, is merely to say the same thing by the use of another set of words, with the effect of affirming that which has just been denied.
>
> . . .
>
> [T]he difficulty is that the contract impairment clause forbids state action under any circumstances, if it has the effect of impairing the obligation of contracts. That clause restricts every state power in the particular specified, no matter what may be the occasion. It does not contemplate that an emergency shall furnish an occasion for softening the restriction or making it any the less a restriction. . . . [24]

The suggestion that emergencies somehow discharge politicians from complying with the text of the Constitution was not new, of course. Seven decades prior to *Blaisdell* the Supreme Court had considered that same argument in the context of restrictions on civil liberties during the Civil War. Justice David Davis gave short shrift to the "emergency" excuse: "The Constitution of the United States is a law for rulers and people, equally in war and in peace, and covers with the shield of its protection all classes of men, at all times, and under all circumstances. No doctrine, involving more pernicious consequences, was ever invented by the wit of man than that any of its provisions can be suspended during any of the great exigencies of government."[25]

After quoting the Davis opinion, Sutherland reminded his colleagues that constitutions can be amended but not changed by events alone. No department of the government may "change a constitution, or declare it changed, simply because it appears ill-adapted to a new state of things."[26] Furthermore, observed Sutherland, the Contracts Clause specifically dealt with exigent circumstances. It was framed and adopted during the post-Revolutionary era for the express purpose of preventing legislation designed to relieve debtors in time of financial distress. The meaning of such a constitutional provision, he added, "is fixed when it is adopted, and it is not different at any subsequent time when a court has occasion to pass on it."[27]

Then, to hammer the point home, Sutherland reiterated:

> A provision of the Constitution . . . does not admit of two distinctly opposite interpretations. It does not mean one thing at one time and an entirely different thing at another time. If the contract impairment clause, when framed and adopted, meant that the terms of a contract for the payment of money could not be altered *in invitum* [against the will of the other party] by a state statute enacted for the relief of hardly pressed debtors . . . it is but to state the obvious to say that it means the same now.[28]

Next, Sutherland assailed the Court's second key argument: that an "essential attribut[e] of sovereign power" is to "safeguard the vital interests of its people" and, therefore, the reservation of that power could be "read into contracts . . . to secure the peace and good order of society."[29] According to the majority opinion, the Blaisdells' financial plight affected "fundamental interests of the State. . . . [T]he question is no longer merely that of one party to a contract as against another, but of the use of reasonable means to safeguard the economic structure upon which the good of all depends."[30] The Minnesota legislature could not permit private parties to "bargain away the public health or the public morals," said the Court.[31]

Sutherland agreed in principle, but he distinguished debt relief from other "police power" functions. Yes, the state could bar the "sale or manufacture of intoxicating liquors," said Sutherland, or prevent private parties from creating harmful nuisances.[32] But debt relief is different. The loan to the Blaisdells was legal when made, and such loans continued to be legal after enactment of the Minnesota Mortgage Moratorium Law. Unlike bootleg liquor and harmful nuisances, mortgage loans were encouraged by the state for the benefit of homeowners and farmers. Minnesota's policy was to promote mortgages, and fulfillment of mortgage contracts entailed no illegal act by either creditor or debtor. The "contract was lawful when made, and it has never been anything else," Sutherland emphasized.[33] What the Minnesota legislature had done, however, was to enable one party, at the expense of the other, to prevent enforcement of an obligation that remained "lawful and possible of performance after the passage of the statute as it was before."[34]

Finally, Sutherland tackled the Court's third rationale: that any restrictions imposed on debtors by the Minnesota moratorium were "reasonable and appropriate" to satisfy a legitimate state purpose.[35] After all, the majority argued, the Blaisdells' mortgage still had to be paid at some point in time; only the remedy for nonpayment had been altered, by extending the time frame. And, meanwhile, the Blaisdells would have to reimburse the bank for the rental value of the property.[36]

Sutherland was unimpressed. Although he acknowledged that the state can alter remedies without impairing the essential obligation of contracts, Sutherland denied that Minnesota's legislature had dealt only with remedies. Instead, the Minnesota statute materially delayed enforcement of the debtor's contractual right of ownership and possession. That change "destroy[ed], for the period of delay, *all* remedy so far as the enforcement of that right is concerned."[37] Besides, said Sutherland, if a contract is impaired, as was the Blaisdell contract, then "it is immaterial whether it is done by acting on the remedy or directly on the contract itself. In either case, it is prohibited by the Constitution."[38] "The phrase, 'obligation of contract,' in the constitutional sense, imports a legal duty to perform the specified obligation of *that* contract, not to substitute and perform, against the will of one of the parties, a different . . . obligation."[39]

As for the payment of rental value, Sutherland dismissed its significance:

> How can such payment be regarded, in any sense, as compensation for the postponement of the contract right? The ownership of the property to which petitioner was entitled carried with it not only the right to occupy or sell it, but, ownership being retained, the right to the rental value as well. So that, in the last analysis, petitioner simply is allowed to retain a part of what is its own as compensation for surrendering the remainder. Moreover, it cannot be foreseen what will happen to the property during that long period of time. The buildings may deteriorate in quality; the value of the property may fall to a sum far below the purchase price; the financial needs of appellant may become so pressing as to render it urgently necessary that the property shall be sold for whatever it may bring.[40]

The Minnesota Mortgage Moratorium Law was not merely remedial, nor did it qualify as a "reasonable" impairment of contract even if such an exception existed in the Constitution, which it does not. Nor did the state's police power extend to altering the terms of preexisting credit arrangements that the state continued to endorse as a matter of public policy. Nor could the Contracts Clause, crafted specifically to address a financial crisis, be set aside whenever a new crisis surfaced. Justice Sutherland put the matter succinctly: "If the provisions of the Constitution be not upheld when they pinch, as well as when they comfort, they may as well be abandoned."[41]

WHAT ARE THE IMPLICATIONS?

After *Blaisdell*, the Supreme Court bent over backwards to validate statutes even though they impaired the obligation of contracts. The original requirements of *Blaisdell*—a temporary emergency that could be alleviated by reasonable regulation consistent with a state's exercise of its police power—gave way to relaxed standards that granted yet more deference to state legislatures. A 1983 case, *Energy Reserves Group, Inc. v. Kansas Power & Light Co.*, summarized the modified rules.[42]

First, the Court determines whether a state law operates as a "substantial" impairment of a contract. The criteria for making that determination are unclear, but a regulation that eliminates "unforeseen windfall profits" will not automatically be invalidated. Apparently, laws that limit parties to realizing their original contract expectations will be upheld even if one of the parties, in accordance with the agreement, is entitled to greater benefits. Moreover, if the signatories operate within a heavily regulated industry, they should anticipate that courts will be especially reluctant to override legislative alterations of a commercial contract.

Second, assuming that "substantial" impairment were established, the state could nonetheless defend its regulation by showing that it had a "significant and legitimate public purpose," such as targeting "a broad and general social or economic problem." Notably, the "problem" no longer had to qualify as an emergency. Indeed, in *Kansas Power* the statute upheld by the Court simply capped price increases under a natural gas supply contract. What had been touted as a dire national crisis in *Blaisdell* became a mere economic hardship in *Kansas Power*.

Third, as in *Blaisdell*, the Court will overturn state-imposed adjustments to the rights and responsibilities of contracting parties only if those adjustments are "unreasonable" when related to the purpose of the legislation. And because the judiciary traditionally rubber-stamps legislative judgments when reviewing commercial and economic regulations, the question whether a particular measure is reasonable in light of its presumed goals will rarely if ever be scrutinized.

That's where the Court stood in 1983, and that's where it stands today. Consider, for example, the insurance industry in south Florida.[43] In August 1992, Hurricane Andrew ripped through the Sunshine State wreaking havoc on an unprecedented scale. With winds up to 180 miles per hour, Andrew destroyed more than sixty thousand homes and left 250,000 people homeless. Property damage was estimated at $16 billion to $18 billion—at the time the costliest natural disaster in U.S. history. After decades of relatively little hurricane activity, the residents of south Florida had become somewhat complacent. So, too, had state and local government officials who had overlooked or ignored significant violations of the building codes.

Property and casualty insurance companies in the state were hit with huge and unanticipated claims. To make matters worse, the insurers had taken advantage of the building boom in south Florida and had written millions of dollars in policies, which in retrospect were priced inadequately to cover losses such as those caused by Andrew. In fact, payouts for the hurricane were nearly twice the amount of premiums that had been collected over the previous twenty years. The upshot: Andrew bankrupted ten of the state's insurers.

Predictably, the companies that survived used their experience from Hurricane Andrew as a model in reassessing their risk exposure in the coastal regions of south Florida. To protect shareholders and remaining policyholders from another catastrophe, large and small insurers alike developed plans calling for substantial cancellations or nonrenewals of existing policies. A few of the hardest-hit companies proposed to withdraw from the state's residential property and casualty market altogether.

Not so fast, said Governor Lawton Chiles and the state legislature. Together they enacted a moratorium statute that barred for six months the cancellation or nonrenewal of any homeowner's insurance policy because of hurricane risk. If an insurer wanted to protect its depleted coffers from the risk of ruinous losses due to another storm like Andrew, tough luck. Never mind that the terms of existing policies, reinforced by laws in effect when those policies were negotiated, allowed for both cancellation and nonrenewal.

A federal appellate court decided the issue in 1998. Based on *Blais-*

dell and related cases, the court dismissed a Contracts Clause challenge by Vesta Fire Insurance: "[T]he statute's impact on existing insurance contracts cannot be said to be an unconstitutional impairment."[44]

Seven years later and nearly one thousand miles westward, the insurance industry suffered another hurricane-related blow even more destructive than Andrew. In August 2005, Hurricane Katrina devastated large parts of Louisiana, Mississippi, and Alabama. In New Orleans, where the levees failed, floodwaters swamped much of the city. A staggering number of homes and businesses were destroyed or severely damaged. Hundreds of thousands of residents were displaced from storm-battered areas.

Less than a month later Hurricane Rita struck southwestern Louisiana, again inundating coastal communities, leveling buildings, breaching levees, and driving residents from their homes. Some losses were not insured, but covered losses from the two storms were estimated to exceed $60 billion.[45] Naturally, the insurance companies were obligated to pay proven claims. In accordance with Louisiana law, insurance contracts had to afford at least twelve months to submit such claims. That wasn't good enough for Governor Kathleen Blanco and the Louisiana legislature, even though it had been part of the bargain between insurers and policyholders when they signed their contracts.

A new, retroactive statute, instigated by the governor and passed by the legislature, extended the minimum period within which Louisianans could file to recover losses from Katrina and Rita. The effect was to double the time frame—to two years instead of one—in return for which the insurance companies received absolutely nothing. Sensibly, the insurers argued that the state was unconstitutionally impairing an obligation of their contracts. But that argument—unassailable to those of us who revere the text of the Constitution—did not convince the Louisiana Supreme Court. Again, citing *Blaisdell* and the cases that it spawned, the court held that "the measures taken by the legislature . . . are both appropriate and reasonable in order to protect the rights of the citizens of Louisiana and their general welfare."[46]

Regrettably, the court did not specify where in the Constitution it found the right that the legislature sought to protect—essentially a right to file an overdue insurance claim that, by contract, was null and void. Neither did the court identify the source of the state legislature's constitutional authority to gut the rights of insurance company shareholders, employees, and those policyholders who honor their contracts and rely on a solvent industry to pay legitimate claims. How could the court promote the "general" welfare of Louisianans simply by transferring benefits from one class of persons (insurance company shareholders already saddled with billions of dollars in losses) to another class (policyholders who had allowed a full year or more to lapse without submitting damage claims)? And how could a legal regime that creates instability and uncertainty somehow foster rebuilding and risk-taking so vital to Louisiana's recovery?

Those questions remain unanswered. Rather than exercising judicial independence and invalidating a plainly unconstitutional statute, the Louisiana Supreme Court—like the U.S. Supreme Court in *Blaisdell*, the *Gold Clause Cases*, and *Kansas Power*—chose to defer to the legislature. That choice may satisfy some legal scholars who embrace so-called judicial restraint, but even University of Texas law professor Lino Graglia, perhaps the foremost apostle of legislative deference, recognized how badly the Court had botched its job. Although Graglia vigorously objects to nine justices, "unelected and life-tenured, making policy decisions for the nation as a whole from Washington, DC,"[47] here is what he wrote about *Blaisdell*: "Examples of enacted law clearly in violation of the Constitution are extremely difficult to find. Perhaps the clearest example in 200 years is Minnesota's 1933 Mortgage Moratorium Act, debtor-relief legislation clearly prohibited by the contracts clause. By a five-to-four vote, however, the Supreme Court held the law constitutional, thereby missing one of its few, if not its only, legitimate opportunities to exercise judicial review to invalidate a law."[48]

Today, the Contracts Clause is moribund, essentially excised from the Constitution by *Blaisdell* and its progeny. States now have broad leeway to alter private contractual arrangements with little regard for the disfavored parties whose rights have been extinguished.

CHAPTER 4

Lawmaking by Administrative Agencies

The Dirty Dozen List: Whitman v. American Trucking Associations, Inc. (2001)

WHAT IS THE CONSTITUTIONAL ISSUE?

"All legislative Powers herein granted shall be vested in a Congress of the United States." —U.S. Constitution, Article I, Section 1.

You probably assume—maybe because the Constitution says so—that Congress enacts all federal laws. Guess again. Our federal administrative agencies actually dwarf Congress when it comes to implementing regulations that control what Americans can and cannot do. In effect, Congress has delegated much of its lawmaking authority to unelected bureaucrats. They, in turn, make thousands of laws prescribing rules of conduct that bind private citizens, state governments, and local governments.

Some of the agencies are components of an executive department. For example, the Census Bureau is part of the Department of Commerce. Other agencies are independent—not wholly accountable to either the president or Congress—such as the Food and Drug Administration, which determines what drugs are sufficiently safe and effective to be sold in the United States. Most important for our purposes, administrative agencies often exercise legislative, executive, and judicial powers. The FDA, for instance, can issue regulations having the same force and effect as a statute, impose penalties for violations, and conduct trial-type proceedings that affect the rights and interests of particular parties.

If the separation-of-powers principle—a cornerstone of our Constitution for more than two centuries—means anything, it means that no government entity should be authorized to pass laws, enforce the laws that it passes, and then judge whether its own actions and the actions of other parties comply with those same laws. In this chapter we will be looking at the legislative role of administrative agencies. Specifically, we will examine this question: If the Constitution states that all legislative power vests in Congress, how can Congress delegate that power to agencies that are neither elected by the people nor accountable to the people's representatives?

First, however, let's consider the scope of the problem. Perhaps you are familiar with the *Federal Register*. It is published every day and provides notice of executive orders as well as actual and proposed new rules by the various federal regulatory agencies. During the twelve-month period ended March 31, 2006, the *Federal Register* contained an astonishing 77,537 pages.[1] At the beginning of each calendar quarter, the executive orders, rules, and regulations in the *Federal Register* that become final law are included in the *Code of Federal Regulations*. If you were to purchase a current edition of the *CFR* from the U.S. Government Printing Office, you would need enough shelf space for more than two hundred bound volumes. By comparison, the entire *U.S. Code*, which contains all the laws passed by Congress and signed by the president, requires roughly thirty-five volumes—about one-sixth the number devoted to the *CFR*.

As of midyear 2005, the *CFR* comprised rules and regulations from 319 independent and executive agencies.[2] The upshot: an alphabet soup of bureaus run by anonymous bureaucrats who tell us how to live our lives. There is the CFTC (Commodity Futures Trading Commission), DEA (Drug Enforcement Administration), EEOC (Equal Employment

Opportunity Commission), FAA (Federal Aviation Administration), FCC (Federal Communications Commission), FDIC (Federal Deposit Insurance Corporation), FEC (Federal Election Commission), FEMA (Federal Emergency Management Agency), FERC (Federal Energy Regulatory Commission), FMC (Federal Maritime Commission), FTC (Federal Trade Commission), IRS (Internal Revenue Service), ICC (Interstate Commerce Commission), OSHA (Occupational Safety and Health Administration), NLRB (National Labor Relations Board), NTSB (National Transportation Safety Board), SEC (Securities and Exchange Commission), SBA (Small Business Administration), and SSA (Social Security Administration).

Had enough? But that's just nineteen agencies—the better-known ones. There are three hundred more, including such household names as OELA (Office of English Language Acquisition), CPPBSD (Committee for Purchase from People Who Are Blind or Severely Disabled), JBEA (Joint Board for the Enrollment of Actuaries), ONHIR (Office of Navajo and Hopi Indian Relocation), and URMCC (Utah Reclamation Mitigation and Conservation Commission). Each of those agencies is alive and well today. Virtually no human activity is exempt from the federal regulatory juggernaut.

Moreover, it is not just the number of agencies that are involved in lawmaking, it is also the burden that their regulations impose. To get a sense of the problem: In 1995, Carol Browner, then head of the Environmental Protection Agency, announced that the EPA had streamlined its regulatory procedures to save businesses and state and local governments 23 million hours of unnecessary paperwork each year.[3] Kudos to Browner. But why did the EPA impose those unnecessary requirements in the first place? How many small businesses went belly-up trying to comply? And how many larger firms supported the onerous regulations because the high cost of compliance would put their smaller rivals at a competitive disadvantage?

Along those same lines, a recent study for the Small Business Administration revealed that small firms pay disproportionately to cope with excessive regulation. For firms with more than five hundred employees, the cost per employee to comply with environmental laws was $717 annually. Firms with fewer than twenty employees spent more than six times as much; their annual compliance cost per employee was $3,228.[4]

Compliance costs are rarely considered when evaluating the presumed benefits of agency rule making. More often than not, the argument in favor of legislative delegation is simply that outside experts, not busy members of Congress, are best equipped to decide complex technical issues. But according to law professor David Schoenbrod, that argument is "hogwash." Schoenbrod points out that there are seldom clear technical answers. Indeed, knowledge in Washington, D.C., is highly politicized; the questions at bottom are not technical but rather value-based. And the people making the final decisions at the agencies tend to be lawyers, just like many members of Congress. When it is necessary and politically convenient, Congress manages to get the technical advice it needs to resolve complex issues.[5]

Of course, even if our senators and representatives are unqualified or too busy to handle the job assigned to them by the Constitution, the answer cannot be to pretend that parts of the Constitution do not exist. Yet in *Whitman v. American Trucking Associations, Inc.*, that is basically what the Supreme Court did.[6] For all practical purposes the Court removed the nondelegation doctrine from the Constitution. That doctrine, which holds that Congress may not freely delegate its legislative powers, traces its roots to John Locke, the distinguished political philosopher whose writings were influential in crafting both the Declaration of Independence and the Constitution. In 1690, Locke stated that "[t]he legislative cannot transfer the power of making laws to any other hands; for it being but a delegated power from the people, they who have it cannot pass it over to others"; the legislative power is "to make laws, and not to make legislators."[7]

In *American Trucking*, the Supreme Court ignored John Locke and more than three hundred years of history. The Court essentially rewrote Article I, section 1, to read: "All legislative Powers herein granted shall be shared between the Congress of the United States and several hundred unelected agencies."

The evisceration of the nondelegation doctrine didn't happen overnight. Not until the 1940s did the real trouble begin. Until then, the Court honored the notion that lawmaking is for the legislative branch, and the legislative branch means Congress.[8] As early as 1825, Chief Justice John Marshall had distinguished between establishing rules of practice for the federal courts—an internal operational function that could therefore be assigned to the judiciary—and passing legislation that concerns the rights and obligations of private parties. "It will not be contended," wrote Marshall, "that Congress can delegate . . . powers which are strictly and exclusively legislative."[9]

Unfortunately, Marshall offered little guidance as to which powers were "strictly and exclusively legislative," but he did lay the groundwork for the "intelligible principle" standard that still controls nondelegation cases today. Marshall explained: If Congress delegates quasi-legislative powers to another body, it must provide a "general provision" by which "those who are to act" can "fill up the details."[10]

In other words, (Congress cannot give an outside agency carte blanche to make law, but it can authorize the agency to flesh out the particulars of a law that Congress has already shaped.) That idea was formalized a century later in *J.W. Hampton Jr. Co. v. United States*. There, the Court unanimously upheld the president's delegated authority to raise or lower duties imposed by the Tariff Act of 1922 in order to equalize differences between foreign and domestic costs of production. The act specified the criteria to be considered, fixed certain limits of change, and required an investigation by the Tariff Commission. Such delegations are constitutional, said the Court, as long as Congress "shall lay down by legislative act an *intelligible principle* to which the person or body authorized . . . is directed to conform."[11]

Obviously, the term "intelligible principle" is itself somewhat wooly, and much of the controversy since *Hampton* has focused on this question: Just how precise does the intelligible principle have to be? The heyday for proponents of nondelegation occurred in 1935 when the Supreme Court threw out two separate legislative delegations under the

National Industrial Recovery Act (NIRA), a centerpiece of President Franklin D. Roosevelt's New Deal.

The first case, *Panama Refining Co. v. Ryan*, concerned the president's authority to prohibit interstate shipment of petroleum in excess of quotas fixed by the states. Chief Justice Charles Evans Hughes, for an eight-member majority, struck down that provision as an unconstitutional delegation of legislative power to the president. Congress, he wrote, "has declared no policy, has established no standard, has laid down no rule."[12] NIRA, he explained, proposed "no criteria to govern the President's course. It does not require any finding by the President as a condition of his action."[13] In effect, Congress had left the matter to the president, "to be dealt with as he pleased."[14]

Several months later, in *A.L.A. Schechter Poultry Corp. v. United States*, the Court rejected another provision in NIRA that authorized Roosevelt to approve codes of fair competition submitted by trade associations and other industry groups. This time the decision was unanimous. Chief Justice Hughes once again wrote for the Court: "Such a sweeping delegation of legislative power" is "unknown to our law and utterly inconsistent with the constitutional prerogatives and duties of Congress."[15] He added that "the discretion of the President in approving or prescribing codes, and thus enacting laws for the government of trade and industry throughout the country, is virtually unfettered."[16] In a concurring opinion, Justice Benjamin N. Cardozo, the lone dissenter in *Panama Refining*, characterized the NIRA codes as "delegation running riot."[17]

Regrettably, the New Deal Court ultimately came to terms with the Roosevelt administration. Although *Panama* and *Schechter* have never been officially overruled—in fact, they have been cited in more than forty subsequent Supreme Court decisions—not a single post–New Deal statutory program has been invalidated as an unconstitutional delegation of legislative power to the executive branch.[18] Quite the contrary, the pendulum has plainly swung in the opposite direction.

In 1943 the Court upheld a delegation to the Federal Communications Commission to regulate the composition of radio broadcasting. The so-called intelligible principle was that the regulation had to be consistent with "public interest, convenience, or necessity."[19] The next year the Court permitted the Office of Price Administration sufficient discretion to set "generally fair and equitable" rent and price ceilings after consulting with industry representatives.[20] There were still other amorphous standards such as "just and reasonable," "unfair methods of competition," and "excessive profits"—whatever those terms might mean.[21]

For an especially egregious example of agency overreaching, consider two cases involving delegation of legislative power to the Army Corps of Engineers under the Clean Water Act (CWA), presumably to protect wetlands. In the first case, *Solid Waste Agency of Northern Cook County v. Army Corps of Engineers*, a consortium of municipalities near Chicago asked the corps for permission to fill several ponds on the site of an abandoned sand and gravel pit, which the municipalities wanted to use for solid waste disposal.[22] The CWA specified that permits were required to fill "navigable waters of the United States." Those waters, according to a special rule adopted by the corps in 1986, included isolated, intrastate, disconnected puddles and pools that provided habitat for birds flying across state lines on their way south and back. Applying the "migratory bird rule," the corps refused to issue a permit, and the U.S. Court of Appeals rejected the municipalities' challenge.

That was too much even for the U.S. Supreme Court. Chief Justice William H. Rehnquist, in a hotly contested 5–4 ruling, reversed the appellate court, concluding that the corps' interpretation of "navigable waters of the United States" was unreasonable. Congress did not intend the CWA to reach an abandoned sand and gravel pit that was non-navigable, cut off from other waters, and wholly within a single state. That was the right outcome, but more important was what the Court did *not* say. Rehnquist did not write that the CWA provided no intelligible principle to guide the corps in interpreting "navigable waters." Nor did Rehnquist hold that excessive discretion in the hands of the corps represented an impermissible delegation of legislative authority. Instead, the Court simply declared that the corps' interpretation was unreasonable, leaving it to the same agency to try again without further clarification from Congress.

Predictably, the corps did try again—in *Rapanos v. United States*—claiming jurisdiction over wetlands near, even if not connected to, tributaries that lead to navigable waters.[23] A developer in Michigan had filled in part of his property without obtaining a permit. The property was twenty miles from the nearest waterway that might be considered navigable. In a fractured opinion, the four more liberal justices wanted to honor the corps' claim of jurisdiction; the four more conservative justices thought that "navigable waters of the United States" should mean relatively permanent streams, oceans, rivers, and lakes connected to interstate waters. Splitting the difference, Justice Anthony M. Kennedy wrote the opinion that would become the holding of the Court: The corps would have jurisdiction over wetlands if they had a "significant nexus" to waters that are, or reasonably could be made, navigable. The end result: more litigation to resolve the wrong question. Rather than asking whether an agency interpretation of a statute is reasonable, the Court should be asking whether the agency is constitutionally authorized to interpret such a vague statute at all.

It is tempting to conclude from the two wetlands cases that the Court can treat each agency interpretation on its merits, rejecting those interpretations that go too far. Tempting, yes, but case-by-case judicial review has not worked. Mostly that is because of *Chevron U.S.A., Inc. v. Natural Resources Defense Council*, a 1984 case in which the Court established a two-part test for reviewing agency interpretations of statutes.[24] First, the court determines whether Congress has spoken directly to the question at issue. If so, the court adopts the express provisions of the statute. But if the statute is "silent or ambiguous," as is frequently the case, then the court examines whether the agency's regulations are "based on a permissible construction of the statute."[25] In practice, the *Chevron* test has been highly deferential; the vast majority of agency interpretations have been deemed "permissible."

That is why opponents of "delegation running riot" were excited when *Whitman v. American Trucking Associations* reached the Supreme Court in 2001. *American Trucking* asked whether Congress in the Clean Air Act (CAA) can delegate legislative power to the Environmental Protection Agency (EPA) to set air quality standards. Under section 109 of the CAA, Congress directed the EPA to apply criteria "requisite to protect the public health" with "an adequate margin for safety."[26] In 1997 the EPA revised its standards for ozone and particulate matter, triggering a challenge by private companies and several states, who sued Christine Todd Whitman, administrator of the EPA.

According to the Court of Appeals, the EPA's exercise of authority under such nebulous guidelines violated the nondelegation doctrine. The EPA, said the appellate court, "lacked any determinate criteria for drawing lines. It has failed to state intelligibly how much is too much."[27] The Supreme Court, unfortunately, disagreed.

Where Did the Court Go Wrong?

Seventy-three years after the 1928 *Hampton* case, the Court had a golden opportunity to breathe new life into the intelligible principle standard. Sadly, it was not to be. Today, administrative agencies still legislate. Driving what may have been the final nail in the coffin of the nondelegation doctrine, *American Trucking* allowed Congress to abdicate its role as the nation's exclusive lawmaker. And by opening the door for unelected bureaucrats to improvise liberally when they construe federal statutes, *Chevron* exacerbated the problem. First the Court permitted agencies to exercise legislative power that the Constitution was designed to withhold. Then the Court stood aside when those same agencies abused their newly conferred power. Now, after *American Trucking*, the best we can wish for is that administrative agencies will use their unconstitutional powers "reasonably." That unlikely outcome would be the triumph of hope over experience.

What makes *American Trucking* so interesting and so outrageous is that the so-called intelligible principle designed to guide the EPA in setting air quality standards under the CAA—namely, "protect the public health" with "an adequate margin of safety"—was not only ambiguous but logically impossible to apply.[28] Here is why: When Congress amended the CAA in 1970, it assumed that air pollutants such as ozone, controlled under section 109, were "threshold" pollutants—meaning that they were a threat to public health above a certain threshold concentration level, but not below that level. Thus, the legislative directive to the EPA—protect the public health with an adequate margin of safety—meant simply that air quality standards should be set sufficiently below the threshold to provide a cushion against adverse health effects.

A few years later, however, it was discovered that most of the section 109 pollutants were the "nonthreshold" variety—meaning that adverse health effects would occur at *any concentration above zero*. By 1977, when Congress again amended the CAA, legislators knew that even minuscule levels of nonthreshold pollutants were unsafe. Yet, recognizing the economic and social consequences of an outright ban, Congress rejected that alternative.[29] And making matters worse, Congress failed to set forth a new intelligible principle. As a result, the principle by which the EPA was directed to set air quality standards for nonthreshold pollutants was not only unintelligible but nonsensical.

Indeed, even a total ban would not have solved the problem. Nonthreshold pollutants occur naturally in the environment. The EPA could not eliminate them if it wanted to. Thus, it was literally impossible for the EPA to set standards that "protect the public health with an adequate margin of safety." As written, the statute required the EPA to engage in an entirely arbitrary and fruitless exercise: determining a level of concentration that would guard against adverse health effects when no such level existed, much less one that would have provided an adequate margin of safety.

Essentially, Congress abdicated its constitutional responsibility to make a fundamental policy choice in a matter that had a significant impact on our health and our economy. Although it could have supplied an intelligible principle to steer the EPA, Congress opted, unconstitutionally, to delegate its legislative power to the agency. The CAA, which should have spelled out how the EPA was to exercise that power, offered no guidance whatsoever. That meant the EPA was faced with two illegitimate choices: Either set the standard for nonthreshold pollutants at zero, in direct contradiction of congressional intent, or arbitrarily select a nonzero standard at which adverse health effects would still exist. The first option was impossible to achieve, flouted Congress, and had severe economic repercussions. Predictably, the EPA chose the second path—despite the adverse health effects.

That folly didn't seem to bother Justice Antonin Scalia, who wrote the *American Trucking* opinion, joined in relevant part by Chief Justice Rehnquist, Justice Kennedy, and Justices Sandra Day O'Connor, Clarence Thomas, Ruth Bader Ginsburg, and Stephen G. Breyer. True to form, given his well-known allegiance to the text of the Constitution, Scalia acknowledged that the "text permits no delegation" of legislative powers.[30] How, then, could he justify delegation to the EPA under section 109 of the CAA? Simple: Congress did not really delegate legislative power; instead, Congress merely delegated a "certain degree of discretion, and thus of lawmaking, [which] inheres in most executive or judicial action."[31] Under section 109, according to Scalia, the scope of discretion was "well within the outer limits of our nondelegation precedents."[32]

Congress, declared Scalia, had to "provide substantial guidance on setting air standards that affect the entire national economy." But the statute did not have to lay out a "determinate criterion" for saying "how much [of the regulated harm] is too much."[33] Therefore, he continued, it was "not conclusive for delegation purposes that . . . ozone and particulate matter are 'nonthreshold' pollutants that inflict a continuum of adverse health effects at any airborne concentration greater than zero."[34] The EPA, exercising its regulatory discretion, could resolve that dilemma without actually legislating. Ergo, the text of the Constitution, which vests all legislative power in Congress, was not violated.

That sleight of hand did not impress Justice John Paul Stevens. Although he agreed with the end result of *American Trucking*, he wrote separately, joined by Justice David H. Souter, to express his disagreement with the Court's reasoning. From Stevens's perspective, the Court had two choices. It could admit that the power delegated to the EPA was "legislative" but nevertheless conclude that the delegation was permissible because the CAA contained a sufficiently intelligible principle. Or the Court could pretend, as did the majority, that the authority delegated to the EPA was somehow not "legislative power."

Ultimately, Stevens was persuaded that "it would be both wiser and

more faithful to what we have actually done in delegation cases to admit that agency rule-making authority is 'legislative power.' "[35] After
all, he explained, if the final standards established by the EPA had been
prescribed by Congress, everyone would agree that those rules were the
product of an exercise of legislative power. In the same fashion, when an
agency exercises rule-making authority pursuant to a permissible delegation from Congress, it, too, exercises legislative power.[36]

Perhaps so, but Stevens still hadn't answered the key question: What
are the limits of "permissible delegation"? He turned to that topic next,
and his rationale tells us a great deal about a Supreme Court that has lost
its compass. "In Article I," wrote Stevens, "the Framers vested 'All legislative Powers' in the Congress, just as in Article II they vested the
'executive Power' in the President. Those provisions," he continued,
"do not purport to limit the authority of either recipient of power to
delegate authority to others."[37] So, according to Justice Stevens, if the
Constitution doesn't expressly prohibit Congress or the president from
delegating their respective powers, then delegation is authorized. But
that turns the Constitution on its head.

The underlying premise is straightforward: All powers not permitted are prohibited—precisely the opposite of Stevens's notion that all
powers not prohibited are permitted. Limited government and enumerated powers are the touchstones. The federal government has only those
powers granted by the Constitution. They are expressly enumerated in
Article I for Congress and in Article II for the executive branch. The
point is repeated, for emphasis, in the Tenth Amendment, which states
that "The powers not delegated to the United States by the Constitution . . . are reserved to the States . . . or to the people." In other words,
if a power is not enumerated, the federal government does not have that
power, and no law may constitutionally be enacted to give the federal
government a power it does not have.

Justice Thomas understood that principle. Legislative power cannot
be delegated by Congress because there is no enumerated power authorizing the delegation. In his concurring opinion, Thomas conceded
that the Court had frequently approved agency directives no more "intelligible" than the directive provided to the EPA under section 109 of

the CAA. Nonetheless, he pointed out, there may be a "genuine constitutional problem." Specifically, the text of the Constitution provides that all legislative power is vested in Congress and "does not speak of 'intelligible principles.' "[38] Even if a directive is deemed to be "intelligible," that does not somehow transform the delegated powers from legislative to nonlegislative. To the contrary, "there are cases in which the principle is intelligible and yet the significance of the delegated decision is simply too great for the decision to be called anything other than 'legislative.' "[39]

Yet, because the litigants in *American Trucking* did not ask the Court to revisit its past delegation precedents, Thomas was not inclined to do so. He did write, however, that he would be willing in a future case "to address the question whether our delegation jurisprudence has strayed too far from our Founders' understanding of separation of powers."[40] Justice Thomas realizes that the nondelegation principle is effectively codified in the Constitution—if only because its opposite, the authority to delegate legislative power, is nowhere to be found.

Are we to conclude, therefore, that agencies such as the EPA may not exercise any discretion when they carry out their duties under statutes such as the CAA? Of course not. Justice Scalia stated the principle correctly: Although Congress may not delegate its legislative power, not all grants of discretion are delegations. To illustrate: If the Food and Drug Administration were to rule, under a broad grant of authority from Congress, that no drug may be produced unless it is "effective," that would be an unconstitutional exercise of legislative power. But if Congress were to pass the same rule and establish clear-cut guidelines for determining "effectiveness," the FDA could be empowered to decide whether a particular drug meets the guidelines. Similarly, the Social Security Administration could not set the level of benefits for retirees or the criteria for eligibility, but it could establish procedures for determining eligibility and verifying claims. And the Internal Revenue Service, while it could not be given authority to set tax rates, could be directed to design appropriate forms for tax reporting and to monitor compliance.

As for the EPA, its functions under the CAA must not include free rein to establish limits on pollutant emissions but could allow discretion to impose a system of measurement and identify those who violate the standards set by Congress. The crucial question is whether a statute grants the kind, quality, and quantity of discretion that makes the statute into a delegation. If so, the statute is improper. But if the statute entailed duties that involved some discretion, short of actual legislation—and did not contravene other background tenets such as federalism, separation of powers, and individual rights—then the statute would be constitutional.

Law professor Gary Lawson, an expert on the nondelegation doctrine, put it this way: "Some measure of . . . discretion is entirely consistent with a 'proper' allocation of governmental powers as that would have been understood in 1789." Lawson then asks: "How can we tell when a statute vests so much discretion . . . that it crosses the line between a 'proper' means of implementing a federal power and an 'improper' delegation of legislative authority?" Lawson would examine two criteria: the degree of discretion and the importance of the issue. "Congress must make the central, fundamental decisions in each statutory scheme, but Congress can leave the detail to others."[41] Admittedly, that leaves substantial wiggle room in assessing whether a statute impermissibly grants legislative power to a government entity other than Congress. Still, says Lawson, line-drawing problems are ubiquitous in constitutional law. That is what the courts are for; that is why judges get paid.

WHAT ARE THE IMPLICATIONS?

Unfortunately, the courts have gotten it wrong. Justice Scalia got it wrong in his *American Trucking* majority opinion when he concluded that the delegation by Congress to the EPA really didn't involve legislative power. Justice Stevens got it just as wrong in his concurring opinion when he concluded that Congress had set out an "intelligible principle" that made the delegation proper even if it *did* involve legislative power. Never mind that the principle was logically impossible to implement.

The practical consequences of those mistakes are not trivial. Joel

Schwartz, former head of California's state pollution control agency, reminds us that "[a]ir pollution reductions are expensive, costing Americans at least tens of billions of dollars each year." He continues: "It would be nice if we didn't have to give up anything in order to achieve additional reductions in air pollution. But in the real world, the costs of air pollution control mean higher prices, lower wages and lower returns on investments, reducing the resources we have available for everything else that affects our health, safety and quality of life."[42]

To be sure, regulators are not typically malevolent, and they don't ordinarily intend to harm the people they are supposed to protect. Still, argues Schwartz: "As a powerful, highly specialized agency with a staff that is passionate about air quality, the EPA unavoidably suffers from tunnel vision: the pursuit of a single-minded goal to the point where it does more harm than good. Environmental regulators will pursue the next increment of air pollution reduction, and the next, regardless of whether the increasingly marginal benefits are worth having or the costs worth bearing."[43]

Sadly, the EPA is only one of the several hundred administrative agencies whose regulations affect our daily lives. Overreaching by the EPA is just the tip of the delegation iceberg. Here are just a few examples of impermissible delegations of legislative authority:

- The Federal Communications Commission has almost total discretion to grant or deny broadcast licenses.
- The Securities and Exchange Commission can bar "deceptive" devices used in connection with the sale of a security. After more than seventy years of administrative rule making and litigation, no one is quite sure what that means.
- The Secretary of Labor has expansive rule-making authority to ensure "occupational safety and health."
- The Department of Transportation has nearly exhaustive power to prescribe automotive safety standards.
- The Federal Trade Commission can define and prosecute "unfair" acts or practices affecting commerce.

If we had to point to one agency that exemplifies the problems inherent in delegated power, our choice would be the FDA. Abuse of its lawmaking role may well have resulted in the deaths of countless Americans. Consider the vague grants of authority and responsibility in the Food, Drug, and Cosmetic Act, which created the FDA. The act forbids the marketing of any drug that has not been proven safe and effective. Applications from drug companies can be denied if the FDA finds "there is a lack of substantial evidence that the drug will have the effect it purports or is represented to have. . . . [T]he term 'substantial evidence' means evidence consisting of adequate and well-controlled investigations . . . on the basis of which it could fairly and responsibly be concluded" that the drug will live up to the manufacturer's claims.[44]

For all intents and purposes, Congress has left it to the FDA to determine the degree of safety and efficacy, the level of certainty required from investigators, the quantity and quality of data to be examined, the meaning of "substantial evidence," and the criteria for reaching conclusions "fairly and responsibly." By relinquishing its lawmaking function, Congress gave the FDA both latitude and incentives to delay drug approvals unnecessarily. And by allowing unelected bureaucrats to exercise such power, Congress left the public without an effective means to protest.

Rarely will a drug be 100 percent safe for all potential users; some uncertainty or risk will always be present whenever a drug is approved. For the FDA, however, avoidance of big and obvious mistakes—such as approving an unsafe drug—too often has higher priority than sensible risk management, which would weigh the huge but not so obvious human costs of drug delays and disapprovals. Let's look at a few of those costs, as compiled by an advocacy group, the Abigail Alliance for Better Access to Developmental Drugs:[45]

- When the leukemia drug Gleevec emerged from initial testing in 1998, it was known to be safe and effective. By the time the FDA approved Gleevec in March 2003, approximately 3,600 patients had been denied access. Many of them died waiting. More than 80 percent of the patients who were treated in preapproval clinical trials are alive today.

- FDA approval of Eloxatin for colorectal cancer was delayed from March 2000 until August 2002 despite approval in at least twenty-nine other countries. During that time about forty thousand Americans died without ever getting the drug.

- Kidney cancer patients faced a choice of certain death or a fifty-fifty chance of getting a placebo during FDA-mandated trials of Nexavar and Sutent. The evidence of Nexavar's efficacy was so compelling that Bayer discontinued the tests for ethical reasons, and the placebo patients finally got the real medicine. About twenty thousand kidney cancer patients died waiting for the two drugs.

- After a delay of several years, the FDA yielded to intense pressure from oncologists and approved Bexxar for non-Hodgkin's lymphoma. About twenty-six thousand people died during the delay.

According to the Abigail Alliance, if those four drugs, and eight others with similar histories, had been available to patients who were barred entry to clinical trials, "more than one million mothers, fathers, sons and daughters" might have lived longer, better lives.[46]

Reasonable people can debate the appropriate standards for drug testing and the number of persons whose lives might have been saved under a different regime. But the job of setting standards is assigned by the Constitution to Congress. Even the most indulgent application of the nondelegation principle would have denied such unbounded discretion to the FDA. The Food, Drug, and Cosmetic Act improperly ceded lawmaking power, not just a ministerial role in implementing a congressional enactment. When a vague directive from Congress tells an agency to measure efficacy by relying on "substantial evidence" from "adequate and well-controlled investigations" leading to conclusions that are reached "fairly and responsibly," that delegation of legislative authority cannot possibly comply with the Constitution.

Yet proponents of delegation—who are adamant despite the FDA horror stories and similar problems with other agencies—offer two major counterarguments. First, they assert that delegation is administratively convenient and fosters governmental efficiency. But the constitutional separation of powers was not intended for those purposes. In fact, a case could be made that distributed powers are specifically designed to put sand in the gears of government—to retard the growth of the leviathan state. "The ultimate purpose of this separation of powers," said the Supreme Court in 1991, "is to protect the liberty and security of the governed."[47] Delegation does just the opposite. It effectively deputizes "tens of thousands of bureaucrats, often with broad and imprecise missions, to 'go forth and legislate.' "[48] Surely it would be convenient and efficient, for example, if Congress authorized the Internal Revenue Service to set tax rates that best "serve the public interest." Only liberty would be sacrificed in the process.

The second argument of delegation advocates is that Congress lacks technical expertise, which administrative agencies can provide. But delegation critics such as David Schoenbrod and Jerry Taylor point out that "most agency heads are not scientists, engineers, economists, or other kinds of technical experts; they are political operatives."[49] Administrative rule making is no less a struggle for political power than is congressional legislation. Moreover, in many respects, government by experts is worse than government by elected officials. "There is no reason to believe that experts possess superior moral knowledge or a better sense of what constitutes the public good. . . . Likewise, specialized expertise provides too narrow a base for the balanced judgments that intelligent policy requires."[50] If Congress needs technical assistance to legislate, it can certainly obtain such assistance from congressional and agency staff, universities, professional associations, think tanks, and other public policy institutes.

Equally important, delegation is a recipe for political irresponsibility. Congress gets to claim credit for the supposed benefits of agency regulation and yet dodge culpability for the associated costs. Ironically, when blame is ultimately assessed, members of Congress are the first to criticize the agencies whose rules were enacted under obtuse guidelines that Congress itself enacted. One remedy, suggested by Justice Breyer, would force Congress to approve each and every administrative regulation that establishes a rule of private conduct.[51] If legislative logjams were to develop, Congress could establish internal rules that would expedite the approval process.

Finally, delegation buttresses the power and influence of special interests. Ordinary citizens are even less well equipped to press their case before administrative agencies than before Congress. National legislators—but not agency heads—are responsive to the needs and desires of voters, who can exact retribution at the polls. By contrast, individual voters have no direct representation in the administrative process, nor do they typically have access to trained legal counsel, expert witnesses, and consultants. "As a result, the general public rarely qualifies as a 'stakeholder' in agency proceedings and is largely locked out of the decision-making process."[52]

Delegation has become a political narcotic—hooking Congress on more and bigger regulatory schemes with scant regard for their costs, little concern over the political repercussions, and most of all, disrespect for a Constitution expressly designed to prohibit what Congress has eagerly promoted.

PART TWO

Eroding Freedom

CHAPTER 5

Campaign Finance Reform and Free Speech

The Dirty Dozen List: *McConnell v. Federal Election Commission* (2003)
Dishonorable Mention: *Buckley v. Valeo* (1976)

WHAT IS THE CONSTITUTIONAL ISSUE?

"Congress shall make no law . . . abridging the freedom of speech."
—U.S. Constitution, First Amendment.

Campaign finance laws attack the heart of our democratic political system. Their purpose is to restrict participation in the political process, which is intended to be freewheeling and open. Yet reformers are convinced that our system is too contentious, too loud, too expensive, too unfair, and too time-consuming for politicians who would prefer not to compete for our votes. To get elected, however, politicians must speak to the voters. That is a good thing, not a bad thing. It is the essence of democracy and a means of ensuring that our government is based on consent of the governed.

Even speaking to a relatively small audience costs money for a suitable venue, staffing, and advertising. Speaking to a larger radio or television audience, as politicians must, costs a lot of money. Accordingly, raising money is an integral part of persuading voters to support a candidate. Money preserves and protects the free discussion of political ideas. That applies both to the politicians who want to speak to voters and to the voters who want to speak to one another about politicians and issues.

In short, in a free society political campaigns are *supposed* to be loud, contentious, expensive, and time-consuming. Although proponents of campaign finance restrictions claim it is unfair for some politicians or voters to spend more money on campaigns than others, fairness has little to do with it. The point of campaigns is for the politician whose ideas are most popular to win the race. Regulating the money that politicians raise and spend is a direct restriction on political speech, in the same way that regulating printing presses is a direct restriction on freedom of the press. The whole point of having a democratically elected government is to ensure freedom. We cannot allow the regulators to destroy freedom in a bungled effort to protect it.

The regulation of political participation in the guise of campaign finance "reform" is often justified in the name of curbing corruption, but the architects of modern campaign finance laws have never produced any evidence of corruption that allegedly results from privately financed campaigns or of wealthy individuals' or companies' "buying" elections. Instead, reformers merely assert a litany of horribles to rationalize their opposition to the current system. They favor a managed system, one that is managed by their rules, according to their standards, and designed to achieve their ends, which do not include a vigorous and free marketplace for political expression.

Essentially, campaign finance laws are a solution in search of a problem. Consider, for example, the demonization of political influence.

It is the first week of December 2003, less than thirty days before the upcoming New Hampshire presidential primary. Fictitious financier George Croesus wants very much to see John Kerry elected president in 2004. In return for providing financial support—say, $500,000—Croesus would like access to the new president and input regarding his foreign policy. Here is how a Croesus-Kerry conversation might have gone:

Kerry: "Hi, George. Nice to see you."

Croesus: "Likewise, but let's not beat around the Bush. If you get elected, I'd like access and influence. In return, I'll have my corporation spend $500,000 on TV advertisements supporting you just before next month's New Hampshire primary."

Later that day Kerry gets a call from fictitious senator John McWayne, who has considerable political clout and might consider crossing party lines to endorse Kerry. McWayne thinks his endorsement could make a big difference—indeed, just as much difference as a financial contribution of, say, $500,000. In return, McWayne, like Croesus, would like access to the new president and input regarding his foreign policy. Here is how a McWayne-Kerry conversation might have gone:

Kerry: "Hi, John. Nice to see you."

McWayne: "Likewise, but let's not beat around the Bush. If you get elected, I'd like access and influence. In return, I'll endorse you just before next month's New Hampshire primary. Believe me, my endorsement should be worth at least $500,000."

Now fast-forward a few days, to December 10, 2003. That is when the U.S. Supreme Court decided *McConnell v. Federal Election Commission*, a constitutional challenge to the Bipartisan Campaign Reform Act of 2002 (BCRA), commonly known as the McCain-Feingold bill.[1] The Court determined in *McConnell* that political expression was entitled to less First Amendment protection than Klan speech, pornography, and flag burning.

As a result, the Croesus-Kerry deal—exchanging a TV ad worth roughly $500,000 shortly before an election in return for political access and influence—would be a crime punishable by a fine and up to five years in prison. On the other hand, the McWayne-Kerry deal—exchanging an endorsement worth roughly $500,000 shortly before an election in return for political access and influence—would be perfectly okay. No doubt, hidden in the Court's mind-numbing 168 pages of multiple opinions, the justices explain that apparent paradox.

Then again, maybe not. Evidently the Court was unable or unwilling to grasp the notion that politics is essentially a bargain between candidates and the electorate. From a constitutional perspective there should be no distinction between the Croesus deal and the McWayne deal. When a candidate promises to pursue an agenda that a voter favors, it should not matter constitutionally whether the voter's return promise is to (1) vote for the candidate, (2) convince his friends to vote for the candidate, (3) write letters to the editor in support of the candidate, (4) pay for an ad that supports the candidate, or (5) donate money to the candidate. Nor should it matter if the candidate's end of the bargain includes a commitment to meet with the voter, listen to his views, or, to put it crassly, give him access and influence.

Whether the voter pledges a single vote, a public endorsement, payment for an ad, or a contribution of money so the candidate can pay for his own ad, each of those acts has the same end: getting the candidate elected. And each act operates through the same means: political speech. The exchange of speech for promised conduct by the candidate if he's elected is not corrupt. It is democracy at work.[2]

There are, of course, important exceptions to the proposition that campaign contributions in return for political considerations are an inherent part of the democratic process: (Donors may not, for example, contribute to a candidate's campaign in order to procure favoritism in the award of government contracts or the receipt of government services, or to promote discrimination against a noncontributor who seeks such contracts or services.) A government official is a fiduciary to his constituents and may not use his station to confer benefits or impose costs by bending rules or procedures contrary to the rights of those constituents. That principle has long been settled under existing laws covering bribery, extortion, kickbacks, and racketeering.

Otherwise, a payoff to a candidate is corrupting only if it is spent for personal pleasure, such as buying a new car. That type of "contribution" does not generate political speech, and it should be illegal. But when a candidate receives something of value and then sets the money aside in a segregated fund that can be used only for political expression, that is not corruption. Rather, it is the kind of speech that the Constitution was designed to protect. [The First Amendment does not allow treating political advocacy as if it were a bribe.]

Regrettably, the Supreme Court did just that in *McConnell*. The huge case was a consolidation of ten separate complaints against BCRA, filed by no less than eighty parties who were represented by fifty high-octane law firms. The most wide-ranging challenge came from Senator Mitch McConnell (R–KY), joined by twenty-six co-plaintiffs. Separate challenges came from the National Rifle Association, Republican National Committee, California state Democratic and Republican parties, National Association of Broadcasters, U.S. Chamber of Commerce, AFL–CIO, and others spanning the political spectrum.

Basically, the Court reaffirmed that prevention of corruption or even the "appearance of corruption" is a sufficiently important government interest for Congress to disregard First Amendment protections of political speech. Armed with that insight, a five-member majority upheld the two most significant provisions of BCRA. First, it is a crime for anyone to give "soft money" to political parties. Soft money consists of contributions for such things as party-wide get-out-the-vote drives—that is, money not designated for a particular candidate's campaign and therefore exempt from limits imposed by pre-BCRA rules. Second, it is a crime for corporations and labor unions to pay for broadcast advertisements that mention a candidate for federal office within sixty days of a general election or thirty days of a primary.

What Were the Facts?

For the first eight years of the Republic, the power of money in politics—at least at the presidential level—was not a paramount issue. After all, George Washington had been elected unanimously in 1789 and was unanimously reelected in 1792. Since the election of 1796, however, no campaign has been free of financial influence. Perhaps recognizing the First Amendment implications, Congress took 129 years before deciding that corrective action was necessary. The Federal Corrupt Practices Act was passed in 1925. It established campaign spending limits for parties in congressional races and required some reporting by national party committees, but its loosely worded provisions had little effect on the use of cash as a means of political expression.

Fast-forward another half century. In 1971, Congress enacted the

Federal Election Campaign Act (FECA) and amended it in 1974, putting teeth in the federal government's crackdown on the financing of political campaigns. Still, one problem remained: Parts of FECA were unconstitutional. That is the conclusion the Supreme Court reached in the 1976 case *Buckley v. Valeo*—a suit by Senator James L. Buckley (R–NY), along with candidates, contributors, and political parties, against government officials, including Francis R. Valeo, who was a member of the Federal Election Commission by virtue of his position as secretary of the U.S. Senate.

Under FECA, political contributions and expenditures were capped, and those above $250 had to be disclosed. "Contributions" included money donated to a candidate ($1,000 limit), spent on a candidate's behalf after consulting or coordinating with him ($1,000 limit), or paid to a political action committee ($5,000 limit), which funnels money to candidates. FECA defined "expenditures" as outlays by the candidate of his own or family money ($25,000 limit), plus outlays by others ($1,000 limit) for advertisements and other promotions that expressly advocate the election or defeat of a clearly identified candidate but were not coordinated with him.

In a fractured opinion with multiple dissents, the *Buckley* Court upheld FECA's disclosure requirements and contribution limits against a First Amendment challenge. According to the Court, the government had a "compelling interest" in avoiding the "actuality and appearance of corruption." Large contributions, reasoned the Court, did not have adequate "expressive content" under the First Amendment to outweigh their possible corrupting influence. Regrettably, none of the justices defined "corruption," although the Court implied that it meant big bucks "given to secure a political quid pro quo from current and potential office holders."[4]

Hence, it would be corrupt for anyone to contribute money intended to affect a politician's position on an issue. Imagine trying to apply that formulation—especially when the mere "appearance of corruption" might justify restrictions on core political speech. That gaping loophole, as we shall see, was used twenty-seven years later by McCain-Feingold supporters to justify eviscerating the First Amendment.

Yet, despite the *Buckley* Court's blind spot on contribution limits, the justices rebuffed FECA's caps on independent expenditures by individuals, political action committees, and some nonprofit corporations. First of all, a candidate could hardly corrupt himself by spending his own or his family's money. Second, said the Court, independent expenditures not coordinated with the candidate are entitled to a higher level of First Amendment protection than contributions. Those expenditures result in direct speech by the paying party, not indirect speech through a candidate to whom the paying party makes a donation. Moreover, the Court added, advocating someone's election or defeat is much the same for First Amendment purposes as discussing a political issue or favoring or opposing legislation. Third, the Court pointedly noted that attempts to level the playing field by capping expenditures of wealthier voters did not pass constitutional muster. "[T]he concept that government may restrict the speech of some elements of our society in order to enhance the relative voice of others is wholly foreign to the First Amendment."[5]

Thus, for fans of free speech, *Buckley* was a mixed bag in the short term but a disaster in the long term. On the plus side, the Court invalidated limits on individual expenditures. On the minus side, the Court affirmed contribution limits and, even worse, gave the government an easy way to circumvent First Amendment guarantees: After *Buckley* any campaign finance regulation designed to inhibit the "appearance of corruption" would likely be condoned by the Court. That is what transpired more than a quarter of a century later in *McConnell v. Federal Election Commission* when the Court negated *Buckley*'s modest liberalization of FECA's expenditure restrictions—and then went even further in affirming virtually all of BCRA.

The key ingredients of BCRA were twofold: First, no more "soft money"—that is, unregulated contributions to political parties for such purposes as get-out-the-vote drives, generic party advertising, and even public communications funded by state and local parties that promote, support, attack, or oppose a clearly identified federal candidate. Never mind that the influence of political parties, exercised through public speech, is an entirely proper consequence of free expression and association.

Second, unions and corporations would no longer be permitted to initiate "electioneering communications"—that is, broadcast ads designed to affect election results but exempt from existing FECA restrictions because the ads did not include so-called magic words (such as "Elect John Smith" or "Defeat Jane Doe"). No matter that corporations and labor unions, like political parties, serve as vital associations based on the shared interests of their members. Those shared interests may be largely economic, but that does nothing to diminish their constitutional value.

BCRA's broad prohibition of electioneering communications was especially shameful. It applied to any broadcast, cable, or satellite communication by a corporation or union—other than news items or editorial commentary by a media corporation—that mentioned a candidate for federal office and aired within thirty days of a primary or sixty days of a general election. Even if the ad did not expressly advocate the election or defeat of the candidate, it was still banned. In effect, punishment would be meted out for saying too much about someone running for federal office. Plainly, the main effect of the ad ban was to protect incumbents from voter scrutiny of positions they had taken while purportedly serving their constituents.

That transparent infringement on First Amendment rights apparently concerned President George W. Bush. He acknowledged that he had "reservations about the constitutionality of the broad ban on issue advertising, which restrains the speech of a wide variety of groups on issues of public import in the months closest to an election." Yet he signed the legislation anyway, rationalizing that "the courts will resolve these legitimate legal questions as appropriate under the law."[6] Sadly, George Bush did not see eye-to-eye with his nineteenth-century predecessor Andrew Jackson, who had a less crabbed view of the president's constitutional responsibility:

Congress, the Executive, and the court must each for itself be guided by its own opinion of the Constitution. Each public officer who takes an oath to support the Constitution, swears that he will support it as he understands it, and not as it is understood by others. It is as much the duty of the . . . President to decide upon the

constitutionality of any bill or resolution which may be
presented to [him] for passage or approval, as it is of the
supreme judges, when it may be brought before them
for judicial decision.[7]

Instead of heeding President Jackson's sage advice, President Bush
preferred to delegate his constitutional responsibility to the nine justices
on the Supreme Court. When BCRA was ultimately tested for constitutionality in *McConnell*, the justices botched the job.

WHERE DID THE COURT GO WRONG?

In December 2003, two months after an unusually long four-hour oral
argument, the Supreme Court issued its decision in *McConnell*. Two
major themes were evident. First, reaffirming *Buckley*, the Court differ-
entiated political speech, which is protected by the First Amendment,
from the money used to pay for the speech, which is supposedly not
protected. That false dichotomy had the effect of treating campaign
contributions as if they were bribes under the Constitution. According
to the *McConnell* majority, the government cannot restrict a candidate's
speech, but contributions of money by voters to generate that speech
can be capped—albeit at a level slightly higher than the limits upheld in
Buckley. It is as if a free press were guaranteed but the amount that
shareholders could invest in a media company were restricted.

Second, the Court suggested that it would be "corrupt" for a voter,
through his campaign finance activities, to garner more political influence than another voter. A candidate who offered political access in
appreciation for a contribution or expenditure would be presumed to
have acted corruptly. A voter who was the beneficiary of a candidate's
gratitude would be presumed to have exercised undue influence. In effect, the Court rewrote the First Amendment so that it mandated *fair*
speech, as perceived by nine justices, instead of ensuring *free* speech, as
intended by the framers. That egalitarian impulse, utterly at odds with
the idea of individual liberty that animates the Bill of Rights, was at the
core of the Court's opinion.

Justices John Paul Stevens and Sandra Day O'Connor, joined by
David H. Souter, Ruth Bader Ginsburg, and Stephen G. Breyer, observed that they were "under no illusion that BCRA will be the last
congressional statement on the matter. Money, like water, will always
find an outlet. What problems will arise, and how Congress will respond, are concerns for another day."[8] In dissent, Justice Clarence
Thomas agreed: "[S]peech regulation will again expand to cover new
forms of 'circumvention,' only to spur supposed circumvention of the
new regulations, and so forth," in a "never-ending and self-justifying
process."[9]

Nonetheless, the majority upheld BCRA's ban on soft money and
its limits on campaign-season political ads. That prompted this scathing
dissent from Justice Antonin Scalia: "Who could have imagined that
the same Court which, within the past four years, has sternly disapproved of restrictions upon such inconsequential forms of expression as
virtual child pornography, tobacco advertising, dissemination of illegally intercepted communications, and sexually explicit cable program-
ming, would smile with favor upon a law that cuts to the heart of what
the First Amendment is meant to protect: the right to criticize the
government."[10]

In discussing BCRA's ban on soft money, the Court concluded that
allowing such donations to remain unregulated would have "enabled
parties and candidates to circumvent FECA's limitations on . . . contributions."[11] Similarly, the majority was concerned that corporate and
union "issue ads" mentioning a candidate close to an election would
exploit FECA's authorization of such ads unless they used "magic words"
expressly advocating the candidate's election or defeat. *Buckley* had distinguished issue ads from express advocacy, but the *McConnell* Court
disagreed, saying they were "functionally identical in important respects."[12]

Interestingly, the new BCRA regulations do not apply to print ads,
Internet blogs and magazines, news stories, commentary, or editorials
aired by media companies. The Court explained that "reform may take
one step at a time,"[13] and went on to rationalize that a "valid distinction . . . exists between the media industry and other corporations that

are not involved in the regular business of imparting news to the public."[14] In other words, a non-media corporation may not pay for electioneering communications unless, of course, it becomes a media corporation by acquiring a newspaper or radio/TV station, in which case unrestricted spending on commentary or editorials is somehow justified.

Even more bizarre, the Court insisted that soft dollars are presumptively associated with corruption, or at least with the appearance of corruption. For evidence the majority pointed to the practice by many large donors of contributing to both political parties.[15] Thus, asserted the Court, the desire for a political bargain must be the motivating factor, not ideology. But there is nothing inherently wrong with political bargains. Justice Anthony M. Kennedy, in dissent, hit the nail on the head: "It is well understood that a substantial and legitimate reason, if not the only reason, to cast a vote for, or to make a contribution to, one candidate over another is that the candidate will respond by producing those political outcomes that the supporter favors. Democracy is premised on responsiveness."[16]

Furthermore, analyses of voting patterns suggest that congressional action is less a function of donations and lobbying than it is of public opinion, ideology, and party affiliation.[17] Contributions normally go to candidates who favor the donor's position. So any cause-effect relationship is more likely to flow from a candidate's views to a voter's donation, not vice versa. Nor do large contributions "cause" candidates to win elections. The typical pattern is for money to go to candidates who are already favored—mostly incumbents.

As for donations to both parties, the explanation is straightforward: Politicians dish out many and diverse favors that donors want, covering a large range of issues.[18] Thus, it is risky business to invest exclusively in a candidate who may be supportive on some issues but not on others. Moreover, major contributors have no reliable way of knowing what issues will be important to them over the coming months and years. If large contributions are perceived as a problem, the answer from a public policy perspective is not to ignore the First Amendment, but to defuse the entire process by limiting the largesse that government dispenses. If

Congress has fewer favors to bestow, the usual suitors will be less gener-
ous in striking their political bargains.

Justice Scalia sums it up nicely:

> If the Bill of Rights had intended an exception to the
> freedom of speech in order to combat this malign pro-
> clivity of the officeholder to agree with those who
> agree with him, and to speak more with his supporters
> than his opponents, it would surely have said so. It did
> not do so, I think, because the juice is not worth the
> squeeze. Evil corporate (and private affluent) influences
> are well enough checked (so long as adequate
> campaign-expenditure disclosure rules exist) by the
> politician's fear of being portrayed as "in the pocket" of
> so-called moneyed interests. The incremental benefit
> obtained by muzzling corporate speech is more than
> offset by loss of the information and persuasion that
> corporate speech can contain. That, at least, is the as-
> sumption of a constitutional guarantee which prescribes
> that Congress shall make no law abridging the freedom
> of speech.[19]

Scalia clearly understood, as the majority did not, that disproportionate influence by large donors—corporate, union, or individual—is
hardly improper. Rather, it is the inevitable consequence of economic
and social disparities. Speech having unequal influence comes in many
shapes: media, celebrities, religious leaders, and the economically successful. Because of differences in access, quantity, or credibility, the
impact of speech will necessarily vary, but the First Amendment places
its trust in the public, not the government, to sort it out.

WHAT ARE THE IMPLICATIONS?

BCRA is unconstitutional.[20] So, too, are provisions of FECA, upheld
by the Supreme Court in *Buckley*, that allow restrictions on campaign

contributions and express advocacy. That means *McConnell* and *Buckley* should both be overturned. In the process, the Court must tackle three of its key campaign finance tenets:

First, limitations on political contributions should be tested by the Court using the same standard—strict scrutiny—that is applied to limitations on expenditures. Accordingly, such limitations should be invalidated unless they serve a "compelling" governmental interest that cannot be satisfied in a less restrictive manner. Second, the artificial distinction between issue ads and express advocacy should be discarded. Third, the Court's confused notion of "corruption," and its willingness to regard the *appearance* of corruption as a compelling governmental interest without evidence of *actual* corruption, should be rejected as an incoherent loophole in the First Amendment.

1. Contributions Versus Expenditures

There is much debate over the question of whether money is protected speech. In fact, the question itself is misstated. While the contribution or expenditure of money is not by itself speech—except in a limited symbolic sense—a contribution or expenditure *for the exclusive purpose of generating speech* is so entwined with the resulting speech that it is, and should be, protected to the same extent as the speech itself. As with many rights, exercising the right to speak almost always costs money, especially to reach a large audience. The right to speak thus encompasses the right to pay for speech or its distribution, just as the right to legal counsel encompasses the right to hire a lawyer, and the right to free exercise of religion includes the right to contribute to the church of one's choice.

In each of those cases, the expenditure or contribution of money is protected, not because "money is speech" or "money is a lawyer" or "money is religion," but because spending money is part of the *exercise of the right to speak*, to counsel, or to religious freedom. For that reason government limits on spending for speech inevitably inhibit the underlying freedom of speech itself. Consider, for example, government restrictions on campaign spending for meeting rooms and microphones.

Surely such restrictions would impede political expression even if there were no constraints on the speaker or his topic.

The Supreme Court in *Buckley* rationalized that contributions spent by the candidate on communication involve "speech by someone other than the contributor."[21] There should be no difference, however, between contributions and expenditures for First Amendment purposes. In both cases speech is mediated through other parties—private groups, advertising agencies, policy experts, or the like. (Rarely does an expenditure involve a speaker voicing his opinions personally.) Proponents of BCRA seized on *Buckley*'s inconsistent treatment of contributions and expenditures to increase regulations on expenditures. Yet the similarity between the two does not suggest that expenditures be regulated but that regulation of contributions be scrutinized with greater rigor. Most often, restrictions on contributions, like restrictions on expenditures, violate the Constitution.

The image of a contributor handing a candidate a large check may seem troublesome at first blush, but FECA requires contributors as well as candidates to identify anyone making more than a minimal donation.[22] If the contribution is fully disclosed and the money is spent *only* on political speech and related activities, voters can reach their own judgments about the candidate's independence. Unlike payola, which is surreptitiously received and then spent on private pleasures such as cars, boats, and jewels, campaign contributions are used only for publicly disclosed and constitutionally favored political speech. What a candidate gains from a contribution is a greater ability to communicate. If his message is well received, he may be elected. In that sense, however, the benefit from a contribution is no different from the benefit of any other political support.

Naturally, problems will remain whether or not contribution limits are relaxed. Politicians will still use "earmarks"—special legislative provisions, sometimes benefiting large donors—artfully added to complex spending bills at the last minute, often avoiding floor debate and skirting public attention. But the answer to that problem is greater transparency, not the suppression of political donations. To the extent that the earmark process is hidden from voters, that situation has to be addressed head-on. Once voters are aware that their senator or representative may have favored a special interest group, they can determine whether he deserves their continued backing.

Similarly, unused campaign funds can become a war chest, spent later for unrelated activities. Under the Ethics Reform Act of 1989, such funds cannot be converted to private use when an elected official steps down from office. That restriction is perfectly appropriate; the money was donated to promote the candidate's election, not his personal aggrandizement. The First Amendment protects the former, not the latter. If the restrictions on unused funds are still too loose—a subject beyond the scope of this commentary—the remedy is to make them tighter. And if voters remain unaware that campaign donations have been diverted to pay for other expenses—even those expenses that are political rather than personal—the remedy is, once again, greater transparency, not a limit on the underlying contributions.

2. Express Advocacy Versus Issue Advocacy

Under *Buckley*, the artificial line between issue advocacy, which was not regulated, and express advocacy, which was treated as a contribution and hence forbidden to labor unions and most corporations, turned on whether the speech urged people to "vote for," "vote against," "elect," or "defeat" a clearly identified candidate. That line makes no sense. It was intended to carve out a narrow exception to the general rule that expenditures, unlike contributions, were immune from regulation. Without that exception, so it was argued, corporations and unions would circumvent the ban on direct contributions by spending money on unregulated expenditures. The *Buckley* Court's "solution": prohibit expenditures that paid for speeches containing such "magic words" as *elect* and *defeat*—that is, speech directed at electing specific candidates rather than promoting issues.

Yet when a corporation or union expressly advocates the election or defeat of a candidate, that act—no less than issue advocacy—lies at the heart of the First Amendment. The Court's willingness to condone limits on express advocacy, applying the same lenient standard as applied to contributions, was never coherent. Even if an ad with the magic words was deemed more valuable to the candidate than other forms of speech—and thus more susceptible to corruption—that would simply command vigilance in uncovering and punishing corruption if it occurred. But heightened vigilance does not translate into preemptive regulation. And if regulations are nonetheless enacted, courts should not apply a lesser standard in determining whether they pass constitutional muster. Restrictions on express advocacy, like restrictions on issue advocacy, ought to be strictly scrutinized.

Unaccountably, BCRA, as affirmed in *McConnell*, moves in the opposite direction. Rather than reject *Buckley*'s diminished regard for express advocacy by corporations and unions, BCRA adds yet another level of regulations aimed at electioneering communications. In effect, BCRA has eliminated the bright-line magic words and instead bans all corporate and union broadcast ads that merely mention a candidate within sixty days of an election or thirty days of a primary. When political speech matters most—close to an election—the *McConnell* Court valued it least.

Fortunately, the Court gave itself some wiggle room by allowing specific ads to be reviewed on a case-by-case basis. By June 2007, only four years after *McConnell*, Chief Justice John G. Roberts and Justice Samuel A. Alito had replaced Chief Justice William H. Rehnquist and Justice O'Connor. The newly constituted Court decided that *McConnell*'s bright-line rule for electioneering communications might have gone too far. The case was *Federal Election Commission v. Wisconsin Right to Life*, in which a nonprofit group (WRTL) wanted to run an ad shortly before the 2004 election asking Wisconsin citizens to contact their two senators, Russ Feingold (D) and Herbert H. Kohl (D), and "tell them to oppose the filibuster" of President Bush's judicial nominees.[23]

WRTL argued that the ad was a genuine effort to speak about an *issue*, not attack a particular *candidate*. Of course, under a strict reading of *McConnell* that wouldn't matter, because Feingold was mentioned in the ad, and he was running (unopposed) for reelection. In *Wisconsin Right to Life*, with Justice Alito providing a critical fifth vote, the Court agreed with WRTL: An ad merely advocating a position, without criticizing a particular candidate, was not an electioneering communication under BCRA. Writing for a five-member majority, Chief Justice Roberts established a new standard for "issue ads": They can be barred "only if the ad is susceptible of no reasonable interpretation other than as an appeal to vote for or against a specific candidate."[24]

If that is progress, it is measured in inches. We began with vague restrictions on "express advocacy" under FECA. Then *Buckley* clarified matters by banning only those corporate and union ads containing certain "magic words." *McConnell* extended the ban to "electioneering communications" that mention candidates near an election. Now we're back to "vague" under *Wisconsin Right to Life*: Apparently it is okay to discuss an issue but not if a "reasonable interpretation" of the discussion might influence someone's vote. The framers must be turning in their graves.

3. Corruption and the Appearance of Corruption

Much of the difficulty in recent campaign finance law stems from an overly broad view of government's interest in regulating corruption. Essentially, government's compelling interest should be limited to quid pro quo bribery of actual or potential officeholders—that is, either (a) the exchange of political promises or deeds by the candidate in return for *personal* favors from his supporters, or (b) contributions to procure favoritism in the award of government contracts or the receipt of government services, in violation of an official's fiduciary obligation to his constituents. But contributions and expenditures exclusively dedicated to generating political speech may not ordinarily be equated with bribes, and the value of speech in persuading or informing the public may not constitutionally be considered corrupt.

Our democratic system in general and the First Amendment in particular assume that politicians and the public may be influenced by the political speech of competing interest groups and individuals. A system under which influential speech costs money entails some risk that politicians will place their self-interest ahead of their constituents. Yet, however imperfect that system may be, it is the one the Constitution established. It may not be redefined simply as "corrupt" to bypass the First Amendment. Nor may voters—even those who make large political donations—be treated presumptively as conspirators against the public.

Occasionally, politicians behave unlawfully, but rarely has government been able to prove actual corruption from campaign contributions. Instead, to justify its regulations, government insists that we must prevent a "perception" of corruption that might shake confidence in our democratic institutions. (Yet mere public suspicions or perceptions afford no basis for ignoring our constitutional scheme.) Rather, the proper answer is either more speech, the election of candidates voluntarily practicing the public's notion of virtue, or, if the existing system cannot hold the public's confidence, a constitutional amendment.

Instead of preventing corruption or even the appearance of corruption, the real effect of the regulations upheld in *McConnell* and *Buckley* has been to protect incumbents from upstart challengers. The careers of sitting politicians can more easily be perpetuated if the speech of their opponents can be repressed.

As for money, it is just a symptom. Overweening government has wormed its way into nearly every aspect of our lives. Our pervasive regulatory and redistributive state creates huge incentives for profiteering. With so many benefits to be doled out, the potential for abuse is enormous. And because there is a big government problem, there is also a big money problem. By cutting government down to size, however, we can minimize the influence of big money.

Until then we need to restore free political speech by razing the ineffective and unconstitutional structure that *McConnell* and *Buckley* have put in place.

CHAPTER 6

Gun Owners' Rights

The Dirty Dozen List: *United States v. Miller* (1939)

WHAT IS THE CONSTITUTIONAL ISSUE?

"A well regulated Militia, being necessary to the security of a free State, the right of the people to keep and bear Arms, shall not be infringed."—U.S. Constitution, Second Amendment.

A tale of two cities: New York, New York, and Anniston, Alabama. "Violent armed robbers take over a restaurant, terrorizing employees and customers. The predators herd the hapless victims into a refrigerator with the intention of killing them. Shots are fired, and the gruesome disaster ends."[1] That ordeal unfolded in both cities nearly a decade apart. The outcomes were vastly different.

In December 1991, at a Shoney's restaurant in Anniston, the robbers discovered that a customer, Thomas Glenn Terry, had hidden under a table. One of the robbers pulled a gun on Terry. Bad idea. Terry, who was legally armed with a .45 semiautomatic pistol, fired five shots into the robber's chest and abdomen, killing him instantly. A second robber, holding the restaurant manager at gunpoint, opened fire on Terry, who suffered a grazing wound to the hip. Terry responded in kind, critically wounding the second robber. Shoney's customers and employees were freed. No one else was injured.[2]

Fast-forward to May 2000. Six men and a woman at a Wendy's restaurant in New York were bound, gagged, and forced into a walk-in refrigerator. Then they were shot in the head. Five died; two were gravely injured. The gunmen "faced no meaningful opposition to their unspeakable cruelty. In fact, under New York's strict gun control laws, any restaurant employee or patron who had armed himself would be considered as guilty as the murderers."[3] New York, unlike Alabama, didn't trust its citizens to arm themselves for self-defense.

Six years later another resident of the Big Apple discovered an antidote to the city's absurd gun laws: She decided to ignore them. In September 2006, fifty-six-year-old Margaret Johnson left her Harlem apartment to visit a nearby firing range. Riding in a wheelchair, accompanied only by her small dog, Ms. Johnson was attacked. She "felt an arm grab her violently from behind, tearing at her pocketbook and her necklace. The man managed to get the necklace, but Ms. Johnson refused to let go of her pocketbook. . . . As the man choked her . . . , Ms. Johnson pulled out her gun and fired a single shot."[4] The unsuccessful mugger, with a gunshot wound to his elbow, had nine previous arrests, mostly for robbery, and had spent several years in prison for narcotics violations. Who knows how many muggings he committed without being caught.

Ms. Johnson had no criminal record and faced no charges because New York authorities chose not to enforce the city's gun laws. She was licensed to carry a .357 handgun to and from a firearms range, but the weapon had to be unloaded and in a locked container—hence worthless against an attacker trying to choke her and steal her property.[5] Ironically, New York mayor Michael Bloomberg had just returned from a trip to Washington, D.C., where he had complained that politicians who oppose measures to crack down on illegal guns have been "cowed or duped" by an "extremist gun lobby." No one should be permitted to possess a gun illegally, added Bloomberg.[6] Tell that to Margaret Johnson. Tell her how New York police—arriving long after she had been mugged and robbed—would have protected her.

Or tell it to Suzanna Gratia, whose mother and father were killed by a crazed gunman in Luby's Cafeteria in Killeen, Texas. It was October 1991, during lunch hour, when George Jo Hennard crashed his Ford pickup through Luby's plate glass doors and then calmly started shooting people with two 9-millimeter semiautomatic pistols. The massacre went on for ten minutes—enough time for Hennard to reload five times. No one returned fire because no one was armed. Texas law at the time barred private citizens from carrying a firearm, either openly or concealed. Before police arrived, Hennard had slaughtered fifteen women and eight men, and wounded another nineteen. Then he killed himself.[7]

Ms. Gratia was there, with a gun stored uselessly in her car 150 feet away. She saw her parents executed while she obeyed the law that protected their killer. Sixteen months later she reflected on the horrific events of that afternoon: "No, I do not absolutely know that I could have hit him or frightened him away. But I do know that I was less than 10 feet away from him, that he was standing while everyone else in Luby's was on the floor, that I was thinking clearly, that I could have braced my handgun against the table my father and I had overturned as a barricade, that with that gun I can hit far smaller targets at far greater distances. I know that my having my handgun would have at least given us a chance."[8]

The list of victims could go on and on. Kitty Genovese in the 1960s was "slowly murdered in the courtyard of her apartment complex in New York City while dozens of people watched from their windows too fearful to come to her aid . . . because [they] had been disarmed by gun control laws."[9] Or thirty years later, Judith Houston Boston, a pediatric nurse in Washington, D.C., "was gunned down outside her apartment building and bled to death while her fearful neighbors cowered behind the locked doors of their apartments."[10] Or Alan Berg, a Jewish talk show host in Denver, who was killed in 1995 after receiving death threats from white supremacists. Berg had applied unsuccessfully for a concealed handgun carry permit. Only applicants with a "true and compelling need" could get permits. According to one police official, "Just because you fear for your life is not a compelling reason to have a permit."[11] Berg never got the chance to show whether a handgun might have saved his life.

More recently, on the Virginia Tech campus in Blacksburg, Virginia, a crazed killer fired hundreds of shots and methodically massacred thirty-two people. Why did nobody stop the madman as he reloaded his handgun time after time? For one possible explanation, consider this report from a *Roanoke Times* article: A bill, introduced on behalf of the Virginia Citizens Defense League, would have overridden university rules and given properly licensed students and employees the right to carry handguns on public college campuses. The bill died in the Virginia General Assembly fifteen months before the April 2007 bloodbath. Virginia Tech spokesman Larry Hincker was pleased with the outcome at the time. "I'm sure the university community is appreciative of the General Assembly's actions because this will help parents, students, faculty and visitors feel safe on our campus." Thirty-two fatalities would prove him dead wrong.[12]

Killers such as the lunatic at Virginia Tech, undeterred by laws against murder, are not going to be deterred by laws against guns. Nor will antigun regulations have any salutary effect on the deep-rooted causes of violent crime, such as illegitimacy, teenage pregnancy, unemployment, dysfunctional schools, and drug and alcohol abuse. The cures are complex and protracted. Yet we need not become passive prey for criminal and psychotic predators while we attack the underlying reasons for their lethal behavior. Americans who want to defend themselves by possessing suitable firearms should be able to do so. Instead, our politicians enact gun controls—misguided and often unconstitutional obstacles to self-defense, helpful only to the armed thugs who commit the violent acts.

An obvious remedy when our legislators engage in such mischief is to convince them that more guns in the hands of law-abiding citizens will reduce crime. That solution would work, but its implementation on a state-by-state basis will be time-consuming and difficult. Another remedy, national in scope, is to educate the Supreme Court on the real meaning of the right to keep and bear arms. Only then will the Court exercise its necessary and proper role in overturning unconstitutional restrictions on firearms—federal, state, and local.

And so we consider in this chapter the question that has divided Second Amendment scholars for decades: Does the right to keep and bear arms belong to us as individuals, or does the Constitution merely recognize the collective right of states to arm the members of their militias? In 1939 the Court had a golden opportunity to resolve that question. The case was *United States v. Miller*, and the challenged statute required registration of machine guns, sawed-off rifles, sawed-off shotguns, and silencers.[13] Lamentably, the Court did little to illuminate, and much to mystify, the meaning of the Second Amendment. Justice James Clark McReynolds's opinion was riddled with ambiguities. It established no definitive legal principle and offered no useful guidance or analysis to inform any modern-day Second Amendment deliberation.

And that is the good news.

Much worse from our perspective—and the reason that *Miller* is included among the Dirty Dozen—is that the Supreme Court provided a rationale for appellate courts across the nation to reject the individual rights view of the Second Amendment. As a result of the Court's abdication in *Miller*, the law of the land in forty-seven states (except Texas, Louisiana, Mississippi, and the District of Columbia) is that individuals have no redress in federal court under the Second Amendment of the U.S. Constitution if a state bans the possession and use of firearms for private (nonmilitia) purposes.

What Were the Facts?

In *Miller*, two mobsters, Jack Miller and Frank Layton, were indicted for knowingly transporting a sawed-off shotgun from Oklahoma to Arkansas in violation of the 1934 National Firearms Act, which required federal registration of such guns and payment of a substantial tax.[14] Neither Miller nor Layton was charged with firing the gun or committing any crime involving use of the gun. Instead, they were indicted for a technical violation of the registration and tax requirements of the act.

The Arkansas trial court dispensed with the case in a single paragraph: "The court is of the opinion that this section [of the National Firearms Act] is invalid in that it violates the Second Amendment."[15]

That was the right decision, but its brevity was both unorthodox and virtually unprecedented. The decision contained no examination of other cases or of constitutional text, structure, purpose, or history. Such cursory analysis meant that the opinion had no teeth. Moreover, the defendant, Jack Miller, and his counsel, Paul Gutensohn, did not present any evidence or extended argument concerning the critical Second Amendment issues before the court.

Then the *Miller* case took an even more bizarre turn. After losing in the lower court, the United States government appealed directly to the Supreme Court.[16] There, the government challenged the ruling that the Second Amendment invalidated the National Firearms Act. On March 15, 1939, the Court directed Miller's counsel, Gutensohn, to appear in Washington, D.C., for oral argument on March 31—giving him a mere two weeks to craft his written brief and prepare for a grueling interrogation by the justices. Gutensohn, who was court-appointed and had not been compensated for his representation of Miller, replied that he had received neither the government's brief nor a copy of the trial court record. He stated further that he wanted to file a written brief but doubted that he could travel all the way to Washington for oral argument.

The Court then offered Gutensohn a delay until late April. Apparently exasperated, he declined by telegram: "Suggest case be submitted on [government's] brief. Unable to obtain any money from clients to be present and argue case." Gutensohn's proposal—that only the government's brief would inform the Court, with no response by the defendants—was arguably malpractice and surely contrary to his clients' interest. He should properly have asked that counsel be appointed and the appeal delayed.

Alternatively, the Supreme Court, on its own volition, could have appointed Gutensohn or someone else as counsel for the defendants and then provided adequate time to prepare briefs and oral argument. That would have offered a semblance of fairness and due process to Miller and Layton. More important, it would have ensured that the Second Amendment question—resolution of which would affect the constitutional rights of all Americans—would get a full briefing and fair hearing before the Court. In fact, the argument for court-appointed paid counsel was even stronger in *Miller* than in most appeals. After all, Miller prevailed in the lower court. The United States, not the defendants, initiated the appeal to the Supreme Court. In effect, the government propelled *Miller* to the High Court, pitting unrepresented defendants against highly qualified Justice Department lawyers.

In any event, Miller and Layton were unable or unwilling to defend themselves on appeal, especially within impossible time constraints. Neither defendant showed up before the Supreme Court; they had no written brief to support them and no legal representation at oral argument. The Court did nothing to appoint other counsel or reschedule the case. Instead, Justice McReynolds produced a muddled opinion that has confused lawyers, law students, judges, and the public for almost seven decades.

When it was all over, the Supreme Court reversed the lower court's holding that the National Firearms Act violated the Second Amendment. Justice McReynolds ruled that only those weapons related to militia use were protected by the amendment. McReynolds's refusal to resolve the key question of whether the Second Amendment protects individual or collective rights has triggered a debate that lasts to this day. In the end, *Miller* was remanded for a new trial. But before the trial could be conducted, Jack Miller was shot and killed. Frank Layton agreed to a plea bargain and was sentenced to five years on probation.

Where Did the Court Go Wrong?

Correctly interpreted, the main clause of the Second Amendment ("the right of the people to keep and bear Arms, shall not be infringed") defines and secures the right.[17] The subordinate clause ("A well regulated Militia, being necessary to the security of a free State") helps explain why we have the right. Thus, membership in a well-regulated militia is a sufficient but not necessary condition to the exercise of our right to keep and bear arms. Imagine if the Second Amendment said, "A well-educated Electorate, being necessary to self-governance in a free State, the right of the people to keep and read Books, shall not be infringed." Surely, no one would suggest that only registered voters (that is, members of the electorate) would have the right to read.[18] Yet that is precisely the effect if the Second Amendment is interpreted to apply only to members of a militia.

If the Second Amendment truly meant what the collective rights advocates propose, then the text would read, "A well regulated Militia, being necessary to the security of a free State, the right of the States to arm their Militias, shall not be infringed." But the Second Amendment, like the First and Fourth Amendments, refers explicitly to "the right of the people." And consider the placement of the amendment within the Bill of Rights, the part of the Constitution that deals exclusively with the rights of individuals. There can be no doubt that First Amendment rights such as speech and religion belong to us as individuals. Similarly, Fourth Amendment protections against unreasonable searches are individual rights. In the context of the Second Amendment, we secure "the right of the people" by guaranteeing the right of each person.

Second Amendment protections were not intended for the state but for each individual against the state—a deterrent to government tyranny. Here is how federal appellate judge Alex Kozinski put it: "All too many of the . . . great tragedies of history—Stalin's atrocities, the killing fields of Cambodia, the Holocaust—were perpetrated by armed troops against unarmed populations."[19] Nearly two centuries before those horrific events, Alexander Hamilton made a similar point in *Federalist No. 29*: "[I]f circumstances should at any time oblige the government to form an army of any magnitude, that army can never be formidable to the liberties of the people while there is a large body of citizens, little, if at all, inferior to them in discipline and the use of arms, who stand ready to defend their own rights and those of their fellow-citizens."

James Madison agreed. In *Federalist No. 46* he declared that a standing army "would be opposed [by] a militia amounting to near half a million citizens with arms in their hands." Alluding to "the advantage of being armed, which the Americans possess over the people of almost every other nation," Madison continued: "Notwithstanding the military establishments in the several kingdoms of Europe, which are carried as far as the public resources will bear, the governments are afraid to trust the people with arms."

Most persons would argue that the threat of tyrannical government is less today than it was when our republic was experiencing its birth pangs. Perhaps so. But government's inability to defend its citizens against foreign and domestic predators remains a serious problem. The demand for police to defend us increases in proportion to our inability to defend ourselves. That is why disarmed societies tend to become police states.

Witness law-abiding inner-city residents, disarmed by gun control, begging for police protection against drug gangs—despite the terrible violations of civil liberties that such protection entails (such as curfews, antiloitering laws, civil asset forfeiture, nonconsensual searches of public housing, and even video surveillance of residents in high crime areas). An unarmed citizenry creates the conditions that lead to tyranny. The right to bear arms is preventive; it reduces the demand for a police state. When people are incapable of protecting themselves, they become either dependents of the state or victims of the criminals.

That is what happened to the five people killed at Wendy's in New York City; to twenty-three more fatalities at Luby's Cafeteria in Killeen, Texas; to Kitty Genovese, Judith Houston Boston, Alan Berg, and thirty-two casualties at Virginia Tech. They became victims, unarmed and defenseless against gun-toting fanatics. Not enough police, too many gun controllers in the legislature, and too few Supreme Court justices willing to declare unambiguously in *United States v. Miller* that the Second Amendment secures an individual right to keep and bear arms.

The Court's focus in *Miller* was on the prefatory clause of the Second Amendment. McReynolds reasoned that the purpose of the amendment was "to assure the continuation and render possible the effectiveness of [militia] forces."[20] Therefore, the amendment "must be interpreted and applied with that end in view."[21] Nowhere did the Court question whether Miller and Layton were members of the militia. The unanimous holding in *Miller* hinged not on the defendants' qualification for militia service but on the particular weapon that was the subject of their indictment.

Here is the crucial passage from McReynolds's opinion:

> In the absence of any evidence tending to show that possession or use of a "shotgun having a barrel of less than eighteen inches in length" at this time has some reasonable relationship to the preservation or efficiency of a well regulated militia, we cannot say that the Second Amendment guarantees the right to keep and bear such an instrument. Certainly it is not within judicial notice that this weapon is any part of the ordinary military equipment or that its use could contribute to the common defense.[22]

In other words, because Miller and Layton had produced no evidence linking the shotgun to the preservation of a militia, they were still subject to the National Firearms Act. The Second Amendment did not guarantee them a right to transport such a weapon across state lines and evade the prescribed tax.

"The Militia," said the Court, "comprised all males physically capable of acting in concert for the common defense."[23] Each person had an obligation "to possess arms, and, with certain exceptions, to cooperate in the work of defence."[24] That suggested a right belonging to each of us individually. But the Court also held that the right extended only to weapons rationally related to a militia—not self-evidently including a sawed-off shotgun. McReynolds's mixed ruling has puzzled legal scholars for nearly seventy years. The obvious inference is that military weapons *are* covered. But if military use is the decisive test, then in today's context, citizens could possess shoulder-launched missiles. Clearly, that is not what the Court had in mind. Indeed, antigun activists would be apoplectic if the Court's military-use doctrine were extended to cover weapons such as the improvised explosive devices now used in Iraq.

A proper reading of the Second Amendment should not attempt to link each and every weapon to militia use—except to note that the grand scheme of the amendment was to ensure that persons trained in the use of firearms would be ready for militia service. That was the view of the Georgia Supreme Court, for example, in a case decided in 1846: "The right of the whole people, old and young, men, women and boys, and not militia only, to keep and bear arms of every description, and not such merely as are used by the militia, shall not be infringed, curtailed, or broken in upon, in the smallest degree; and all this for the important end to be attained: the rearing up and qualifying a well-regulated militia, so vitally necessary to the security of a free State."[25]

Perhaps McReynolds would have cited the Georgia case if the Court had benefited from legal briefing on behalf of the defendants. But that is not what transpired. Rather, McReynolds endorsed the strange notion that the Second Amendment protects only weapons with a defined military use—a rocket-propelled grenade for every household.

Because the *Miller* opinion is so murky, unless and until the opinion is overturned, it must be interpreted narrowly, allowing restrictions on such weapons as machine guns and silencers, with slight value to law-abiding citizens and high value to criminals. Thus, *Miller* applies to the type of weapon, not to the question of whether the Second Amendment protects all individuals, only members of a militia, or just states.

That is not, however, the manner in which *Miller* has been cited by trial and appellate courts in ten of twelve judicial circuits—all but the Fifth Circuit and the D.C. Circuit (about which more in a moment). From border to border, courts have seized on Justice McReynolds's unfortunate pronouncement in *Miller* that the aim of the Second Amendment was to "assure the continuation and render possible the effectiveness" of the militia.[26] *Miller's* plain message, according to those courts, was that the constitutional right to keep and bear arms must relate to the militia and does not apply to individuals who want to possess and use firearms for private purposes. Here is a sampling of quotations from ten federal appellate courts interpreting *Miller*:

- First Circuit: According to *Miller*, the "second amendment applies only to weapons that have a 'reasonable relationship to the preservation or efficiency of a well regulated militia.' "[27] *Miller* did not establish a general rule protecting military weapons when they are used for private nonmilitary purposes.[28]

- Second Circuit: "[T]he right to possess a gun is clearly not a fundamental right."[29]

- Third Circuit: The *Miller* Court "found no conflict between federal gun laws and the Second Amendment, narrowly construing the latter to guarantee the right to bear arms as a member of a militia."[30]

- Fourth Circuit: "[T]he Second Amendment only confers a collective right of keeping and bearing arms."[31]

- Sixth Circuit: Although "the Supreme Court did not lay down a general rule in *Miller*, . . . [i]t is clear that the Second Amendment guarantees a collective rather than an individual right."[32]

- Seventh Circuit: "*Miller* and its progeny do confirm that the Second Amendment establishes no right to possess a firearm apart from the role possession of the gun might play in maintaining a state militia."[33]

- Eighth Circuit: "[T]he Supreme Court held in *Miller* that the Second Amendment protects the right to bear arms in 'some reasonable relationship to the preservation or efficiency of a well-regulated militia.' "[34]

- Ninth Circuit: *Miller* "found that the right to keep and bear arms is meant solely to protect the right of the states to keep and maintain armed militia."[35]

- Tenth Circuit: "*Miller* has been interpreted by this court and other courts to hold that the Second Amendment does not guarantee an individual the right to keep and transport a firearm where there is no evidence that possession of that firearm was related to the preservation or efficiency of a well-regulated militia."[36]

- Eleventh Circuit: "[T]he *Miller* Court understood the Second Amendment to protect only the possession or use of weapons that is reasonably related to a militia actively maintained and trained by the states."[37]

Happily, the U.S. Court of Appeals for the Fifth Circuit—covering Texas, Louisiana, and Mississippi—reached a different conclusion. In a 2001 Texas case, *United States v. Emerson*, the court decided that *Miller* upheld neither the individual rights model of the Second Amendment nor the collective rights model.[38] According to the Fifth Circuit, *Miller* simply determined that the weapons at issue were not protected. Thus, liberating itself from *Miller*'s muddy reasoning, the Fifth Circuit held, unequivocally, that the Constitution "protects the right of individuals, including those not then actually a member of any militia . . . to privately possess and bear their own firearms . . . suitable as personal individual weapons."[39]

That individual right is not absolute, said the court. For example, killers do not have a constitutional right to possess weapons of mass destruction. Some persons and some weapons may be restricted. Indeed, the court held in 2001 that Dr. Timothy Joe Emerson's Second Amendment rights could be temporarily curtailed because there was reason to believe he might have posed a threat to his estranged wife. But Emerson's personal situation aside, the Fifth Circuit—alone at that time among all the federal appellate courts that had tried to unravel *Miller*'s tangled logic—subscribed to the individual rights model of the Second Amendment.

Enter then–U.S. Attorney General John Ashcroft. First, in a letter to the National Rifle Association, he reaffirmed a long-held opinion that all law-abiding citizens have an individual right to keep and bear arms.[40] Ashcroft's letter was supported by eighteen state attorneys general, including six Democrats, and was followed by a Justice Department brief filed with the Supreme Court in the *Emerson* case.[41] The brief expressly argued, for the first time in formal court papers, against the collective rights position.[42] Then in 2004 the Justice Department affirmed its view of the Second Amendment in an extended and scholarly staff memorandum opinion prepared for the attorney general. The opinion concluded that "The Second Amendment secures a right of individuals generally, not a right of States or a right restricted to persons serving in militias."[43]

Despite the Justice Department's individualist interpretation of the

Second Amendment, the government had maintained in its brief that the outcome in *Emerson* was correct and need not be reviewed by the Supreme Court. According to the brief, even though Dr. Emerson had an individual right to bear arms, a federal government restriction on persons subject to a domestic violence restraining order was a permissible exception to Second Amendment protection.

Many legal scholars are now taking that same position—namely, the Second Amendment secures an individual right that can, however, be limited in some circumstances. Harvard's Alan Dershowitz, a former American Civil Liberties Union board member, says he "hates" guns and wants the Second Amendment repealed. But he condemns "foolish liberals who are trying to read the Second Amendment out of the Constitution by claiming it's not an individual right. . . . They're courting disaster by encouraging others to use the same means to eliminate portions of the Constitution they don't like."[44] Harvard's Laurence Tribe, another respected liberal scholar, and Yale professor Akhil Amar acknowledge that there is an individual right to keep and bear arms, albeit limited by "reasonable regulation in the interest of public safety."[45]

In that respect, Tribe and Amar agree with the *Emerson* court and with the Justice Department on two fundamental issues: First, the Second Amendment confirms an individual rather than a collective right. Second, that right is not absolute; it is subject to regulation. To the extent there is disagreement, it hinges on what constitutes permissible regulation—that is, where to draw the line.

The Supreme Court declined to review *Emerson*. Although the Fifth Circuit's interpretation of the Second Amendment differed fundamentally from the interpretation by other federal courts, the High Court sidestepped the question—possibly because Dr. Emerson had lost. In the end, the federal statute at issue in *Emerson* was upheld by the Fifth Circuit, notwithstanding the appellate court's view that the Second Amendment secures an individual right. Thus, the statute is still invoked in all U.S. jurisdictions; hence, the Supreme Court had no practical need to resolve the Second Amendment debate.

WHAT ARE THE IMPLICATIONS?

That meant *Miller* remained on the books despite its misleading reading of the Second Amendment that had effectively gutted the amendment in almost every state. Fortunately, help was on the way. In the District of Columbia, the only judicial circuit that had not fleshed out its view of the Second Amendment, the U.S. Court of Appeals for the D.C. Circuit had an opportunity to interpret *Miller*. The case was *Parker v. District of Columbia*, a straightforward constitutional challenge to D.C.'s draconian gun control laws.[46] *Parker* was filed by six law-abiding D.C. residents who wanted to possess functional firearms to defend themselves where they lived and slept. *Parker* was not about machine guns and assault weapons. It was about the right to own ordinary, garden-variety handguns. Nor did the plaintiffs argue for the right to carry a gun outside the home. That is a more complicated question for another day. The *Parker* litigation was about a pistol in the home for self-defense.

Off and on over the years, Washington, D.C., has reclaimed its title as the nation's murder capital. Yet the D.C. government has been feckless in disarming violent criminals. At the same time, however, it has done a superb job of disarming decent, peaceable residents.

For starters, all firearms must be registered in D.C., but handgun registration has been banned since 1976. Even those pistols registered prior to the 1976 ban cannot be carried from room to room in the home without a license, which is never granted. Moreover, all firearms in the home, including rifles and shotguns, must be unloaded and either disassembled or bound by a trigger lock. In effect, no one in the district can possess a functional firearm in his or her own residence. The law applies not just to "unfit" persons such as felons, minors, and the mentally incompetent, but across the board to ordinary, honest, responsible citizens.

More than three dozen challenges to the D.C. law had already been filed—but mostly by criminals serving long sentences for gun possession. The *Parker* case was different. The lead plaintiff, Ms. Shelly Parker, lived in a high-crime neighborhood in the heart of the district. People living on her block were harassed relentlessly by drug dealers and addicts. Ms. Parker decided to do something about it. She called the police—time and again—then encouraged her neighbors to do the same. She organized block meetings to discuss the problem. For her audacity, Shelly Parker was labeled a troublemaker by the dealers, who threatened her at every opportunity.

In 2002 the back window of her car was broken. Then a large rock was thrown through her front window. Her security camera was stolen from the outside of her house. A drug user drove his car into her back fence. A year later a dealer pounded on her door and tried to pry his way into her house, repeatedly yelling, "Bitch, I'll kill you. I live on this block, too." Ms. Parker knew that the police were "not going to do very much about the drug problem" on her block. She wanted to possess a functional handgun within her home for self-defense but feared arrest and prosecution because of D.C.'s unconstitutional gun ban.

A second plaintiff was a special police officer who carried a handgun to provide security for a federal office building, the Thurgood Marshall Judicial Center. But when he applied for permission to possess a handgun within his home, to defend his own household, the D.C. government turned him down. Other plaintiffs included a gay man who was assaulted in another city on account of his sexual orientation. While walking to dinner with a coworker, he encountered a group of young men who started yelling "faggot," "homo," "queer," "we're going to kill you, and they'll never find your bodies." He pulled his handgun out of his backpack, and his assailants retreated. He could not have done that in Washington, D.C.

The six plaintiffs in *Parker v. District of Columbia* asked a federal judge to prevent D.C. from barring the registration of handguns, banning the possession of functional firearms within the home, and forbidding firearms from being carried from room to room. The plaintiffs lived in the district, paid their taxes in the district, and obeyed the laws in the district. But the District of Columbia said that if someone broke into their houses, their only choice was to call 911 and pray that the police would arrive in time. That is not good enough. The right to keep and bear arms includes the right to defend your property, your family, and your life.

For several reasons Washington, D.C., was a unique and appropriate venue to affirm that the Second Amendment secures an individual right to keep and bear arms. First, the city's rate of gun violence was among the highest in the nation, yet D.C. had the most restrictive gun laws of any major city. If "reasonable" regulations are those that prohibit bad persons from possessing massively destructive firearms, then the district's blanket prohibition of handguns was patently unreasonable.

Second, until 1868 when the Fourteenth Amendment was ratified, the Bill of Rights applied only to the federal government. Since then, the Court has held that most of the other ten amendments apply to the states as well. But the applicability of the Second Amendment to the states has not been resolved. That complex and widely debated question need not be addressed when a Second Amendment challenge is raised in Washington, D.C. That is because the U.S. Congress, not a state, is constitutionally empowered "To exercise exclusive Legislation in all Cases whatsoever" over the nation's capital.[47]

Third, felonies under D.C. law are prosecuted by the U.S. Attorney for the District of Columbia, an employee of the Justice Department—the same Justice Department that is now on record favoring an individual rights theory of the Second Amendment.

The D.C. litigation strategy worked. In March 2007, in a block-buster opinion, the *Parker* plaintiffs prevailed in the U.S. Court of Appeals. A three-judge panel held, two-to-one, that "the Second Amendment protects an individual right to keep and bear arms."[48] Moreover, the court continued, activities protected by the amendment "are not limited to militia service, nor is an individual's enjoyment of the right contingent upon his or her continued or intermittent enroll-ment in the militia."[49] In fact, said the court, "the right to arms existed prior to the formation of the new government" in 1789.[50]

At this writing, *Parker* (under a new name, *District of Columbia v. Heller*) is headed to the Supreme Court, and that is where it belongs. The citizens of this country deserve a foursquare pronouncement from the nation's highest court about the real meaning of the Second Amendment. Presently, because courts in forty-seven states have used *Miller's* opaque holding to deny Second Amendment rights, individuals who seek to keep and bear arms for private use can depend only on state constitutions and statutes. That is unacceptable. A disputable Second Amendment right without a legally enforceable federal remedy is, in some states, no right at all.

For those of us eagerly awaiting a comprehensive and comprehensible Supreme Court statement on the Second Amendment—overturning or at least defogging *Miller*—the Constitution is on our side. But meanwhile the implications of the *Miller* decision are dangerous and far-reaching. Armed and violent criminals have turned many inner-city neighborhoods into combat zones. Yet the evidence is clear: More guns in the hands of responsible owners yield lower rates of violent crime. Gun control does not work. In fact, gun control prevents weaker people from defending themselves against stronger predators. Two think-tank scholars put it this way: "Reliable, durable, and easy to operate, modern firearms are the most effective means of self-defense ever devised. They require minimal maintenance and, unlike knives and other weapons, do not depend on an individual's physical strength for their effectiveness. Only a gun can allow a 110-pound woman to defend herself against a 200-pound man."[51]

Examining the past half century, civil liberties lawyer Don B. Kates reminds us that guns are not correlated with criminal violence. In the 1950s the U.S. murder rate was steady although the number of guns increased annually by roughly 2 million. From the mid-sixties until the early seventies, the murder rate doubled along with the additional 2.5 to 3 million new guns each year. But the late seventies saw a steady and then a declining murder rate accompanied by 4 to 5 million more guns annually. That decline preceded an explosion of violent killings during the crack cocaine epidemic of the late eighties—followed, however, by a dramatic decrease in murder through the nineties, even as Americans acquired 50 million guns. Long-term, considering the thirty-year period from 1974 to 2003, guns in circulation doubled, but murder rates declined by a third. "So much for the quasi-religious faith that more guns mean more murder," observed Kates.[52]

The residents of Washington, D.C., experienced the perverse effects of gun control firsthand. Before the district banned handguns in 1976, the murder rate had been declining, but soon thereafter the rate climbed to the highest of all large U.S. cities. During the thirty-one-year life of the D.C. gun ban, with the exception of a few years during which the city's murder rate ranked second or third, there have been more killings per capita in D.C. than in any other major city.[53] Naturally, antigun advocates have an explanation: Single-city gun regulations are unenforceable because guns are imported from surrounding areas where controls are lax. Yet that notion is refuted when we examine countrywide data.

Guns and murder rates are uncorrelated among nations. Indeed, the tendency is that more guns go hand in hand with lower murder rates. For the nine nations having the most guns (16,000 to 39,000 per 100,000 population), 1.17 persons per 100,000 are murdered on average each year. By contrast, the murder rate is 5.5, almost five times higher, for the nine nations having 5,000 or fewer guns per 100,000. Handguns are allowed in the four European countries lowest in violence: Switzerland, Germany, Norway, and Austria. Handguns are banned in Luxembourg (with a murder rate nine times higher), Lithuania and other former Soviet nations (ten or more times higher), and Russia (twenty times higher).[54]

Within the United States approximately 460,000 gun crimes are committed each year, but guns are also used to ward off gun criminals. Estimates of defensive gun use—typically, weapons are merely brandished, not fired—range from 1.3 million to 2.5 million per year. That means defensive uses occur about three to five times as often as violent gun crimes.[55] Just as important, armed victims who resist gun criminals get injured less frequently than unarmed victims who submit. In more than eight out of ten cases where the victim pulls a gun, the criminal turns and flees even if he is armed.[56]

Finally, two federal government agencies recently examined gun controls and found no statistically significant evidence to support their effectiveness. In 2004 the National Academy of Sciences reviewed 253 journal articles, 99 books, 43 government publications, a survey of 80 gun-control measures, and its own empirical work. The researchers could not identify a single gun-control regulation that reduced violent crime, suicide, or accidents.[57] A year earlier the Centers for Disease Control and Prevention reported on an independent evaluation of firearms and ammunition bans, restrictions on acquisition, waiting periods, registration and licensing, child access prevention laws, and zero tolerance laws. Conclusion: None of the laws had a meaningful impact on gun violence.[58]

Proponents of gun control are not persuaded by the evidence, nor are they persuaded by the text of the Second Amendment; the history, purpose, and structure of the Constitution; or the intent of the framers. The enactment of antigun regulations has become an article of faith in some cities and states. Regulations persist and even spread in the face of compelling legal and policy arguments for their demise. Regrettably, in *United States v. Miller*, the Supreme Court abdicated when asked to verify that Americans, including those not serving in a militia, have a right to possess and bear their own firearms as personal individual weapons. That right is essential to sustain a free society. The Constitution does not permit our government to take the right away.

CHAPTER 7

Civil Liberties Versus National Security

The Dirty Dozen List: *Korematsu v. United States* (1944)

WHAT IS THE CONSTITUTIONAL ISSUE?

"No person shall be . . . deprived of life, liberty, or property, without due process of law." —U.S. Constitution, Fifth Amendment.

On December 7, 1941, "a date which will live in infamy," Japanese planes attacked the U.S. naval base at Pearl Harbor, killing more than 2,300 Americans and destroying nearly two hundred ships and aircraft. The next day President Franklin D. Roosevelt requested and received from Congress a formal declaration of war against Japan. Three months later the president issued an executive order that gave certain military commanders nearly total discretion to exclude persons from designated areas that had military significance. Soon thereafter the commanding general of the Western Defense Command, John L. DeWitt, decided that the prevention of espionage and sabotage necessitated forcible removal of all Japanese Americans from "military areas" within selected western states.

Thus began a two-year process during which 120,000 Japanese

Americans, including 70,000 U.S. citizens, were subject first to curfews, then to exclusion from their homes, and finally relocation to internment camps. None of the 120,000 victims was convicted of espionage or sabotage, or even accused of disloyalty. Not until mid-1946 did the last residents of the internment camps return to their homes. Meanwhile, Congress had passed Public Law 503, which partly ratified Roosevelt's executive order and, by implication, DeWitt's directive.

Toyosaburo "Fred" Korematsu was one of the internees victimized by both the executive and legislative branches of the U.S. government. We will learn more about him shortly. His most enduring deed was to seek judicial relief by challenging the constitutionality of his treatment. Korematsu insisted that the exclusion of all persons of Japanese ancestry from selected western areas discriminated against those persons in violation of their Fifth Amendment rights. Ordinarily we might think of such a challenge, based on discrimination, as implicating the Equal Protection Clause of the Constitution. But that clause is part of the Fourteenth Amendment, which can be invoked only against the states, not against the federal government. By contrast, the Fifth Amendment contains no equal protection clause, but it does contain a Due Process Clause, which the courts have sometimes used to restrain discriminatory federal acts.[1]

In any event, the claim by Korematsu unmistakably raised the specter of racial and ethnic profiling—a hot-button issue that has vexed Americans in the wake of the civil rights debates and continues to vex Americans as we confront Muslim terrorists more than six decades after the Japanese internments. What, then, is racial profiling all about, and what lessons can we learn from the *Korematsu* case?

Let's start with a definition. Racial or ethnic profiling involves the selection by government officials of persons—for investigation or stronger action—based on race, nationality, or ethnicity. Few Americans would argue that the United States, under attack by Japan, should be forbidden from considering Japanese ancestry as one of the criteria in developing a list of persons that the government might want to investigate. After all, nationality combined with evidence of misbehavior may add materially to the predictive power of a profile designed to identify and apprehend spies and saboteurs.

But the Roosevelt administration did not combine nationality with evidence of misbehavior, nor did the administration confine its profile to identifying targets for further investigation. Instead, Japanese ancestry was the sole criterion, and incarceration, not investigation, was the resultant government act. Perhaps the questioning of Japanese Americans could be justified in light of military exigency. But when unrefined racial profiling, with no indication that a single suspect had been disloyal, is used to deny liberty to 120,000 innocent persons, we should be outraged.

Sadly, the Supreme Court was not outraged. Its 6–3 decision in *Korematsu v. United States*, written by Justice Hugo L. Black, absolved the Roosevelt administration from an unconscionable violation of civil liberties.[2] Dissenting justice Robert H. Jackson cautioned that "guilt is personal and not inheritable."[3] By condoning Korematsu's mistreatment, he continued, "the Court for all time has validated the principle of racial discrimination. . . . The principle then lies about like a loaded weapon ready for the hand of any authority that can bring forward a plausible claim of an urgent need. . . . [Each] passing incident becomes the doctrine of the Constitution."[4]

The "plausible claim of an urgent need," mentioned by Jackson, was conjured up in a 1942 internal government memorandum citing three alleged facts: First, detention would protect Japanese Americans against vigilante violence. Second, "resident Japanese cannot well be distinguished from a disguised Japanese soldier"; in other words, all Japanese persons look alike. Third, Japanese Americans were much more likely to engage in sabotage than other Americans.[5] Imagine, in a modern context, if those same three justifications, without any supporting evidence, were advanced in support of raw racial profiling against African Americans after a terrorist incident sponsored by, say, Sudan. Revulsion at such a racist policy would sweep the nation.

Yet the Japanese internment policy triggered no indignation from the Court's majority or from many prominent Americans who on other occasions might be outspoken defenders of civil rights. Walter Lippmann led the anti-Japanese clamor; Earl Warren, then attorney general of California and later chief justice of the United States, advocated a Japanese American roundup (although he later repented); and President Roosevelt was apparently uninterested in doubts expressed by his attorney general, Francis Biddle, and his wife, Eleanor.[6] Interestingly, some well-known conservatives—normally proponents of far-reaching wartime powers—opposed internment. J. Edgar Hoover thought that alleged sabotage by Japanese Americans should be handled on a case-by-case basis, requiring probable cause to take action and proper judicial processes.[7] Senator Robert Taft, the conservative Republican from Ohio, was alone in objecting on the Senate floor to enactment of Public Law 503, which was then passed by voice vote.[8]

On the Court itself, only Justice William O. Douglas later expressed regret for his support of the majority opinion. Its author, Hugo Black, insisted several years before he died that he "would do precisely the same thing today."[9] Considering Roosevelt's successful efforts to reconstitute the New Deal Court, some observers speculated that the *Korematsu* decision was more the politically motivated work of Roosevelt loyalists than a rigorous legal analysis. Justice Felix Frankfurter's law clerk in 1943 noted that Frankfurter was "very close and devoted to Roosevelt" and "saw himself as a member of the President's war team."[10] With the exception of Chief Justice Harlan Fiske Stone, every member of the *Korematsu* majority was a certified New Dealer; and Stone, although a nominal Republican, had generally voted to uphold New Deal programs.[11]

Regarding Roosevelt's own motives, political science professor Peter Irons, a former ACLU board member who wrote *Justice at War*, the definitive account of the Japanese internment cases, had this to say: "Roosevelt's desire for partisan advantage in the 1944 elections provides the only explanation for the delay in ending internment. Political pressure influenced the evacuation and internment debates in 1942, and political concerns held up the release of Japanese Americans almost three years later. Between these two episodes, they received a cruel and unnecessary civics lesson in the power of politics to dictate military and judicial decisions."[12]

If our stake in the outcome of *Korematsu* were limited to its implications for racial and ethnic profiling, that would be bad enough, but there is another aspect of the case that is just as important: the scope of the federal government's wartime powers. By conferring on the president the prerogative to incarcerate 120,000 innocent Americans based solely on their Japanese ancestry, the Congress set the stage for other presidential power grabs, culminating in President George W. Bush's unprecedented claims of executive authority in the war on terror. And the Supreme Court, by rejecting Korematsu's constitutional challenge, missed a golden opportunity to establish a legal regime that would have foreclosed, or at least deterred, later abuses.

Shortly, we will discuss a post–9/11 example of executive power run rampant. That case involves Jose Padilla, also an American citizen of foreign descent, imprisoned indefinitely, without charges filed. But, first, the distressing saga of Fred Korematsu.

What Were the Facts?

A narrative of Fred Korematsu's early adult years could broadly describe many other Americans. He worked after school to earn his way through college, but when he couldn't make ends meet, he left college to work as a shipyard welder. Later, he applied for military service but was rejected for medical reasons. Then came Pearl Harbor, and Korematsu's tale took an ominous turn. First, he lost his shipyard job when his union expelled all members of Japanese descent. Then he worked at various short-term welding jobs until ordered by the U.S. government to evacuate his home.[13]

Most important from a legal perspective, Korematsu was a U.S. citizen. He had never been to Japan, did not claim Japanese citizenship, did not read Japanese, and spoke the language poorly.[14] Nonetheless, his lineage gave rise to legal troubles that began just two months after the Pearl Harbor attack. Here is an abbreviated account, adapted from Justice Owen Roberts's dissenting opinion:[15]

- February 19, 1942: Roosevelt issued Executive Order No. 9066, presumably to protect against espionage and sabotage. The order provided that certain military commanders might, in their discretion, "prescribe military areas" and define their extent, "from which any or all persons may be excluded," subject to whatever restrictions the military commander might impose.

- March 2, 1942: General John L. DeWitt, military commander of the Western Defense Command, issued a series of proclamations identifying the areas potentially subject to exclusion: all of California (including San Leandro, where Korematsu resided), Washington, Oregon, Idaho, Montana, Nevada, Utah, and the southern portion of Arizona.

- March 21, 1942: Congress enacted Public Law 503, which specified that anyone who knowingly "shall enter, remain in, leave, or commit any act in any military area or military zone prescribed . . . by any military commander . . . contrary to the restrictions applicable to any such area" shall be guilty of a crime.

- March 27, 1942: General DeWitt barred "all alien Japanese and persons of Japanese ancestry who are within the limits of Military Area No. 1," where Korematsu lived, "from leaving that area for any purpose." At that point in time, Korematsu had not been excluded from his home. Quite the contrary, he would have committed a crime if he had left the area.

- May 3, 1942: General DeWitt issued another order excluding all persons of Japanese ancestry from specified areas, including San Leandro. The order required Korematsu to go to a nearby assembly center for reassignment. Catch-22! If Korematsu remained at home, he would be liable to prosecution under the new order. And if he left the area, he would be liable to prosecution under the earlier March 27 order. The obvious purpose of the two orders, taken together, was to drive all Japanese Americans into assembly centers—in effect,

prisons from which no one was permitted to leave
without permission.

Korematsu elected to stay home. A month later he was charged with
violating Public Law 503 because he had knowingly remained within
an area covered by the exclusion order and had not reported to the assembly center. He was convicted, given a suspended sentence, and
placed on probation for five years. The conviction was affirmed on appeal.[16] But the suspended sentence from a civil court did not stop the
military from taking Korematsu into custody and enforcing the exclusion order; he was sent to an assembly center.

Meanwhile, on March 18, 1942, Roosevelt had issued Executive
Order No. 9102, which launched the War Relocation Authority, an
agency responsible for establishing so-called Relocation Centers. Korematsu found himself transferred to one of the new centers, subsequently
described as "concentration camps" by Justice Roberts.[17] Thus, from the
date of his conviction until internment officially ended in 1944, Korematsu was imprisoned—first in an assembly center and then in a relocation center. No question was ever raised regarding his loyalty to the
United States.

Thanks to Peter Irons, we now know more facts, which were not
presented to the courts. Irons is the political scientist and legal historian
who in 1981 used the Freedom of Information Act to obtain from the
Justice Department archival documents related to the internment cases.
Most important, he found documents that were intentionally withheld
by the government; they cast considerable doubt on the main rationale
for the exclusion and relocation orders: namely, that Japanese Americans
were high risk to engage in espionage and sabotage.

For example, Irons discovered a fifty-seven-page memorandum on
the "Japanese Question," prepared by the Office of Naval Intelligence.
The author of the memo estimated that the number of Japanese Americans "who would act as saboteurs or agents" of Japan was "less than
three percent of the total." He concluded that "the entire 'Japanese
Problem' has been magnified out of its true proportion, largely because
of the physical characteristics of the people, [and] should be handled on

the basis of the *individual*, regardless of citizenship, and *not* on a racial basis."[18]

Irons also learned that Attorney General Francis Biddle had written to Roosevelt on December 30, 1943: "The present practice of keeping loyal American citizens in concentration camps on the basis of race for longer than is absolutely necessary is dangerous and repugnant to the principles of our Government."[19] Concerned more with partisan politics than legal principle, Roosevelt ignored Biddle's evident distress.[20]

A month later Biddle instructed the FBI to analyze a massive document, prepared under General DeWitt's direction, titled *Final Report, Japanese Evacuation from the West Coast, 1942*. Among its accusations the *Final Report* averred a possible connection between the sinking of U.S. ships by Japanese submarines and Japanese espionage activity on the West Coast. J. Edgar Hoover responded to Biddle in a "Personal and Confidential" memorandum on February 7, 1944. He wrote that the bureau had no information that "attacks made on ships or shores in the area immediately after Pearl Harbor have been associated with any espionage activity ashore."[21] Moreover, the chairman of the Federal Communications Commission, also at Biddle's request, documented that DeWitt and his staff had been continuously informed that there were no unidentified or unlawful radio signals during the period in question.[22]

Aware of those memos, a Justice Department lawyer who was preparing the *Korematsu* legal brief wrote to the solicitor general: "We are now therefore in possession of substantially incontrovertible evidence that the most important statements of fact advanced by General DeWitt to justify the evacuation and detention were incorrect, and furthermore that General DeWitt had cause to know, and in all probability did know, that they were incorrect."[23] Despite that admission, the government's final brief glossed over the bogus espionage charges in DeWitt's *Final Report*. Instead, the brief cryptically stated in a footnote: "We have specifically recited in this brief the facts relating to the justification for the evacuation, of which we ask the Court to take judicial notice; and we rely upon the *Final Report* only to the extent that it relates to such facts."[24]

Even as the Justice Department dissembled in its brief to the Court,

Japanese American troops were on their way toward eighteen thousand declarations for valor by war's end. Newspapers reported their exploits and reminded readers that many of the Japanese Americans had volunteered for service from internment camps.[25]

Where Did the Court Go Wrong?

Justice Black began his *Korematsu* opinion on a high note: "[A]ll legal restrictions which curtail the civil rights of a single racial group are immediately suspect. . . . [C]ourts must subject them to the most rigid scrutiny."[26] That was a new and important pronouncement. Just a year earlier, in *Hirayabashi v. United States*, a unanimous Court had upheld the conviction of another Japanese American for violating General DeWitt's curfew order.[27] In that case the Court had required only a "rational basis" for the government-imposed race-based curfew.[28] The new standard of review—"rigid scrutiny"—was a significant step forward in protecting against discrimination. Indeed, over the ensuing years, racial classifications would almost never survive such exacting judicial review.

Under "rigid" or strict scrutiny, courts will invalidate challenged legislation unless it serves a compelling government interest and is narrowly tailored to attain its objective. When legislation restrains many more people than necessary, or fails to restrain large numbers of persons who are similarly situated, it typically fails the test for narrow tailoring. General DeWitt's exclusion directive did both. It was overinclusive in covering 120,000 persons, none of whom had been shown to be disloyal. And it was underinclusive in exempting other racial groups—such as German Americans and Italian Americans—who, like Fred Korematsu, could trace their ancestry to countries with which we were then at war.

In the 1943 case, the *Hirayabashi* Court, using the more lenient "rational basis" standard, refused to second-guess "the judgment of the military authorities and of Congress that there were disloyal members of [the Japanese American] population, whose number and strength could not be precisely ascertained."[29] That was enough for Justice Black in *Korematsu*, even though he purported to apply "rigid scrutiny" and conceded that a curfew was mild when compared to exclusion from one's home:

> In the light of the principles we announced in the Hirabayashi case, we are unable to conclude that it was beyond the war power of Congress and the Executive to exclude those of Japanese ancestry. . . . True, exclusion from the area in which one's home is located is a far greater deprivation than constant confinement to the home from 8 p.m. to 6 a.m. . . . But exclusion from a threatened area, no less than curfew, has a definite and close relationship to the prevention of espionage and sabotage.[30]

Citing General DeWitt's *Final Report* and accepting his judgment that exclusion of all Japanese Americans was a military imperative, Justice Black dismissed the charge that exclusion was group punishment based on antagonism to those of Japanese origin. He insisted that "Korematsu was not excluded from the Military Area because of hostility to him or his race. He was excluded because we are at war with the Japanese Empire."[31] Black noted that "investigations made subsequent to the exclusion" confirmed that Japanese Americans retained loyalties to Japan. Moreover, he added, "Approximately five thousand American citizens of Japanese ancestry refused to swear unqualified allegiance to the United States and to renounce allegiance to the Japanese Emperor, and several thousand evacuees requested repatriation to Japan."[32]

But Black had reached beyond the record of the *Korematsu* case. The "investigations" to which he referred were not in evidence; the Japanese Americans who refused to swear allegiance were, in many cases, protesting their internment and their treatment; the evacuees who requested repatriation were mostly aliens, not American citizens.[33] And even if Black were justified in relying on his so-called evidence, how could the asserted misconduct of "several thousand" individuals possibly excuse the imprisonment of seventy thousand American citizens and nearly fifty thousand other loyal Japanese Americans?

Black's answer to that question was evasive. Essentially, he insisted that the issue in the case was not detention. Korematsu's conviction was for remaining within the area covered by the exclusion order, and only that infraction was to be considered by the Court. In other words, if Korematsu had reported to the assembly center as ordered, rather than remaining at home, he might not have been detained. Black put it plainly: "[W]e cannot say, either as a matter of fact or law, that his presence in that center would have resulted in his detention in a relocation center. Some who did report to the assembly center were not sent to relocation centers."[34] Never mind that only a few elderly, ill, or institutionalized Japanese Americans avoided transfer to relocation centers.[35] And never mind the government's admission in its Supreme Court brief that Korematsu, if he had obeyed DeWitt's exclusion order, "would have found himself for a period of time, the length of which was then not ascertainable, in a place of detention."[36]

According to Black, if Korematsu wanted to challenge his detention, he should have waited until he was actually detained and then filed a petition for a writ of habeas corpus on the ground that there was no valid basis for his detention. Indeed, Mitsuye Endo had done just that, and the Supreme Court, in an opinion released on the same day as *Korematsu*, unanimously ordered her to be freed.[37]

In a hard-hitting dissent, Justice Owen Roberts made short shrift of Black's disingenuous argument. First, he observed, "We cannot shut our eyes to the fact that had the petitioner attempted to . . . leave the military area in which he lived he would have been arrested and tried and convicted" for violating General DeWitt's order of March 27, 1942.[38] Next, Roberts pointed out that the "two conflicting orders, one which commanded him to stay and the other which commanded him to go, were nothing but a cleverly devised trap to accomplish the real purpose of the military authority, which was to lock him up in a concentration camp."[39] Finally, Roberts mocked Black's suggestion that Korematsu (and the other evacuees) should have followed Mitsuye Endo's lead and petitioned for a writ of habeas corpus:

> [I]t is a new doctrine of constitutional law that one in-
> dicted for disobedience to an unconstitutional statute
> may not defend on the ground of the invalidity of the
> statute but must obey it though he knows it is no law
> and, after he has suffered the disgrace of conviction and
> lost his liberty by sentence, then, and not before, seek,
> from within prison walls, to test the validity of the
> law.[40]

Roberts emphasized that the detention issue, at the root of the *Ko-rematsu* case, was a deprivation of liberty far more severe than the mere exclusion that the majority opinion condoned or the curfew that was upheld in *Hirayabashi*:

> This is not a case of keeping people off the streets at
> night . . . nor a case of temporary exclusion of a citizen
> from an area for his own safety or that of the commu-
> nity. . . . On the contrary, it is the case of convicting a
> citizen as a punishment for not submitting to imprison-
> ment in a concentration camp, based on his ancestry,
> and solely because of his ancestry, without evidence or
> inquiry concerning his loyalty and good disposition
> towards the United States.[41]

A second dissent, by Justice Frank Murphy, was equally biting. Murphy had written a concurring opinion in the *Hirayabashi* case, al-though his concurrence read much like a dissent. He had protested that "distinctions based on color and ancestry are utterly inconsistent with our traditions and ideals. . . . [I]t bears a melancholy resemblance to the treatment accorded to members of the Jewish race in Germany. . . . In my opinion this goes to the very brink of constitutional power."[42] Pick-ing up in *Korematsu* where he left off in *Hirayabashi*, Murphy's dissent charged that the exclusion of Japanese Americans "goes over 'the very brink of constitutional power' and falls into the ugly abyss of racism."[43]

With regard to General DeWitt's *Final Report*, Murphy was utterly contemptuous: In support of his "blanket condemnation of all persons of Japanese descent," DeWitt cites "no reliable evidence."[44] DeWitt's reasons for the forced evacuation were "largely an accumulation of much of the misinformation, half-truths and insinuations that for years have been directed against Japanese Americans by people with racist and economic prejudices—the same people who have been among the foremost advocates of the evacuation."[45] Murphy added that "every charge relative to race, religion, culture, geographic location, and legal and economic status has been substantially discredited."[46]

He concluded, as do we, that "no reasonable relation to an 'immediate, imminent, and impending' public danger [was] evident to support this racial restriction which is one of the most sweeping and complete deprivations of constitutional rights in the history of this nation."[47]

WHAT ARE THE IMPLICATIONS?

Fast-forward four decades to February 1983. That is when the Commission on Wartime Relocation, in its report to Congress, finally acknowledged that the internment program was a "grave injustice," which was "conceived in haste and executed in an atmosphere of fear and anger at Japan." The commission found unanimously that Roosevelt's "Executive Order 9066 was not justified by military necessity" but was the product of "race prejudice, war hysteria and a failure of political leadership."[48]

At roughly the same time, Peter Irons, joined by several other lawyers, filed a lawsuit to reverse Fred Korematsu's criminal conviction. Korematsu had been offered a pardon, but he wanted a new trial. Soon thereafter a federal court threw out his conviction, finding that it had been based on flawed evidence. A decade later President Ronald Reagan authorized reparations of $20,000 each to thousands of internees, including Korematsu. Then, in 1999, President Bill Clinton awarded Korematsu a presidential Medal of Freedom, the nation's highest civilian honor. Fred Korematsu died at age eighty-six on March 30, 2005.[49]

Although Korematsu's conviction was set aside by a federal court in 1983, that court had no authority to overturn the Supreme Court's 1944 opinion. And so the opinion stood for more than a half century, and still stands today—discredited to be sure, but lying about, as Justice Jackson warned, "like a loaded weapon ready for the hand of any authority that can bring forward a plausible claim of an urgent need."[50]

Justice Jackson was indeed prescient. The events of 9/11 certainly gave rise to an "urgent need," and President George W. Bush has been more than willing to wield the "loaded weapon" of wartime power. He has claimed authority to convene military tribunals without congressional approval, establish secret CIA prisons, declare that all battlefield detainees are enemy combatants without conducting hearings as required by the Geneva Conventions, and employ interrogation techniques that may have violated our treaty commitments banning torture.[51] Are those activities outside the scope of executive powers? If not, what are the bounds that constrain the president's conduct?

Those questions remain unanswered, in part because the Supreme Court declined to draw a line in *Korematsu*. The problem is not that courts are invoking *Korematsu* to justify executive power. The holding in that case is an anachronism, "overruled in the court of history" even if not officially repudiated by the Supreme Court.[52] But Fred Korematsu's challenge, if it had been upheld, would have stood as a formidable barrier to excessive concentrations of power in the executive branch. Instead, the Court condoned President Roosevelt's unconstitutional internment and passed up its chance to establish legal precedent that might have dissuaded future executive misbehavior.

Today, suspensions of constitutional protections are defended on the same grounds that the Japanese internment was justified: national security. Indeed, our courts are now grappling with the treatment of Jose Padilla who, like Fred Korematsu, is a U.S. citizen of foreign descent, imprisoned indefinitely without charges filed. Padilla supposedly plotted to detonate a "dirty bomb" and use natural gas to blow up apartment buildings in New York, Washington, D.C., and Florida. He was captured in the spring of 2002—not on the battlefields of Afghanistan or Iraq but at Chicago's O'Hare Airport. He was held incommunicado in a South Carolina military brig from June 2002—unable to see a lawyer until the government acceded to outside pressure almost two years later. Finally, in November 2005, after nearly three and a half years in prison, Padilla was indicted—not for his supposed bomb plot but for conspiring to commit crimes outside the United States. He was convicted on those unrelated charges in August 2007.

From a tactical perspective the Bush administration accomplished its objective: It kept a person perceived to be dangerous off the streets. But for those of us concerned about the rule of law and the Constitution, the parallels to *Korematsu* are troublesome. Reasonably construed, the president's status as commander-in-chief authorizes him to seize and detain enemy soldiers found in a zone of active combat. But he cannot order the incarceration, without charge, of an unarmed nonsoldier far from active combat, especially a U.S. citizen on our own soil. Otherwise, anyone could wind up imprisoned by the military without incriminating evidence.

Yes, Padilla may deserve the treatment he is receiving—maybe worse—but that isn't the point. We cannot permit the executive branch to declare that a U.S. citizen is an enemy combatant, whisk him away, detain him indefinitely without charges, deny him legal counsel, and prevent him from arguing to a judge that the whole thing is nothing but a mistake.

Of course, advocates of expanded executive power remind civil libertarians that our presidents have been honorable men who understand that the Constitution is made of more than tissue paper. Perhaps so. But the policies that are put in place by one administration—whether under President Franklin D. Roosevelt or George W. Bush—are precedent-setting. Supporters of expanded wartime authority need to reflect on such power in the hands of future presidents who may want to jettison the carefully conceived separation of powers that has been a cornerstone of our Constitution since 1789.

Suppose, however, that President Bush had released Padilla, who then proceeded to blow up parts of New York. The potential for such tragedies exists whenever anybody is discharged for lack of evidence and then commits a crime. In the case of suspected terrorists, the stakes are immense. So a powerful argument can be made for changing the rules and establishing a preventive detention regime—tilting toward national security even though some civil liberties might be compromised. But if we do change the rules, the process cannot be implemented by executive edict without congressional or judicial input. And it cannot be law on the fly, with no knowledge of the rules by anyone other than the executive officials who are responsible for their enforcement.

In 1866, after a war that cost a half million American lives, the U.S. Supreme Court underscored the importance of adhering to constitutional principles no matter how exigent the circumstances:

> The Constitution of the United States is a law for rulers and people, equally in war and in peace, and covers with the shield of its protection all classes of men, at all times, and under all circumstances. No doctrine, involving more pernicious consequences, was ever invented by the wit of man than that any of its provisions can be suspended during any of the great exigencies of government. Such a doctrine leads directly to anarchy or despotism, but the theory of necessity on which it is based is false; for the government, within the Constitution, has all the powers granted to it, which are necessary to preserve its existence.[53]

It took seventy-eight years for a less enlightened Court to determine that the rights of 120,000 Japanese Americans did not stand in the way of a wartime president who chose to disregard the Constitution. The recent case of Jose Padilla suggests that constitutional government has not yet been fully restored.

CHAPTER 8

Asset Forfeiture Without Due Process

The Dirty Dozen List: *Bennis v. Michigan* (1996)

WHAT IS THE CONSTITUTIONAL ISSUE?

"[N]or shall any State deprive any person of life, liberty, or property, without due process of law." —U.S. Constitution, Fourteenth Amendment.

Consider the following names of actual legal cases: *Marbury v. Madison, Brown v. Board of Education, United States v. One 1970 Pontiac GTO.*[1] Undoubtedly that third name must strike the reader as more than a little odd; after all, it suggests that the government is suing an automobile. One might be surprised to learn that cases in which property is named as a defendant are quite common.[2] Equally surprising, this "guilty property" fiction has existed in one form or another for thousands of years.[3] In its modern American form it is known as "civil forfeiture."

American civil forfeiture is derived from the law of admiralty.[4] At the time of the Founding, the owner of a smuggling ship might be half a world away, far beyond the reach of the courts. As a pragmatic solution, courts created the legal fiction that the ship itself was the "defendant," and the government would literally bring charges against the ship. Upon a showing of "guilt," the property would be forfeited to the government.[5]

In the admiralty context, the "guilty property" fiction must have seemed quite reasonable. Without the power of civil forfeiture, the government would have had little hope of enforcing customs laws or policing crimes on the high seas. During the Civil War, however, civil forfeiture laws were released from these historical moorings. The Confiscation Acts allowed the Union to seize and forfeit the rebels' northern property and the property of those who aided the Confederacy.[6] When the Supreme Court upheld these acts against constitutional challenges, it worked "a revolution in forfeiture law that persists to this day."[7]

Starting in the twentieth century, civil forfeiture found new application in major government efforts to eliminate undesired social behavior such as alcohol and drug abuse. As the war on drugs has escalated, so, too, has the use of civil forfeiture. This modern application, however, ignores the rationale underlying the legal fiction of "guilty property." At admiralty, property was seized as an *alternative* means of punishing property owners whom the courts could not reach personally. In the typical modern forfeiture case, property is seized as *additional* punishment of a person whom the courts could easily punish directly.

While this expansion is profoundly troubling, there are certain instances, even in the modern context, in which forfeiture seems reasonable. The most obvious example is the seizure of "pure contraband" or "objects the possession of which, without more, constitutes a crime."[8] If the mere possession of the object is illegal, then the seizure of such an object deprives the owner of nothing to which he has a right. So, for example, an individual found to be in possession of child pornography cannot allege a violation of his rights when the government seizes the material. Similarly, when the purpose of confiscation is to return stolen property to its owner, forfeiture is easily justified. It would be a curious result indeed if it were held that thieves had a constitutional right to retain the proceeds of their criminal activity. Thus forfeiture to recapture "ill-gotten gains," such as money obtained from the sale of contraband, is likewise legitimate.

More concern is warranted, however, when forfeiture is premised on the "use" of property to "facilitate" the commission of a crime. This concern is exacerbated by the fact that courts have been unclear as to just what it means to "use" property to "facilitate" the commission of a crime. Generally, courts have favored expansive definitions, capturing property with even the most tenuous connection to the actual crime.[9]

Even so, it is usually difficult to feel sorry for the criminal whose property is confiscated because it was used in the commission of a crime. One must remain mindful, however, that it is the connection to the *crime* and not the connection to the *criminal* that taints the property in a civil forfeiture action. As a result, troubling questions arise when property is borrowed or rented and subsequently used in a criminal act. Can the government, consistent with due process, confiscate the innocent owner's property for no other reason than that a third party has used that property in the commission of a crime? What if the property owner does not and cannot know how his property is being used?

In 1974 the Supreme Court suggested that "it would be difficult to reject the constitutional claim of . . . an owner who proved not only that he was uninvolved in and unaware of the wrongful activity but also that he had done all that reasonably could be expected to prevent the proscribed use of his property."[10] Despite this tantalizing pronouncement, the Court's 1996 decision in *Bennis v. Michigan* disallowed an "innocent owner" defense.

One of the remarkable things about that case is how low the stakes were for Tina Bennis and how enormous they were for the government. Tina Bennis stood to lose less than $300. It is to her credit that she nevertheless spent eight years fighting the government over a matter of constitutional principle.

While Ms. Bennis had little to lose, the state and federal governments stood to lose millions or even billions of dollars in potential profit from innocent owners. The ability to seize any innocent owner's property upon a showing of the most tenuous connection with criminal activity would grant the government wide latitude to confiscate property on an unprecedented scale.

Also hanging in the balance were the answers to fundamental

questions about the nature of the relationship between the sovereign and its citizens. How can the goals of criminal law be achieved and at what cost? Who shall bear that cost? What are the incentives for police to restrain or increase enforcement actions? The answers to these questions determine in no small part whether we remain a free society or begin the slow descent into a police state.

What Were the Facts?

In September 1988, John and Tina Bennis bought a second car, an eleven-year-old 1977 Pontiac. The couple, who were both employed, had split the $600 cost of the Pontiac. It probably was not much of a car, but no doubt they appreciated the convenience of being able to split the driving duties. It was a convenience they would not enjoy for long.

Three weeks later, on October 3, 1988, Detroit police witnessed a woman "flagging" passing vehicles on the corner of Eight Mile and Sheffield, an area known for prostitution.[11] Soon thereafter they witnessed a 1977 Pontiac slow to a stop and allow the woman to enter. The police followed the Pontiac until it stopped again. Upon approaching the vehicle, they witnessed the woman, a recidivist prostitute, performing a sex act on the driver, John Bennis. Mr. Bennis was arrested and later convicted of gross indecency.

One might imagine Tina Bennis's roller coaster of emotions starting late on that October evening: first, concern for the whereabouts of her husband, then relief at the sound of his voice on the phone, followed shortly thereafter by shock and outrage upon hearing where he had been all evening. Unfortunately for Tina Bennis, the roller-coaster ride did not end on October 3. Despite *her* innocence, the events of that night would cause her to spend the next seven years in court.

Simultaneous with the criminal charges against John Bennis, the county prosecutor brought a forfeiture action under a Michigan statute that allowed for the confiscation of property used for the purpose of "lewdness, assignation or prostitution." Notably, this case was the first time in the seventy-year history of the statute that the law had been invoked to forfeit an *automobile* used for prostitution.

At trial, Tina Bennis protested that she was an innocent co-owner—she had, after all, paid for half of the car—and that was a distinct and protectable property interest under common law. Therefore, she argued, the forfeiture of *her* interest in the car violated both the Due Process Clause of the Fourteenth Amendment and the Takings Clause of the Fifth Amendment. While she lost at trial, the Michigan appellate court found her argument convincing and reversed. Unfortunately, the Supreme Court of Michigan reversed the Court of Appeals, upholding the trial court's original order. Ms. Bennis then appealed to the Supreme Court of the United States.

WHERE DID THE COURT GO WRONG?

By a bare 5–4 majority, the Supreme Court upheld the forfeiture of Ms. Bennis's car. Chief Justice William H. Rehnquist, writing for the Court, began with an extended discussion of historical forfeiture cases, all of which, he contended, not only supported upholding the forfeiture in Ms. Bennis's case but also compelled such a holding. While these cases, involving admiralty and prohibition-era liquor smuggling, bear a resemblance to Ms. Bennis's case, they can be distinguished, as Justice John Paul Stevens would spend the bulk of his dissent demonstrating.

Yet the majority did not even attempt to distinguish the previous cases. Instead of examining the false premise on which civil forfeiture is based, the chief justice merely established that forfeiture had been used extensively in the past. Yes, the courts have historically allowed property to be considered "guilty" for pragmatic reasons, but its actual guilt is a legal fiction. Accordingly, courts should always be careful not to allow this fiction to expand unchecked. Most troubling, the majority erroneously concluded that its opinion would not unnecessarily expand the power of the state to confiscate private property. The chief justice seems not to have even considered that this expansion was in fact a likely outcome.

After discussing historical precedent, Rehnquist turned to two recent cases relied on by Ms. Bennis, *Foucha v. Louisiana* and *Austin v. United States*.[12] *Foucha* dealt with the indefinite confinement of criminal defendants found not guilty by reason of insanity. The Court held that

Foucha's continued detention in a psychiatric facility was unconstitutional once it was determined that he was no longer mentally ill, even if the state thought he remained dangerous. If Louisiana persisted in detaining Foucha, his confinement would be equivalent to criminal punishment of a person not convicted of any offense.

Rehnquist's only response was that *Foucha* "did not purport to discuss, let alone overrule," historical forfeiture cases. While this observation is plainly true, it disregards Ms. Bennis's more important argument: "[A] criminal defendant may not be punished for a crime if he is found to be not guilty."[13] That basic notion is particularly applicable to Ms. Bennis's case. Not only was she "not guilty," she had never been accused of complicity in her husband's crime.

In *Austin*, the Court had held that "because 'forfeiture serves, at least in part, to *punish* the owner,' forfeiture proceedings are subject to the limitations of the Eighth Amendment's prohibition against excessive fines."[14] Without elaboration Rehnquist distinguished *Austin* by noting the Michigan supreme court's characterization of the forfeiture proceeding as "an equitable action"—that is, a lawsuit that seeks relief other than money damages. One might naturally think that when determining whether a statute was equitable or punitive in nature, one would look to the operation of the statute rather than the arbitrary label attached to it by the state. This seems particularly true where the state has a profit motive in one label being attached rather than another. Nevertheless, the Court was willing to declare the Michigan statute "equitable" based on nothing more than the state court's say-so.

Rehnquist next drew an analogy to Michigan negligence law, which "[makes] a motor vehicle owner liable for the negligent operation of [a] vehicle by a driver who had the owner's consent to use it."[15] The critical difference between that statute and Michigan's civil forfeiture statute—a difference ignored by Rehnquist—is that civil liability and civil forfeiture serve different purposes. For common negligence, civil damages are awarded for the sole purpose of compensating the injured party, not for the purpose of "punishing" the negligent defendant. Punitive damages, which *are* intended to punish the defendant, are only available when a defendant has acted in a particularly wanton or reckless manner.

That is why the Michigan statute, which imputed only common negligence against the vehicle owner, allowed recovery of compensatory damages but not punitive damages.[16] The Court's previous admission—"forfeiture serves, at least in part, to punish the owner"— should have been the end of the matter. Just as the state could not recover punitive damages from a non-negligent automobile owner, the state should not be able to achieve a similar end through forfeiture.

The chief justice attempted to cure this defect by noting that "forfeiture also serves a deterrent purpose distinct from any punitive purpose."[17] While this may be true for guilty owners, it is irrelevant in Ms. Bennis's case. An innocent owner is not being deterred from anything; by definition she could not have foreseen the use to which her property would be put and therefore could not have adjusted her behavior to avoid forfeiture. Moreover, Rehnquist's argument would prove too much. Many, if not all, punitive measures also serve to deter future wrongful activity, yet due process forbids their application to those who, by the state's own admission, are innocent of any wrongdoing.

Rehnquist concluded that "the cases authorizing actions of the kind at issue are 'too firmly fixed in the punitive and remedial jurisprudence of the country to be now displaced.'"[18] However one feels about a manifest injustice being premised on nothing more than past precedent, this appeal to history—which lawyers call *stare decisis*—ultimately lacks force because the case could have been decided in Ms. Bennis's favor *without* displacing long-standing precedent. It is entirely possible, as demonstrated by Justice Stevens in dissent, to draw principled distinctions between the historical cases cited by Rehnquist and Ms. Bennis's case.

After first noting the sweeping scope of the majority's ruling, which "would permit the States to exercise virtually unbridled power to confiscate vast amounts of property where professional criminals have engaged in illegal acts,"[19] Justice Stevens went on to distinguish the past cases relied on by the majority.

First, he noted that early admiralty law presumed "that the owner of valuable property is aware of the principal use being made of that property."[20] Indeed, early admiralty decisions held that "forfeiture of a ship was inappropriate if an item of contraband hidden on board was 'a trifling thing, easily concealed, and which might fairly escape the notice of the captain.' "[21] This fact, not mentioned at all in the majority opinion, helped mitigate the potential unfairness of civil forfeiture. While the distant shipowner might not receive his day in court if his entire cargo consisted of smuggled goods, it was likely in such circumstances that he knew or should have known the use to which his ship was being put. As Stevens correctly pointed out, none of the Court's historical cases "would justify the confiscation of an ocean liner just because one of its passengers sinned while on board."[22] It follows that the "isolated misuse" of Ms. Bennis's car should be similarly insufficient to justify its forfeiture.

Stevens also identified a second way in which earlier cases were distinguishable from Ms. Bennis's case. In earlier cases involving vehicles, transportation was an element of the offense itself. So, for example, a car with concealed compartments for carrying liquor might be used in violation of a statute prohibiting the transportation of alcohol, or a ship might be used to smuggle narcotics.[23] In either of those cases, there exists a strong nexus between the property and the crime. Indeed, the crime could not have existed without a means of transportation. Seizure of these conveyances (particularly those that have been specially modified to conceal contraband) may be justified on the ground that, if not seized, they would again be an integral part of a similar crime. The same cannot be said of Ms. Bennis's Pontiac. While it was the site of an illicit act, the car was hardly necessary, nor was transportation an element of the crime. John Bennis's tryst could just as well have occurred in a motel room or a dark alley. While the seizure of a drug-smuggling ship will materially impede future drug smuggling, the seizure of the Pontiac does nothing to combat prostitution; it merely affects where it will occur.

Finally, Stevens turned to the Court's then-recent holding in *Austin* and the Excessive Fines Clause of the Eighth Amendment.[24] After noting that the majority's opinion was "dramatically at odds" with *Austin*, he found Ms. Bennis's punishment "plainly excessive."[25] He concluded by noting that while he was "not prepared to draw a bright line" between permissible and impermissible forfeitures, he was "convinced that the blatant unfairness of this seizure places it on the unconstitutional side of that line."[26]

Justice Anthony M. Kennedy also issued a brief dissent, which focused on the anachronistic application of hoary admiralty rules to automobiles. As an alternative he suggested that "a strong presumption of negligent entrustment or criminal complicity" would serve the government's interest equally well "where the automobile is involved in a criminal act in the tangential way that it was here."[27] This approach is somewhat less charitable than Justice Stevens's, for it would place the burden on the owner to prove her non-negligence or innocence. Nevertheless, it would provide a remedy for those owners, such as Tina Bennis, who can easily demonstrate their innocence or whose innocence the government concedes.

WHAT ARE THE IMPLICATIONS?

The most immediate and obvious implication of the *Bennis* decision is that it expanded the power of government to confiscate property. Even before *Bennis* that power was vast and threatening. Property owners who managed to recover their seized property stood to lose a great deal because there was no remedy if the property was damaged while in the government's hands. Now, after *Bennis*, property owners have even less protection.

To its credit, Congress has taken some action. In 2000 it passed the Civil Asset Forfeiture Reform Act (CAFRA), which addressed a number of the most troubling aspects of civil forfeiture in the wake of *Bennis*.[28] Notably, CAFRA created a federal innocent-owner exception; expanded the Federal Tort Claims Act to compensate owners for property damage when forfeitures are successfully contested; and shifted the burden to prove negligence in a forfeiture proceeding from the owner to the government.

While it was a step in the right direction, CAFRA is somewhat cold comfort for those offended by the result in *Bennis*. For one thing, it should always be cause for concern when fundamental rights are protected by statute rather than by the Constitution. A right secured by the Constitution can properly be taken away only through the extraordinarily difficult process of amendment. Statutes have no such permanence; they can, and often are, changed out of a perceived sense of urgency, with insufficient regard for the consequences. Moreover, the modicum of security offered by CAFRA applies only to the federal government; state forfeiture laws, like the one at issue in *Bennis*, remain unaffected. An innocent-owner exception rooted in the Constitution would have applied equally at the state and federal levels.

Another significant cause for concern following *Bennis* is the way in which forfeiture distorts our separation of powers scheme and its attendant checks and balances. When the legislature establishes the budget for law enforcement, it is effectively making a declaration as to what the socially optimal amount of law enforcement is.[29] One of the roles of the legislature is to determine, through the power of the purse, the degree to which the executive branch will intrude upon the public through the execution of the laws. Civil forfeiture allows the executive branch unilaterally to increase this level of funding. When property having only the most tangential connection to the commission of a crime is made subject to forfeiture, law enforcement efforts and the attendant intrusions upon private citizens are allowed to expand with no legislative check.

Expansive civil forfeiture also creates a perverse economic incentive for law enforcement agencies to focus on apprehending the least dangerous criminals. Ideally, law enforcement spending should be prioritized according to the danger posed by various criminal activities. But when civil forfeiture enters the picture, these priorities become distorted. Under federal law and most state laws, law enforcement officials sell forfeited property to increase their budgets or they keep property for official use. Rather than encouraging a focus on objective threats, civil forfeiture shifts the focus to revenue generation and budget maximizing. Simply put, government agencies are encouraged to police for profit. That, in turn, can be expected to shift law enforcement priorities toward nonviolent "vice" offenses such as drug possession, illegal gambling, or—as seen in *Bennis*—prostitution.

The human cost of this shift from law enforcement to revenue generation is readily apparent. Even before *Bennis* expanded the range of forfeitable property, there was no shortage of horror stories illustrating the dangers of profit-motivated law enforcement. Take, for example, Sheriff Bob Vogel of Volusia County, Florida, who established a "forfeiture squad" in 1989 to patrol I-95. During the next three years, the forfeiture squad managed to seize more than $8 million. How was it done? The squad stopped thousands of motorists and, under Sheriff Vogel's guidance, seized any moneys in excess of $100 as assumed drug profits. As if that meager basis for "probable cause" were not enough to call the program into question, it was then "regular police practice to bargain with motorists on the spot—stopped on the side of I-95, taking part of their cash in exchange for an agreement not to . . . take legal action against the Sheriff's department or the police." Additionally, lest one think the outrageousness of the program ended there, 90 percent of drivers from whom money was seized were black or Hispanic.[30]

While Sheriff Vogel's exploits were obscene, they pale in comparison to the truly horrific story of Donald Scott. On October 2, 1992, thirty local, state, and federal agents stormed Scott's ranch after a confidential informant accused Scott of growing marijuana. During the ensuing chaos, Scott was shot dead in front of his wife. No marijuana was ever found. The Ventura County district attorney would later determine that "the Los Angeles County Sheriff's Department was motivated, at least in part, by a desire to seize and forfeit the ranch for the government."[31]

Bear in mind that these examples illustrate the zeal and recklessness with which the government will pursue the property of "criminal suspects" (in the very loosest sense of that term). But consider how many innocent people and how much valuable property a criminal might come into contact with daily. As Justice Stevens noted, "Some airline passengers have marijuana cigarettes in their luggage; some hotel guests are thieves; some spectators at professional sports events carry concealed weapons; and some hitchhikers are prostitutes."[32] In our vastly interconnected society living under the cloud of undefined but ominous terrorist threats, it seems impossible in the wake of *Bennis* to impose any meaningful limits on what property law enforcement officials may seize. Given their history, it seems naïve to expect law enforcement agencies to provide any limits of their own.

Although law enforcement will adapt to the new incentives created by an expanded civil forfeiture power, ordinary citizens are unlikely to do so. Owners could protect their property only by refusing to allow

anyone else to use it. This is particularly true in the case of the truly innocent owner who, by definition, does not anticipate his property being
used illicitly. Moreover, it is safe to assume that many, if not most, ordinary citizens will be unaware of the holding in *Bennis* and its consequences. Property owners do not know and could not logically deduce
that their innocence is no defense. Indeed, as Justice Clarence Thomas
admitted in his concurring opinion, "One unaware of the history of forfeiture laws and 200 years of [Supreme Court] precedent regarding such
laws might well assume that such a scheme is lawless."[33] That the forfeiture in *Bennis* would appear lawless to the vast majority of American
citizens strongly suggests that whatever process Ms. Bennis was afforded,
it was not "due process" within the meaning of the Fourteenth Amendment, two centuries of forfeiture jurisprudence notwithstanding.

Justice Oliver Wendell Holmes famously observed, "It is revolting
to have no better reason for a rule of law than that so it was laid down
in the time of Henry IV. It is still more revolting if the grounds upon
which it was laid down have vanished long since, and the rule simply
persists from blind imitation of the past."[34] Revolting it may be, but
blind imitation of the past is the only explanation for the Supreme
Court's decision in *Bennis v. Michigan*. The Court perpetuated and *expanded* the anachronistic doctrine of "guilty property" for no better
reason than that the doctrine was an ancient one. In so doing, the Court
ignored another doctrine, one nearly as old as our republic: "The Legislature . . . may *command* what is right, and *prohibit* what is wrong; but
they cannot change *innocence* into *guilt*; or punish *innocence* as a *crime*."[35]

Tina Bennis was an innocent woman whose property was confiscated as punishment for the crime of another. Perversely, it was a crime
in which *she* was the victim. If to describe her case is not to decide it,
then "due process" has lost much of its meaning. In the wake of *Bennis
v. Michigan*, so it has.

CHAPTER 9

Eminent Domain for Private Use

The Dirty Dozen List: *Kelo v. City of New London* (2005)
Dishonorable Mention: *Berman v. Parker* (1954)

WHAT IS THE CONSTITUTIONAL ISSUE?

"[N]or shall private property be taken [except] for public use...."
—U.S. Constitution, Fifth Amendment.

On the day before Thanksgiving in 2000, Susette Kelo was living in her lovingly restored Victorian home in New London, Connecticut, when a notice was tacked on her front door from the New London Development Corporation (NLDC). The notice informed Susette that she had ninety days to vacate the premises because her home was being condemned. NLDC, using a grant of power from the town, planned to seize land belonging to Susette and her neighbors. Even worse, the land would be transferred to a private developer who would in turn build an expensive hotel, high-end condos, an office building, and other unspecified and upscale amenities on the property. There was nothing wrong with either Susette's home or her working-class neighborhood. It simply was not generating the taxes that the city decided it needed.

Susette and six of her neighbors decided to fight back, arguing that the Fifth Amendment prohibits the use of eminent domain to transfer property from one private party to another solely for so-called economic development—the promise of more jobs and tax revenues. During the seven years it took for her case to reach the U.S. Supreme Court, Susette's pink house came to symbolize the fight to reimpose limits on government's eminent domain power under the Fifth Amendment, limits essential to protecting homeowners and small businesses from unchecked condemnations for private gain.

Eminent domain is the power of government to take a person's land, home, or business. It has rightly been called a "despotic" power of government.[1] Because of the vast potential for abuse of such a drastic power, the words of the Connecticut and U.S. constitutions state clearly that private property shall not be "taken for public use without just compensation."[2] This constitutional provision, known as the Takings Clause, imposes two important limits on the taking of private property: First, the use must be public, and second, just compensation must be paid.[3] If private property could be taken for any use at all, the term "public" would not have been included.

Originally, "public use" was understood by everyone—courts, local governments, and the general citizenry—to have its ordinary meaning, and eminent domain was used only for projects that would be owned by and open to the public, such as roads and public buildings. Courts further explained that government was limited to taking only that property "necessary" for public use.[4] It could not simply grab additional land to increase its holdings.

The "public use" restriction in the Takings Clause fundamentally changed with the Supreme Court's 1954 decision in *Berman v. Parker*.[5] In *Berman*, the Court upheld the constitutionality of "urban renewal"— misguided efforts by federal and local government officials to revitalize urban areas, supposedly to remove slums and eliminate "blight."[6] The case arose in southwest Washington, D.C., in a poor area populated largely by minorities. Congress granted the district government the ability to acquire tracts of land through eminent domain for the purpose of redevelopment, including the resale of the land to private developers.[7] A department store owner objected to his land being taken and given to another private party. His executor, Berman, asked the Supreme Court to review a decision in favor of Parker and other government officials.

In *Berman* the Court read "public use" broadly enough to transform its meaning. "Public use" would now mean "public purpose," as loosely defined by a legislature or administrative agency. Although the circumstances in *Berman* were extreme—the area lacked plumbing and had the highest infant mortality rate in the District of Columbia—the decision had much broader legal implications.[8] Thereafter, courts routinely deferred to legislatures and planning commissions in eminent domain actions to uphold virtually any use of eminent domain, even for private development. What was once a narrow exception to the Constitution's public use requirement, born in a time of concern about urban decline, became a means for governments to take property from one private owner and transfer it to other private parties for their financial gain.

Two things happened in the wake of *Berman*. First, the use of "blight" as a rationale for eminent domain was expanded dramatically. Highly subjective findings would suffice to justify a blight determination. For many cities the concept of "blight" was no longer limited to run-down slums; instead, it could be applied to virtually any area that the government determined was no longer "functionally" viable or was "economically obsolete." Cities declared neighborhoods blighted or "deteriorating" using such criteria as lack of adequate planning, no central air-conditioning, less than two full bathrooms, and even "diversity of ownership."[9]

Second, some governments pushed even further to seize well-maintained property in the name of "economic development." Initially they condemned slums, then blighted areas, then not very blighted areas, then perfectly fine areas. The Michigan Supreme Court's *Poletown* opinion in 1981 was the first to sanction this new trend.[10] In that case the city of Detroit took an entire neighborhood that everyone admitted was not blighted on the grounds that expansion of the nearby

General Motors plant would create "public benefits" in the form of higher tax revenue and more jobs.[11] The Michigan Supreme Court bought this argument, ruling that eminent domain could be used for public benefit.[12] Detroit soon discovered that the closely knit community could not be replaced, and the plant did not live up to its promise of bringing economic prosperity to the city.[13]

For years public officials invoked *Poletown* to justify ever expansive uses of eminent domain. Then in a stunning reversal of legal precedent, in July 2004, the Michigan Supreme Court unanimously overturned the *Poletown* decision. In *County of Wayne v. Hathcock,* the court decisively rejected the notion that "a private entity's pursuit of profit was a 'public use' for constitutional takings purposes simply because one entity's profit maximization contributed to the health of the general economy."[14] In *Hathcock,* the court called *Poletown* a "radical departure from fundamental constitutional principles."[15] "We overrule Poletown," the court wrote, "in order to vindicate our constitution, protect the people's property rights and preserve the legitimacy of the judicial branch as the expositor, not creator, of fundamental law."[16]

A year later the U.S. Supreme Court considered the plight of Susette Kelo. The Court had not looked at a development case since *Berman* in 1954.[17] Meanwhile, public use became public purpose, which then became public benefit. What that meant was that government served the highest bidder—advancing the interests of the financially powerful rather than protecting the rights of citizens.

Indeed, the practice became so routine and widespread that Institute for Justice senior attorney Dana Berliner was able to document more than ten thousand instances of filed or threatened condemnations for private parties in the five years from 1998 through 2002.[18] This number was drawn from public records, however, and thus represents only a fraction of the actual number of cases where private property was condemned in order to become someone else's private property. There is no official database for such condemnations, and many, if not most, go unreported in public sources.

Kelo v. City of New London put the issue to the U.S. Supreme Court in the clearest possible terms.[19] What protection does the Fifth Amendment's public use requirement provide for individuals whose property is being condemned, not to eliminate slums or blight, but for the sole purpose of "economic development" that will allegedly increase tax revenues and improve the local economy?

If private property can be condemned and given to another private entity for private profit and if the determination of which properties are to be condemned can be delegated to a private group unaccountable to the electorate, then are there any limits on the exercise of this government power? Without accountability or constitutional constraints, all the incentives promote aggressive, unbridled use of the eminent domain power, regardless of the impact on the rightful property owners. Regrettably, that is what the Supreme Court condoned in *Kelo.*

WHAT WERE THE FACTS?

Overlooking the Thames River and Long Island Sound, the Fort Trumbull area of New London, Connecticut, was the site of a well-maintained, comfortable, working-class neighborhood. Fort Trumbull was home to many families that traced their roots back to the wave of Italian immigration in the late nineteenth and early twentieth centuries. One such family was the Dery family, headed by matriarch Wilhelmina Dery, who was born in her Fort Trumbull house in 1918. Her parents, the Ciavaglias, arrived from Italy in the 1880s. Like her neighbor, Susette Kelo, Wilhelmina Dery wanted to stay in her home and decided to fight the notice of condemnation that she had received.

In February 1998, Pfizer Inc. announced it was developing a research facility at a site near Wilhelmina Dery's and Susette Kelo's homes in Fort Trumbull. Although the neighborhood was in no way blighted, the city was struggling economically and saw an opportunity to capitalize not only on the new Pfizer facility but also on the land where Susette and her neighbors lived. With the city's approval, the NLDC prepared a plan, purportedly designed to revitalize the Fort Trumbull area but actually intended to complement Pfizer's plans. The NLDC was a private, nonprofit corporation not subject to election by the voters. All of its directors and employees were privately appointed.

The NLDC plan covered ninety acres next to the Pfizer site. In total, 115 land parcels were combined into seven larger parcels to include everything from a waterfront hotel and conference center to a marina, eighty new residences, a large office complex, space for research and development, and a variety of water-dependent commercial uses. The city estimated that the development plan would produce many new jobs as well as between $680,000 and $1,250,000 in new property tax revenue.

The plan contained all the requirements set forth by Pfizer when it agreed to build its global research facility in New London: a luxury hotel for its clients, upscale housing for its employees, and office space for its contractors. Other upgrades to the area, such as renovation of a nearby state park and improvements to the sewage treatment plant, coincided with Pfizer's wishes. Such clout led the city's expert at trial to call Pfizer the "10,000-pound gorilla."[20]

With little concern for area residents, the NLDC decided that the Fort Trumbull neighborhood adjacent to the Pfizer facility would be "redeveloped." Faced with the threat of condemnation, many Fort Trumbull residents agreed to sell their property to the NLDC. Susette Kelo, Wilhelmina Dery, and five others refused. They rightfully wondered how the government could justify taking their property for a "public" use. The contested homes were on only two parcels of land: Parcel 3, which was slated for private office space, and Parcel 4A, which was to provide "park support." Curiously, during the *Kelo* trial, not a single witness could explain what "park support" meant. In total, the contested homes comprised 1.54 acres of the ninety-acre project.

Under the plan discussed at the time of the trial, the NLDC would own the land but lease it to private developers for one dollar per year. The developer selected by the NLDC received a ninety-nine-year lease, but the plans for the contested property were far from definite. The developer's own marketing study found that new office construction on Parcel 3 was "uncertain," "not feasible at this time," and "speculative." Similarly, by trial date, no plan specified what would happen with Parcel 4A—apart from knocking down the existing homes. That omission persists seven years later, as this book is written.

The NLDC, having been delegated the government's power of eminent domain, began condemnation proceedings, which were interrupted when the trial judge rejected the takings in Parcel 4A while upholding the takings in Parcel 3. He enjoined all the condemnations while the appellate courts reviewed his decision. After the Connecticut Supreme Court reversed the trial court in part and ruled 4–3 to uphold all the takings, Susette Kelo, Wilhelmina Dery, and their neighbors asked the U.S. Supreme Court to step in. The Court agreed to revisit takings in the context of economic development for the first time in fifty years. In a sharply divided 5–4 decision, the Court ruled against the property owners.

Where Did the Court Go Wrong?

Justice John Paul Stevens wrote the majority opinion, and from the outset he worked to portray the case as a routine application of prior Court holdings. To do so, Justice Stevens had to overcome explicit precedent that held condemnation for the purpose of taking property from private party A and giving it to private party B was unconstitutional.[21] Despite extensive evidence in the record that the homeowners' property was to be transferred to private parties who would derive significant benefit from the transfer, Justice Stevens rejected that notion. Instead, he insisted that the record did not establish who the beneficiaries would be. Nor did it establish an intent to redevelop the area *solely* to benefit Pfizer or another private party. Therefore, he wrote, it would be "difficult to accuse the government of having taken A's property to benefit the private interests of B when the identity of B was unknown."[22]

Although Justice Stevens recognized that the property would not be used by the public, he dismissed that as a limitation on the government's condemnation authority. Since the close of the nineteenth century, he argued, the Court had "embraced the broader and more natural interpretation of public use as 'public purpose.'"[23] He framed the issue this way: "The disposition of this case therefore turns on the question of whether the City's development plan serves a 'public purpose.' Without exceptions, our cases have defined that concept broadly, reflecting our longstanding policy of deference to legislative judgments in the field."[24]

Not surprisingly, Justice Stevens next turned to *Berman v. Parker,* where he seized upon sweeping Court statements to validate essentially unfettered deference to legislative prerogative:

> The concept of the public welfare is broad and inclu-
> sive. . . . It is within the power of the legislature to de-
> termine that the community should be beautiful as well
> as healthy, spacious as well as clean, well balanced as
> well as carefully patrolled. . . . If those who govern the
> District of Columbia decide that the Nation's Capital
> should be beautiful as well as sanitary, there is nothing
> in the Fifth Amendment that stands in the way.[25]

Then he quoted a 1984 opinion, *Hawaii v. Midkiff,* for the proposition that "it is only the takings purpose, and not its mechanics" that matters in determining public use.[26]

Justice Stevens noted that although the Fort Trumbull area was not blighted, the city overall was economically distressed and had developed a plan to rejuvenate itself:

> Given the comprehensive characteristics of the plan,
> the thorough deliberation that preceded its adoption,
> and the limited scope of our review, it is appropriate for
> us, as it was in *Berman,* to resolve the challenges of the
> individual owners, not on a piecemeal basis, but rather
> in light of the entire plan. Because that plan unques-
> tionably serves a public purpose, the takings here satisfy
> the public use requirement of the Fifth Amendment.[27]

In other words, explained Justice Stevens, the fact that property is taken from one person and immediately given to another does not diminish "the public character of the taking."[28] Even though an area containing several of the homes would be leased to a private developer at one dollar per year for ninety-nine years, the Court had no problem concluding that the taking was for "public use."[29] To reach that conclusion Stevens employed an essentially subjective test: Was the governing body motivated by a desire to benefit a private party or by concern for the public? Because the New London city officials intended that the plan would benefit the city in the form of higher taxes and more jobs, the homes could be taken.

The *Kelo* decision means that cities can take homes or businesses and transfer them to developers if they think the developers *might* generate more economic gains with the property. No controls need be in place to ensure that the project live up to its promises. According to the Court majority, requiring controls would be "second-guess[ing]" the wisdom of the project.[30]

Worse yet, cities need not have any use for the property in the foreseeable future in order to take it. In fact, *Kelo* encourages cities to condemn first and find developers later. From now on, cities can negotiate a sweetheart deal but wait until after the condemnation to actually sign it. Or they can simply take property first and market it to developers later. In *Kelo* some of the homes were taken for an unidentified use and others for an office building that the developer had no plan to construct in the foreseeable future.[31]

Thus, according to the Supreme Court, cities can take property to give to a private developer with no idea of what will ultimately be built and no guarantee of any public benefit.

The decision, particularly Justice Anthony Kennedy's concurrence, suggests but a few minor limits on the use of eminent domain for private development. If a city doesn't bother to prepare a plan, fails to follow its own procedures, or engages in outright corruption, property owners may still find some hope under the U.S. Constitution.[32] But there is almost always a plan; cities are quite adept at following their own procedures; and most cases of eminent domain abuse do not involve blatant corruption such as bribes. Consequently, the vast majority of individuals are left entirely without federal constitutional protection.

Some commentators claimed that *Kelo* didn't change anything and therefore no one needs to worry about it. But *Kelo* did change the law by redefining "public use" to mean "public benefit." To the extent that governments were already taking homes and businesses for private commercial development, that is cause for greater concern, not less. Moreover, *Kelo* threw a spotlight on an already-existing practice that an overwhelming majority of people find outrageous and un-American. And by declaring that there are virtually no constitutional limitations on the ability of cities to take property from A and give it to B, the Court invited more abuse and thus made the problem much worse.[33] Under *Kelo*, government may condemn anyone's property as long as there is a plan to put something more expensive in its place.

The law before *Kelo* sometimes allowed condemnation of property that would result in private ownership, but each situation was extremely limited.[34] None necessitated the sweeping decision of the majority in *Kelo*. Indeed, four members of the Court agreed that its prior decisions did not dictate the result in *Kelo*. Dissenting justice Sandra Day O'Connor, joined by Chief Justice William H. Rehnquist and Justices Antonin Scalia and Clarence Thomas, divided previous cases into three categories: (1) transfer of property from private ownership to public ownership, (2) transfer of property to a privately owned common carrier or similar entity, and (3) transfer of property to eliminate an identifiable public harm.[35] As Justice O'Connor pointed out, "economic development" fits into none of these categories.[36]

Because we have a written Constitution and its text does not change except by amendment, the question in most constitutional cases is how the Court will apply that text to the facts. How far will the Court go in either enforcing or ignoring constitutional rights? For example, we know that the First Amendment protects free speech, but the Court has applied different free speech protection in areas ranging from advertising to the Internet, criticism of the government, and Nazi marches.[37] Although the text of the First Amendment did not change, in each of those areas the Court's decisions changed the law because they applied it to a new situation. Similarly, in *Kelo*, the Court applied the Fifth Amendment's Takings Clause to a different and far more extreme use of eminent domain. By upholding the condemnations in *Kelo*, the Court went to extraordinary lengths to ignore the constitutional mandate that property be taken only for "public use." Never before had the Court gone so far.

When some law professors say that nothing has changed, what they mean is that the Court's general statements about public use have not changed. The Court has said for a number of years that it grants considerable deference to government determinations that a condemnation serves a public use. But at the same time the Court had generally prevented government from taking A's property in order to give it to B for B's private use.[38] In constitutional law, however, the application of general statements to specific facts tells us how seriously the Court takes constitutional rights. The question, therefore, is whether the courts will rubber-stamp virtually all uses of the eminent domain power or intervene when the legislature goes too far. Before *Kelo*, government could take property in deeply troubled, almost uninhabitable areas and transfer it to private developers. Now government can transfer just about any property to private developers. Some lawyers are apparently unable to tell the difference.

WHAT ARE THE IMPLICATIONS?

Home and business owners should view *Kelo* with alarm. As Justice O'Connor noted in her dissent, "The specter of condemnation hangs over all property. Nothing is to prevent the state from replacing any Motel 6 with a Ritz-Carlton, any home with a shopping center, or any farm with a factory."[39] Justice O'Connor also recognized the fundamental injustice at the heart of eminent domain abuse: "Any property may now be taken for the benefit of another private party, but the fallout from this decision will not be random. The beneficiaries are likely to be those citizens with disproportionate influence and power in the political process, including large corporations and development firms. As for the victims, the government now has license to transfer property from those with fewer resources to those with more. The Founders cannot have intended this perverse result."[40]

The *Kelo* decision opened the floodgates of abuse, spurring local governments to press forward with more than 117 projects involving the use of eminent domain for private development in just one year.[41] In the first year after the decision was handed down, local governments threatened with eminent domain or condemned at least 5,783 homes, businesses, churches, and other properties so that they could be transferred to another private party.[42] Even before the Supreme Court's decision, cities had regularly abused the power of eminent domain, but *Kelo* became the green light that Justice O'Connor and Justice Thomas (in a separate dissent) warned about. The decision emboldened officials and developers, who started new projects, moved existing ones forward, and, especially, threatened and filed condemnation actions. Some courts, too, relied on *Kelo* in upholding projects that took the property of one private party only to turn around and give it to another.[43] Sadly, the decision profoundly discouraged many owners who wanted to fight the loss of their home or business but believed, after *Kelo*, it would be hopeless to fight.

At the same time that *Kelo* encouraged the use of eminent domain for private development, it also became a catalyst for national reform. One year after what appeared to be a total victory for local governments allied with private developers, the struggle to limit eminent domain abuse raged more intensely than ever. Many state legislatures responded to the public outcry by restricting eminent domain in a variety of ways. For example, Florida expressly prohibited the use of eminent domain to eradicate so-called blight, while Minnesota narrowed the definition of blighted property.[44] City officials and developers lobbied heavily against substantive limits while simultaneously trying to find ways around the new laws.

Justice Stevens noted in his opinion that states were free to provide greater protection against eminent domain.[45] This could be accomplished legislatively or by amending state constitutions. What seemed like a throwaway line from Stevens quickly took on profound significance, however, when the American public expressed unprecedented outrage over the *Kelo* opinion. Poll after poll found that 70, 80, and even 90 percent and higher of the respondents strongly disagreed with the decision.[46] The more people learned about the decision and its implications, the more the outrage grew. Indeed, a year after the decision was handed down, the polling levels had not changed significantly.[47]

The outrage crossed demographic boundaries. Friend-of-the-court briefs supporting the property owners had been filed in *Kelo* by the NAACP, AARP, Mexican American Legal Defense Fund, urbanologist Jane Jacobs, the National Federation of Independent Businesses, and the American Farm Bureau, among others. Reaction to the decision brought together a similarly wide array of nontraditional allies.

As soon as state legislatures began to convene in the fall of 2005, many introduced legislation to curb eminent domain abuse. Trained and inspired by the Institute for Justice's Castle Coalition, property owners organized to secure passage of legislation that would address the problems in their respective states. Developers and mayors fought tenaciously against these reforms, but one year after *Kelo*, thirty-four states had enacted legislation that placed limits on previously unbridled authority.[48]

Citizen outrage persisted as the fall 2006 elections approached. Measures designed to amend nine state constitutions to limit eminent domain abuse by addressing "public use" were placed on the ballot. All nine passed overwhelmingly, with anywhere from 55 to 86 percent of the vote.[49] Clearly, *Kelo* is the most reviled Supreme Court decision in decades.

In the first major state supreme court decision to address eminent domain for economic development after *Kelo*, the Ohio Supreme Court unanimously struck down Ohio's eminent domain law.[50] The decision saved property owners in Norwood, Ohio, from having their property taken to expand a shopping mall. The court noted, "A primordial purpose of the public use clause is to prevent the legislature from permitting the state to take private property from one individual simply to give it to another. Such a law would be a flagrant abuse of legislative power . . . and to give it deference would be a wholesale abdication of judicial review."[51]

The court closed by saying, "Although the judiciary and the legislature define the limits of state powers, such as eminent domain, the ultimate guardians of the people's rights, as evidenced by the appellants in these cases, are the people themselves."[52]

That kind of activism by property owners and others who recognize the importance of secure property rights to a free society will be necessary in coming years. Ultimately, the Supreme Court must overrule *Kelo*, but until that day the action will be in state courts and legislatures. Victories will have to be protected from relentless counterattacks by developers and mayors; legislatures that have insufficiently secured property rights will need to be emboldened; reforms will need to be passed in the dozen or so states yet to act; and constitutional protections will have to be effected through courts or initiatives.

Meanwhile, in New London, Connecticut, Susette Kelo's old neighborhood has been razed, but no redevelopment has occurred. Dozens of acres of land stand vacant where once a close-knit community lived. But Susette's little pink house, which will be moved to a nearby lot, will stand as an inspiration to all who work to protect property rights.

CHAPTER 10

Taking Property by Regulation

The Dirty Dozen List: *Penn Central Transportation Co. v. New York* (1978)
Dishonorable Mention: *Tahoe-Sierra Preservation Council, Inc., v. Tahoe Regional Planning Agency* (2002)

WHAT IS THE CONSTITUTIONAL ISSUE?

"[N]or shall private property be taken . . . without just compensation."
—U.S. Constitution, Fifth Amendment.

To most people, property means homes, cars, and other tangible assets; however, the phrase "private property" as used in the Fifth Amendment is broader than its lay usage. It encompasses not just the tangible, physical element of private property, but also the intangible bundle of rights associated with the ownership of property. For example, property carries with it the right to make ordinary use of it, to exclude others from use or ownership, and to dispose of it. Thus, rights in property are themselves a form of property; they have value and can be bought and sold. Like all private property, these rights may not be "taken" by the government except for public use and with just compensation.

While takings must be compensated, it has long been held that regulations for the health, safety, and welfare of the public—exercises of the so-called police power—are not takings. If the value of private property is diminished by a valid regulation, the Fifth Amendment's Just Compensation Clause is inapplicable, and there is no requirement that the government compensate the property owner. As Justice Oliver Wendell Holmes Jr. noted, "Government hardly could go on if to some extent values incident to property could not be diminished without paying for every such change in the general law."[1] While this may sound like common sense, its implication for property owners has changed profoundly over the course of the last century as states have asserted their police powers expansively.

At the intersection of the power to take property and the power to regulate it lies the murky concept of *regulatory takings*. Judges and scholars have struggled to formulate a precise definition of the term, but the concept is simple enough: At some point a *regulation* diminishes the value of property so much that it ceases to be a *regulation* and becomes a *taking*. The concept was recognized by the Supreme Court of the United States as far back as 1872. Justice Samuel F. Miller, writing for the Court in the case of a landowner whose property had been flooded by the construction of a dam, noted: "It would be a very curious and unsatisfactory result [if] . . . it shall be held that if the government refrains from the absolute conversion of real property to the uses of the public it can destroy its value entirely, can inflict irreparable and permanent injury to any extent, can, in effect, subject it to total destruction without making any compensation, because, in the narrowest sense of that word, it is not taken for the public use."[2]

The Court later recognized that the line between regulations and takings is crossed at some point before "total destruction" of the property's value, but the precise location of the line remained a mystery. The Court's only guidance was that "while property may be regulated to a certain extent, if regulation goes too far it will be recognized as a taking."[3] In *Penn Central Transportation Co. v. New York*, the Court would undertake to define just how far was "too far."[4]

When government deprives a property owner of the use of his or her property, the cost must be borne by someone. Deciding how far a regulation may go before it becomes a taking is, in effect, deciding who will bear the cost. If property is taken for public use, it makes sense—both morally and economically—to spread the cost of obtaining the property over the entire public. Indeed, this is precisely the conclusion reached by the Founders and articulated in the Fifth Amendment; the "just compensation" provided to the property owner is supplied by the taxpayers. Everyone pays a little bit, but in exchange they enjoy their share of the benefit of the "public use" of the taken property. If property is taken without compensation, the entire cost is borne by the individual property owner.[5]

The allocation of these costs also has political implications. If the government is required to pay for the benefits it seeks to provide, taxpaying voters can weigh the costs they incur against the benefits they receive. Legislators will then have an electoral incentive to engage in takings only when the net benefit to society exceeds the net cost. Voters who must bear the additional cost will punish legislators who abuse takings.

In contrast, if legislators are free to enrich a large group of voters at the expense of a single property owner or a small group of owners, it is in their electoral best interest to do so. Voters can be expected to accept and even demand any benefit, no matter how insignificant, if it costs them nothing to obtain it. Legislators who routinely supply voters with these benefits— that is to say, those legislators who confiscate the most property—can expect political rewards to follow. Under such a system, politicians need be careful only to avoid confiscating property under conditions that are so outrageous as to offend the morals of a majority of voters.

With so much at stake, where the Court draws the line between regulations and takings is not a dry legal exercise. It is a decision that has profound real-world consequences.

WHAT WERE THE FACTS?

On February 1, 1968, the Pennsylvania and New York Central railroads merged to create the Penn Central Transportation Co., the largest railroad in American history. Among its varied holdings and more than twenty thousand miles of rail, the newly formed giant was also the owner of the famous Grand Central Terminal in New York City. While those familiar with Grand Central recognize it in the form it has existed since first opening in 1913, the original design included a twenty-story office building atop the terminal. The office building was never constructed.

Already strapped for cash, Penn Central initially decided to take advantage of the terminal's reinforced structure. Contemporaneous with the merger, the railroad entered into a renewable fifty-year lease with a corporation that wished to construct an office building on top of the terminal. The corporation, UGP Properties, Inc., guaranteed Penn Central $1 million annually during the construction and a minimum of $3 million annually thereafter. For Penn Central it was a highly attractive opportunity in otherwise trying times.

But there was a catch. In 1965, New York City adopted its Landmarks Preservation Law.[6] Under that law, the eleven-member Landmarks Preservation Commission was charged with identifying properties and areas that have "a special character or special historical or aesthetic interest or value as part of the development, heritage or cultural characteristics of the city, state or nation." Having identified properties with these characteristics, the commission also had the authority to designate as a landmark any such property that was also at least thirty years old. As then–Justice William H. Rehnquist would note in his dissent: "The owner of a building might initially be pleased that his property has been chosen by a distinguished committee of architects, historians, and city planners for such a singular distinction. But he may well discover, as appellant Penn Central Transportation Co. did here, that the landmark designation imposes upon him a substantial cost, with little or no offsetting benefit except for the honor of the designation."[7]

The "substantial cost" referred to by Rehnquist was twofold. First, designation as a landmark imposed on the property owner a duty to keep the exterior features of the building in good repair. Second, and more important to Penn Central, the law required that the commission give advance approval to any proposal "to alter the exterior architectural features of the landmark or to construct any exterior improvement on the landmark site."

Penn Central and UGP submitted two plans to the commission that would have significantly altered the appearance of the terminal but otherwise satisfied all applicable zoning laws. The first plan would have left the terminal intact but provided for the construction of a fifty-five-story office building atop it. The second called for tearing down a portion of the terminal and constructing a fifty-three-story office building. The commission found both plans wholly unsatisfactory and refused to approve either. In the commission's opinion, "to balance a fifty-five-story office tower above a flamboyant Beaux-Arts façade seems nothing more than an aesthetic joke" and would "reduce the Landmark itself to the status of a curiosity."[8]

Penn Central, having seen the promise of $150 million in additional revenue vanish with a stroke of the commission's pen, filed suit. Its legal theory, that application of the Landmarks Preservation Law had deprived it of "air rights," was not a novel one. The right to make use of the airspace above one's property was itself considered a valuable form of "property" and enjoyed robust legal protection. The ancient maxim at common law was *"Cujus est solum, ejus est usque ad coelum et ad inferos"* (Whosoever owns the land, owns to the heavens and to the depths). While the rise of commercial air traffic had undermined the literal application of the rule, property owners in 1968 still held most of the air rights they had traditionally enjoyed under Anglo-American law.

Penn Central met with initial success in the New York trial court, winning an injunction barring the city from using the Landmarks Law to impede the construction of the additions. This success was short-lived, however, as the case was reversed on appeal in a decision later affirmed by New York's highest court. Having wound its way through the state court system and lost, Penn Central appealed to the Supreme Court of the United States.

WHERE DID THE COURT GO WRONG?

The question before the Court was whether the New York City Landmarks Preservation Law had crossed the line between regulation and taking. Justice William J. Brennan, writing for the majority, noted the difficulty that the Court had in drawing this line:

> While this Court has recognized that the "Fifth
> Amendment's guarantee . . . [is] designed to bar Gov-
> ernment from forcing some people alone to bear public
> burdens which, in all fairness and justice, should be
> borne by the public as a whole," this Court, quite sim-
> ply, has been unable to develop any "set formula" for
> determining when "justice and fairness" require that
> economic injuries caused by public action be compen-
> sated by the government, rather than remain dispro-
> portionately concentrated on a few persons.[9]

Brennan's characterization of this inquiry is profoundly troubling.
Although allowing that these disproportionate burdens are compensable
when fairness and justice require it, he implies that they are *not* compensable when fairness and justice dictate otherwise. This distinction
may seem subtle, but it has significant consequences. Rather than compensation being the default rule, Brennan's characterization makes compensation depend on the elusive notion of what is just and fair. But the
language of the Fifth Amendment presupposes that compensation is required unless the government can demonstrate otherwise. By opening
the door to the notion that fairness and justice may dictate that property
owners bear the cost, the Court effectively shifted the burden of proof
from the government to the property owner. Once the Court placed
the onus of proving injustice on the property owner, the outcome—that
Penn Central and other property owners would go uncompensated—was
virtually preordained.

With the debate thus framed, Penn Central's prospects for victory
were bleak. Yet they became bleaker still as Brennan explained the process for ad hoc determination of whether fairness and justice require
compensation:

> [T]he Court's decisions have identified several factors
> that have particular significance. The economic impact
> of the regulation on the claimant and, particularly, the
> extent to which the regulation has interfered with

distinct investment-backed expectations are, of course, relevant considerations. So, too, is the character of the governmental action. A "taking" may more readily be found when the interference with property can be characterized as a physical invasion by the government.[10]

The government had not physically invaded Penn Central's airspace by erecting a public building on top of Grand Central Terminal, so the last factor did not weigh in Penn Central's favor. Penn Central's hopes, if any, hung entirely on the economic impact of the regulation.

Surely, the railroad must have thought, the loss of $150 million was a sufficient economic impact that fairness and justice required the loss not be borne by Penn Central alone. Justice Brennan wasted no time in disabusing the company of this notion. Calling Penn Central's position "untenable," Brennan continued:

> "Taking" jurisprudence does not divide a single parcel into discrete segments and attempt to determine whether rights in a particular segment have been entirely abrogated. In deciding whether a particular governmental action has effected a taking, this Court focuses rather both on the character of the action and on the nature and extent of the interference with the rights in the parcel as a whole. . . . [11]

The application of the so-called parcel as a whole doctrine extinguished any remaining hope for Penn Central. In effect, the Court said, "Sure, you lost $150 million, but look at all the things the government let you keep!" Apparently, in the Court's view, $150 million was small change when one considers that Penn Central was allowed "to use the property precisely as it [had] been used for the past 65 years: as a railroad terminal containing office space and concessions."[12]

Ultimately, and unconvincingly, the Court attempted to soften the blow. First, the Court noted that it wasn't literally true that Penn Central had been denied all use of its air rights. The commission might, after all, approve the construction of some smaller addition provided it "would harmonize in scale, material, and character" with Grand Central. Second, the New York law provided for "transferable development rights"—essentially a right that the company could transfer to a different parcel awarded in return for restrictions imposed on Grand Central. The mechanics of "TDRs," as they are known, are complex and well beyond the scope of this work. Suffice it to say that neither TDRs nor the vague promise that the commission might one day approve some addition came close to compensating Penn Central for the loss of its property rights.

Justice Rehnquist, joined by Chief Justice Warren E. Burger and Justice John Paul Stevens, issued a strong dissent. In Rehnquist's view there was no question that the Landmark Law had resulted in a taking. New York City had "destroyed—in a literal sense, 'taken'—substantial property rights of Penn Central."[13] According to Rehnquist, the only remaining inquiry was whether either of two very specific exceptions applied: the nuisance exception or the zoning exception.

Certainly, Penn Central's planned addition could not be considered a "nuisance" within the legal meaning of the term. The planned addition complied with all applicable building laws, other than the Landmarks Preservation Law itself, and did not violate established rights of other parties. Moreover, "[o]nly in the most superficial sense of the word [could] this case be said to involve 'zoning.'"[14] As it is typically understood, zoning involves limitations spread equally over a large area. Although everyone affected by the zoning is equally burdened, they also benefit equally from the enhanced value supposedly offered by the restrictions. In effect, there are reciprocal burdens and benefits from zoning experienced by all affected property owners. Rehnquist, distinguishing the situation in *Penn Central*, noted:

> Where a relatively few individual buildings, all separated from one another, are singled out and treated differently from surrounding buildings, no such reciprocity exists. The cost to the property owner which results from the imposition of restrictions applicable only to his property and not that of his neighbors may be

substantial . . . with no comparable reciprocal benefits. And the cost associated with landmark legislation is likely to be of a completely different order of magnitude than that which results from the imposition of normal zoning restrictions.[15]

With neither exception applicable, Penn Central had, in the dissent's view, unquestionably suffered a taking for which just compensation was due. After strongly suggesting that Penn Central had not been justly compensated, Rehnquist concluded that the case should be remanded to the Court of Appeals "for a determination of whether TDR's [*sic*] constitute a 'full and perfect equivalent for the property taken.'"[16]

WHAT ARE THE IMPLICATIONS?

Writing less than a decade after Grand Central Terminal opened, and more than fifty years before the decision in *Penn Central,* Justice Holmes observed: "The protection of private property in the Fifth Amendment . . . provides that it shall not be taken . . . without compensation. . . . When this seemingly absolute protection is found to be qualified by the police power, the natural tendency of human nature is to extend the qualification more and more until at last private property disappears."[17]

Justice Holmes could hardly have been more prescient if he had identified Penn Central by name. Justice Brennan's opinion so far extended this qualification that Penn Central's "air rights"—$150 million worth of valuable property—were rendered as insubstantial as the air they encompassed.

Had the effects of the *Penn Central* decision been limited to Penn Central itself, the case would be unfortunate although hardly noteworthy; the decision came six years after Penn Central had already declared bankruptcy. Considering the long decline of the American rail industry and the company's many internal problems, Penn Central may have been doomed from the start.[18] What really matters, however, is not what the loss of $150 million meant to Penn Central but what the

Supreme Court's decision meant—and continues to mean—for property owners.

With the perspective afforded by the passage of time, it is now clear that the Penn Central decision was more than the final nail in a deceased railroad's coffin. It was also a dangerous precedent for further erosion of property rights. The extent of that erosion became painfully evident twenty-four years later in *Tahoe-Sierra Preservation Council, Inc. v. Tahoe Regional Planning Agency*.[19]

Tahoe-Sierra dealt with the rights of property owners in the Lake Tahoe basin. Over time, construction around the lake had increased runoff of organic material, and the ensuing algae growth threatened the lake's famed clarity.[20] The blame for this environmental damage might fairly be attributed to a number of different parties, but one group was indisputably innocent: the owners of undeveloped lots. Despite their innocence, the entire cost of preserving Lake Tahoe's clarity would be placed on these property owners; a series of rolling moratoria were put in place by the Regional Planning Agency that prevented any new home construction.

Thus, the *Tahoe-Sierra* plaintiffs—owners affected by the moratoria and an association representing them—brought to the Court strong claims for fairness and justice. Moreover, the case arose in the wake of a trend in Supreme Court jurisprudence that seemed to offer the prospect for revived protections for property rights. While the Court in *Penn Central* had been persuaded by the fact that the railroad was not prevented from earning a "reasonable return" on its investment, here the lots were rendered entirely worthless.

Additionally, much had happened in the law of takings since the decision in *Penn Central*. In *Lucas v. South Carolina Coastal Council*, the Court had held that a similar—but permanent—prohibition on construction deprived owners of all economically viable use of their land and was therefore a per se regulatory taking.[21] In *First English Evangelical Lutheran Church of Glendale v. County of Los Angeles*, the Court had held that "temporary takings which . . . deny a landowner all use of his property are not different in kind from permanent takings, for which the Constitution clearly requires compensation."[22] If temporary takings are compensable and regulations that deprive property of all economically viable use are per se "takings," it should follow logically that temporary regulations that impose similar burdens—say, twenty years of rolling building moratoria—are compensable. Despite the force of this argument, the Court was unconvinced. "Logically," declared Justice Stevens, property like the plaintiffs' "cannot be rendered valueless by a temporary prohibition on economic use, because the property will recover value as soon as the prohibition is lifted."[23]

Recall that in *Penn Central* the Court measured the scope of the deprivation with reference to the value of the "parcel as a whole." Although this test may often create unjust results, as it did for Penn Central, at least it contemplates that sometimes a plaintiff will be compensated. After all, the parcel as a whole has a finite value against which the deprivation may be measured. In *Tahoe-Sierra,* Justice Stevens did not concern himself with the degree of deprivation, which was total, but instead with the length of deprivation. In effect, the Court rejected any diminution in value caused by the "temporary" twenty-year moratoria, because over the infinite course of time the moratorium could conceivably be lifted.

In a triumph of form over substance, *Tahoe-Sierra* gives legislatures virtually free rein to deprive property of its entire value for an unlimited amount of time without compensation, provided they style each successive deprivation as "temporary" in nature. As Justice Clarence Thomas correctly pointed out in dissent, "[T]he 'logical' assurance that a 'temporary restriction . . . merely causes a diminution in value,' . . . is cold comfort to the property owners in this case or any other. After all, 'in the long run we are all dead.'"[24] This observation is not hyperbole; writing shortly after *Tahoe-Sierra* was decided, one legal scholar noted, "Of the 700 or so ordinary people who started on this journey, 55 have since died."[25]

Beyond their legal repercussions, the *Penn Central* and *Tahoe-Sierra* decisions also create perverse economic incentives for future development. The message the two cases send to property owners is "build now, before the regulators rob the property of its value."[26]

The economic implications of *Penn Central* extend even to the design of future buildings. As Rehnquist noted in his *Penn Central* dissent, "Penn Central [was] prevented from further developing its property basically because too good a job was done in designing and building it."[27] For corporations—planning on thirty-, forty-, or fifty-year timescales—the *Penn Central* decision creates an incentive to blend in as "just another office building," rather than invest in architecture that is unique, beautiful, or, as Justice Brennan described Grand Central, "magnificent."[28] It is a popular myth that a system with robust protection for property rights disdains these qualities, that ruthless market efficiency promotes nothing but austere functionality. There could be no more striking refutation of that argument than Grand Central Terminal itself, an American cathedral produced in an age before the regrettable decision in *Penn Central*.[29]

Near the end of his opinion, Justice Brennan observed that holding the restrictions placed on Penn Central to be a taking would "invalidate not just New York City's law, but all comparable landmark legislation in the Nation."[30] Surely Brennan was not arguing that unconstitutional laws become constitutional merely through force of numbers. This puzzling argument could perhaps be explained most charitably as judicial modesty. Brennan seemed to ask, "Who am I to say fifty states are wrong?" The obvious answer is that Brennan was a justice of the United States Supreme Court. As a justice he was not merely permitted but obligated to invalidate unconstitutional state actions without regard to whether or not the states might find it inconvenient.[31] That he and the five justices who joined the majority opinion failed to meet that obligation in *Penn Central Transportation Co. v. New York* has—at the ongoing expense of property owners—earned the Court's decision a place among the Dirty Dozen.

CHAPTER 11

Earning an Honest Living

The Dirty Dozen List: *United States v. Carolene Products Co.* (1938)
Dishonorable Mention: *Nebbia v. New York* (1934)

What Is the Constitutional Issue?

"The enumeration in the Constitution of certain rights shall not be construed to deny or disparage others retained by the people." —U.S. Constitution, Ninth Amendment.

Every day across America thousands of individuals engage in the most massive expression of civil disobedience this nation has ever seen. You will not find them on picket lines or in marches. Instead, you will find them working hard at honest occupations to provide for themselves and their families. Tragically, they do so under laws and regulations that treat them as outlaws. Such is the legacy of the Supreme Court's evisceration of constitutional protection for economic liberty—the right to earn an honest living free from excessive or arbitrary government regulation.

What sort of people persevere in the face of such adversity? They are people like New York commuter van entrepreneur Hector Ricketts. When Ricketts lost his job as director of support services in a hospital, he was worried about supporting his wife and three young children. Instead of losing hope, he devoted all his energies to running Queens Van Plan, Inc., a company that provided van service in Queens, New York. He also became a community leader, serving as president of the Interborough Alliance for Community Transportation, and an outspoken advocate for community-based transportation services. Soon, more than fifty men and women made a living driving for Queens Van Plan, and thousands of customers depended on his vans for reliable and secure transportation services. Dozens of other van companies sprang up, and by the mid-1990s, sixty thousand low-income riders per day were using vans in New York to meet their daily transportation needs. Vans both put people to work and took people to work.

Given the demonstrable demand for van service and the highly subsidized, woefully inadequate public bus service in the community, one might assume that vans would have been a welcome addition to New York City's transportation network. But that was emphatically not the case. Instead, rivals such as the New York Metropolitan Transit Authority, private bus companies with city franchises, and the union representing public transportation workers viewed vans as a competitive threat. Van service opponents used their sizable political clout to convince state legislators and the New York City Council to pass laws that relegated Hector and his fellow van operators to the status of economic outlaws.

The laws purported to set up a process for awarding van permits, but existing companies were given the right to object to any new applicants. Even worse, city bureaucrats had unfettered discretion to deny an application for any reason or no reason at all. Not surprisingly, virtually every application was denied. Meanwhile, Hector and his colleagues continued to provide van service subject to periodic arrest and impoundment of their vans.

More than one thousand miles away, in Tupelo, Mississippi, Melony Armstrong had her own entrepreneurial ambitions. Regrettably, her business was deemed so dangerous that she needed 3,200 hours of classes—about three academic years of school—to train others how to practice her trade without harming their customers. Was she trying to teach future paramedics or nurses? No. She wanted to teach African-style hair braiding.

Welcome to the tangled mess of cosmetology licensing in Mississippi. Hair braiders—and those who want to teach braiding—had to be licensed, but Mississippi offered no licenses specifically for braiding or for braiding instruction. Instead, to practice hair braiding, Melony had to spend three hundred hours in class to earn a license in something called "wigology," even though wigology programs do not emphasize braiding. When Melony wanted to teach her craft to others, the state said she was not allowed unless she spent 3,200 hours in cosmetology and cosmetology instructor programs.[1] Neither of those programs taught braiding.

In the 3,200 classroom hours it would have taken for Melony to get a license to teach hair braiding, she could instead become licensed in *all* of the following professions: emergency medical technician (122 hours plus five emergency runs), paramedic (1,322 hours), ambulance driver (8 hours), law enforcement officer (ten weeks), firefighter (six weeks), real estate appraiser (75 hours), and hunting education instructor (18–20 hours).[2] All those requirements together take 1,000 hours *less* than the time required to get a hair-braiding license.

Mississippi's regulatory scheme left anyone who wanted to teach or to learn the art of African hair braiding out in the cold. Perversely, the state allowed cosmetology instructors with no experience in braiding to teach braiding, even as the state barred experienced braiders from teaching their craft unless they sacrificed three years and thousands of dollars to learn unrelated skills. The result was that students of braiding had no skilled and legal instructors to learn from. In effect, the State of Mississippi outlawed both the teaching and learning of African-style braiding as a business.

Only one group benefited from Mississippi's regulatory regime: the cosmetology establishment. Practicing cosmetologists—led by the State Board of Cosmetology, whose five members were required to have been practitioners for at least ten years—were able to set the bar for entry to their profession high enough to keep competition to a minimum.[3] And cosmetology schools signed up captive customers. Not surprisingly, the board was officially advised by other practicing cosmetologists and cosmetology schools.[4]

The sad experiences of Hector Ricketts and Melony Armstrong demonstrate how burdensome occupational licensing laws can be and how easily they can become barriers to entrepreneurship. Nearly five hundred occupations are regulated by states, and about half of those require state licenses.[5] Occupations requiring government licenses include not only the medical, legal, and other highly specialized professions, but also occupations in which restrictions on entry make little or no sense, such as beekeepers, lightning rod salespeople, fence installers, flower arrangers, and septic tank cleaners.

Entry into many nonprofessional occupations does not require a great deal of capital or education; the only barriers to entry are often those imposed by government. Occupational licensing laws now govern entry into about 20 percent of all jobs in America.[6] Sometimes these laws create outright monopolies, as in the taxicab industry. Other times, as in hair braiding, they restrict entry so onerously that few applicants are approved. Either way, the typical result is a cartel that provides consumers with more costly and less responsive service.

Carving out a better life for oneself through hard work and ingenuity is the heart of the American dream. That dream, "the pursuit of happiness," is enshrined in the Declaration of Independence, but many of the Founding Fathers thought that recognition in the Declaration wasn't enough. They wanted constitutional protection for individual rights. One of the great debates during the ratification of the Constitution was over how best to secure those rights.

The Federalists, who supported ratification, believed individual rights would be sufficiently protected by a system of enumerated powers, and they argued against an injudicious zeal for a bill of rights. First, the Federalists saw any meaningful enumeration of rights as being literally impossible; our rights were simply too numerous to list. James Iredell, who would later sit on the Supreme Court, spoke at the North Carolina ratifying convention in 1788: "[I]t would be impossible to enumerate every [right]. Let any one make what collection or enumeration of rights he pleases, I will immediately mention twenty or thirty more rights not contained in it."[7]

Beyond finding a complete enumeration impracticable, the Federalists also feared that an enumeration of rights might backfire, expanding the power of government:

> [A bill of rights] would contain various exceptions to powers which are not granted; and, on this very account, would afford a colorable pretext to claim more than were granted. For why declare that things shall not be done which there is no power to do? Why, for instance, should it be said that the liberty of the press shall not be restrained, when no power is given by which restrictions may be imposed? I will not contend that such a provision would confer a regulating power; but it is evident that it would furnish, to men disposed to usurp, a plausible pretense for claiming that power. They might urge with a semblance of reason that the Constitution ought not to be charged with the absurdity of providing against the abuse of an authority which was not given.[8]

Despite these objections, the Anti-Federalists insisted on a bill of rights. They remained skeptical that enumerated powers alone would be sufficient to restrain the federal government under the proposed Constitution. It would be better, they thought, to have an incomplete enumeration than none at all, for at least then certain fundamental rights would be guaranteed protection. As Thomas Jefferson wrote to James Madison, "Half a loaf is better than no bread," and "If we cannot secure all our rights, let us secure what we can."[9]

The Anti-Federalists ultimately prevailed, and the Constitution was ratified with the promise that it would be amended to include a bill of rights. It was Federalist James Madison, however, who answered Iredell's challenge that a complete enumeration would be impossible. Under Madison's approach, a number of our most fundamental rights were

specifically enumerated in what became the first eight amendments to
the Constitution. In addition, Madison drafted what became the Ninth
Amendment, which provided that "The enumeration in the Constitution of certain rights shall not be construed to deny or disparage others
retained by the people." In essence, the Ninth Amendment was a
catch-all clause; it encompassed all the common law and natural rights
that Iredell claimed eluded enumeration.

In addition to the Ninth Amendment, the Privileges and Immunities Clause found in Article IV of the Constitution and the Due Process
Clause of the Fifth Amendment protected unenumerated rights, including the right of people like Hector Ricketts and Melony Armstrong to
earn an honest living.[10] Indeed, unlike the Ninth Amendment, these
provisions were actually cited by courts to secure unenumerated rights.[11]
Unfortunately, the efficacy of the Privileges and Immunities Clause and
the Due Process Clause for such purposes was short-lived. In particular,
the use of the Due Process Clause to protect underlying rights from
governmental violation—a constitutional doctrine known as "substantive due process"—experienced a judicial roller-coaster ride beginning
shortly after the Civil War when the Fourteenth Amendment was added
to the Constitution.[12]

Over the years the Fourteenth Amendment became the vehicle by
which the Bill of Rights would be enforced against the states. Among
other things, the amendment said that states could not deprive citizens
of the privileges or immunities of citizenship. Although applicable to all
citizens, this provision was intended to ensure in particular that newly
freed slaves would not be denied economic liberty: the right to contract
and the right to own property. Sadly, a mere five years after the Fourteenth Amendment's ratification, the Privileges and Immunities Clause
was stripped of its intended meaning in the *Slaughter-House Cases*, which
upheld a Louisiana law that required all butchering of animals in New
Orleans to be done by one private corporation—owned, of course, by
politically connected businessmen who had curried favor with the
state.[13]

In an opinion by Justice Samuel F. Miller, the Court held that the
Privileges and Immunities Clause secured only the rights of *national*

citizenship, including those rights that had already been recognized by the Court prior to ratification of the Fourteenth Amendment, or rights such as protection on the high seas that were not within state government jurisdiction. By contrast, the Privileges and Immunities Clause did not secure the rights of *state* citizenship, which according to the Court comprehend "nearly every civil right for the establishment and protection of which organized government is instituted."[14] Conspicuously omitted from the *Slaughter-House* list of protected rights were the rights to contract, compete, and earn an honest living.

Without the Privileges and Immunities Clause to defend unenumerated rights from state encroachment, states during the Progressive era of the early 1900s enacted more and more laws regulating commercial transactions and abridging economic liberties, including the notorious Jim Crow laws. The courts, including the U.S. Supreme Court, turned to other provisions of the Constitution—notably the Due Process Clauses of the Fifth and Fourteenth Amendments—to strike down these laws.[15]

The high-water mark of this practice occurred in *Lochner v. New York*, in which the Court overturned a law that regulated the number of hours that bakery employees could work.[16] Smaller bakeries had gained a competitive edge by having employees willingly work more hours. The challenged law was actually intended to protect larger bakeries from their smaller rivals. Justice Rufus W. Peckham, author of the majority opinion, inquired whether the regulation was a reasonable use of the state's police power or an "unreasonable, unnecessary, and arbitrary interference with the right of the individual . . . to enter into those contracts . . . appropriate or necessary for the support of himself or his family."[17] The Court held that there were no reasonable grounds for violating the employees' and employers' right to contract. Using similar reasoning, between 1905 when *Lochner* was decided and the mid-1930s, the Court struck down nearly two hundred economic regulations as violating substantive due process.

Not surprisingly, during this period—known as the *Lochner* Era—pro-regulation Progressives became increasingly frustrated with the Supreme Court's enforcement of unenumerated rights, particularly the right to enter into private contracts and to pursue lawful occupations free from government interference. It became clear that Progressive—and, later, New Deal—policies would not survive constitutional scrutiny if unenumerated rights were strictly enforced.

But then in 1934, nearly three decades after *Lochner*, the Court reversed course on economic liberties. The case was *Nebbia v. New York*, which dealt with the constitutionality of a law fixing the price at which milk could be sold.[18] Mr. Nebbia was a shopkeeper charged with selling two quarts of milk and a five-cent loaf of bread for eighteen cents, at a time when the state's Milk Control Board had set the price of milk at nine cents a quart. In other words, "He was convicted of a crime for selling his own property—wholesome milk—in the ordinary course of business at a price satisfactory to himself and the customer."[19]

The Court upheld Nebbia's conviction by a vote of 5–4, taking a very narrow view of the rights protected by the Fourteenth Amendment: "[A] state is free to adopt whatever economic policy may reasonably be deemed to promote public welfare, and to enforce that policy by legislation adapted to its purpose. The courts are without authority either to declare such policy, or, when it is declared by the legislature, to override it. If the laws passed are seen to have a reasonable relation to a proper legislative purpose, and are neither arbitrary nor discriminatory, the requirements of due process are satisfied. . . ."[20]

The right to earn an honest living, gutted in *Nebbia*, had been recognized in one form or another as far back as the Magna Carta.[21] The right was reiterated in the courts of England, where Lord Coke observed that "at the common law, no man could be prohibited from working in any lawful trade, for the law abhors idleness."[22] Even Justice William O. Douglas, one of the leading liberals of the twentieth century, described the right to work as "the most precious liberty that man possesses" and eloquently defended it: "Man has indeed as much right to work as he has to live, to be free, to own property. . . . It does many men little good to stay alive and free and propertied, if they cannot work. To work means to eat. It also means to live. For many it would be better to work in jail, than to sit idle on the curb. The great values of freedom are in the opportunities afforded man to press to new horizons, to pit his strength against the forces of nature, to match skills with his fellow man."[23]

Like all rights, the right to earn an honest living is meaningful only if it can be enforced and protected. Thanks to the inclusion of the Bill of Rights, the Constitution provides Americans with two layers of protection: the enumeration of powers, which constrains the ends that the federal government may seek, and the Bill of Rights, which constrains the means by which the government may pursue those ends. During the New Deal, both of these layers of protection came under attack. By condoning a vast expansion of government powers (see especially Chapters 1 and 2), the Supreme Court allowed Congress to pursue virtually any ends. And by ignoring the mandate of the Ninth Amendment, the Court allowed Congress to employ virtually any means.

What Were the Facts?

Between 1934 and 1938 the composition of the Court shifted left. New Dealers, who had already garnered a majority in the *Nebbia* case, were further emboldened by the retirements of Justices Willis Van Devanter and George Sutherland, both of whom had repeatedly voted to strike down New Deal economic regulations. The new Court, with replacement appointees Hugo L. Black and Stanley Reed, had its first opportunity in *United States v. Carolene Products Co.* to consider whether unenumerated rights should continue to be strictly enforced or whether they merited a lower level of protection.[24]

Like *Nebbia*, *Carolene Products* also dealt with milk, which may give some indication of how powerful the dairy lobby was at the time. But while *Nebbia* focused on price-fixing, the issue in *Carolene Products* was the exclusion of competitors. And while the regulation in *Nebbia* was state-imposed, *Carolene* related to a federal law.

In the early twentieth century, despite advances in refrigeration and transportation systems, there was still a great demand for fluid milk that resisted spoilage. Particularly in poorer areas, where refrigerators were uncommon, that demand was met by canned milk, of which there were two principal varieties: condensed milk, preserved with sugar, and evaporated milk, preserved through heat sterilization.

"Filled milk" was a variety of evaporated milk made by compounding skim milk with vegetable oil, generally coconut oil. While it contained no butterfat, filled milk had the same taste, odor, color, consistency, specific gravity, and cooking qualities as ordinary evaporated whole milk. Filled milk did enjoy, however, a decided advantage in price. The retail cost of filled milk was 7½ cents per can compared to 10 cents per can for whole milk.[25]

The dairy industry reacted to this competition by pushing for legislation prohibiting the manufacture or sale of filled milk. Many states enacted such legislation, but the dairy industry remained unsatisfied; filled milk could still be manufactured in some states and transported across state lines into states where manufacture but not sale had been prohibited. The "problem" of filled milk would require a national solution, or so it was argued.

Congress responded by passing the Filled Milk Act, forbidding and penalizing the interstate shipment of compounded milk and declaring that filled milk was "an adulterated article of food, injurious to the public health, and its sale constitute[d] a fraud upon the public."[26] At the time, the Commerce Clause of the Constitution had not been interpreted to allow the federal government to regulate purely intrastate activity, so production of filled milk for intrastate sale continued in the few states that had not outlawed it (or whose courts had struck down the prohibitions).[27] Thus, the Filled Milk Act was not a total prohibition, but the ban on interstate shipments was nearly enough to shut down the entire industry.

After the act's passage, Carolene Products, an Illinois company that manufactured filled milk sold as "Milnut," became the leading (and perhaps the only) manufacturer of filled milk in the country.[28] In 1931, after a successful challenge to the Illinois filled milk statute, Carolene continued operating in its home state.[29] The federal government then charged the company with violating the federal Filled Milk Act by shipping its product across state lines.

In 1934 a federal trial court in Illinois dismissed the charges and invalidated the act. As the court observed, Carolene Products had been engaged in "a well-known lawful industry, one which theretofore was entitled to and had the protection of the Constitution and laws of the United States."[30] The act therefore "amount[ed] to a taking of private property ostensibly for the public good without compensation, and deprive[d] the defendant and others similarly situated of liberty and property, without due process of law."[31] The Supreme Court finally heard the case more than four years later, on April 6, 1938, and Chief Justice Harlan Fiske Stone issued his opinion on April 25, 1938, just nineteen days after oral argument.

WHERE DID THE COURT GO WRONG?

Only seven justices participated in the decision, and six of them voted to uphold the Filled Milk Act.[32] Justice James Clark McReynolds was the sole dissenter, but he did not issue a written opinion. Fellow conservative Justice Pierce Butler, concurring in the end result but not in the Court's reasoning, avoided the constitutional question and argued instead that the statute should be construed to apply only to products that the government could prove were unwholesome or tended to deceive consumers, both of which were questions of fact to be determined by a jury at trial. Justice Hugo L. Black also concurred, without writing separately, in all of the majority opinion except the part that would prove to be most critical. The unusual result of this voting split is that Chief Justice Stone's opinion commanded a majority of the Court while receiving only four votes.

Moreover, Stone's opinion was less than ten pages. His brevity reflected the Court's new approach to reviewing unenumerated rights. After reciting the facts, the Court quickly dismissed Carolene Products' argument that the Filled Milk Act exceeded Congress's power to regulate interstate commerce. The Court also upheld the act against a Fifth Amendment Due Process challenge, holding that the risks of malnutrition and consumer fraud posed by filled milk were sufficient to sustain the statute.

In reaching its conclusion, the Court did not conduct any searching inquiry of the actual risk of malnutrition or consumer confusion posed by filled milk. Had the Court performed even a cursory inquiry, it would have found these risks to be illusory; filled milk was perfectly healthful, and there was no evidence that consumers were mistaking it for regular canned milk. Indeed, "[t]he consequence of the decision was to expropriate the property of a lawful and beneficial industry: to deprive working and poor people of a healthful, nutritious, and low-cost food; and to impair the health of the nation's children by encouraging the use as baby food of a sweetened condensed milk product that was 42 percent sugar."[33] There was another consequence, of course. The Court's decision allowed the whole milk lobby to use the force of government to remove any competition it might face from the filled milk industry.

Under the Court's approach, no inquiry need be made and no evidence need be proffered to support the statute: "Even in the absence of such aids the existence of facts supporting the legislative judgment is to be *presumed*, for regulatory legislation affecting ordinary commercial transactions is not to be pronounced unconstitutional unless in the light of the facts made known or generally assumed it is of such a character as to preclude the assumption that it rests upon some rational basis within the knowledge and experience of the legislators."[34]

This standard of review would come to be known as "rational basis scrutiny": Unless a challenger can demonstrate that a challenged regulation is wholly irrational—that there is no possible justification, no matter how attenuated, for the government's action—the regulation will be upheld. Taken at face value, such a standard would allow the government to regulate with virtually unfettered discretion. Luckily, even the most ardent New Dealers were not prepared to abandon the entire Bill of Rights so that the government could control economic matters. Without deciding the issue—because it was not before the Court—Chief Justice Stone suggested in a footnote that some rights might be entitled to more protection:

> There may be narrower scope for operation of the presumption of constitutionality when legislation appears on its face to be within a specific prohibition of the

Constitution, such as those of the first ten Amendments. . . .

It is unnecessary to consider now whether legislation which restricts those political processes which can
ordinarily be expected to bring about repeal of unde-
sirable legislation, is to be subjected to more exacting
judicial scrutiny. . . .

Nor need we enquire whether similar considerations enter into the review of statutes directed at particular religious, or national, or racial minorities. . . . [35]

In time, Stone's superfluous comments—the legal term is *dicta*—in footnote four of *Carolene Products* became law. The Court accomplished
precisely what the Federalists had feared: It declared, in essence, that
only those rights specifically enumerated in the Constitution, plus selected rights associated with political processes (such as voting) or with
protection of minorities, would be judicially enforced. The innumera-
ble remainder of our rights, including the right to earn an honest living,
would be enjoyed at the pleasure of the government. No result could be
more at odds with the Ninth Amendment's command that "The enumeration in the Constitution, of certain rights, shall not be construed to
deny or disparage others retained by the people."

What Are the Implications?

Carolene Products represented the beginning of a two-tiered approach to
enforcing rights. Those rights that had fortunately been specifically
enumerated would receive meaningful protection, but unenumerated
rights, such as the right to enter into contracts or the right to practice a
trade, would receive only "rational basis" scrutiny. Sadly, the Court has
repeatedly reaffirmed that holding, and with each iteration the language
of the test has become more and more deferential to government
power.

By the time the Court decided *Williamson v. Lee Optical* in 1955,
support for the *Nebbia* and *Carolene Products* approach pervaded the

judiciary.[36] In *Lee Optical* the Court voted 8–0 to uphold an Oklahoma law that barred opticians from fitting or duplicating lenses without a prescription from an ophthalmologist or optometrist.[37] The law made then-common practices illegal, such as fitting old lenses into new frames and replacing broken lenses by measuring the prescription strength of the fragments. In addition, the law prohibited anyone from advertising the sale of lenses, frames, mountings, or any other optical appliances. Even worse, the advertising prohibition extended beyond radio and television to include window displays and even telephone directories.

What rationale could possibly have justified such sweeping prohibitions? None was asserted by the Oklahoma lawmakers because, according to the Court, none need be asserted. Instead, the Court engaged in fanciful speculation as to what might have motivated the legislature:

> The legislature might have concluded that the frequency of occasions when a prescription is necessary [to properly fit frames] was sufficient to justify this regulation of the fitting of eyeglasses. Likewise, when it is necessary to duplicate a lens, a written prescription may or may not be necessary. But the legislature might have concluded that one was needed often enough to require one in every case. Or the legislature may have concluded the eye examinations were so critical, not only for correction of vision but also for detection of latent ailments or diseases, that every change in frames and every duplication of a lens should be accompanied by a prescription from a medical expert.[38]

Again, the Court did not consider whether any of these concerns *actually* motivated the legislature: "It is enough that there is an evil at hand for correction, and that it *might* be thought that the particular legislative measure was a rational way to correct it."[39] The obvious protectionist motivation behind the law was ignored.

Support for the extremely deferential rational basis standard has remained strong, even as the Supreme Court has become significantly more conservative than it was when *Lee Optical* was decided. In 1993, Justice Clarence Thomas, writing the eight-vote majority opinion in *Federal Communications Commission v. Beach Communications, Inc.,*[40] noted that regulations subject to rational basis review come to the Court

> bearing a strong presumption of validity, and those attacking the rationality of the legislative classification have the burden to negative *every conceivable basis* which might support it. Moreover, because we never require a legislature to articulate its reason for enacting a statute, it is entirely irrelevant for constitutional purposes whether the conceived reason for the challenged distinction actually motivated the legislature. . . . In other words, a legislative choice is not subject to court-room factfinding and may be based on rational speculation unsupported by evidence or empirical data.[41]

Justice John Paul Stevens, while agreeing with the outcome, was the only member of the Court to take issue with this formulation. As he correctly observed, "[I]t is difficult to imagine a legislative classification that could *not* be supported by a 'reasonably conceivable set of facts.' Judicial review under the 'conceivable set of facts' test is tantamount to no review at all."[42] The current state of rational basis review is best described by Clark Neily, senior attorney at the Institute for Justice: "Most of us have a drawer or a closet in our home where we put things that are not important enough to have their own place but are not quite worthless enough to throw away either. That is what the rational basis test is for the Supreme Court—a junk drawer for disfavored constitutional rights the Court has not explicitly repudiated, but that it prefers not to enforce in any meaningful way. Like any other junk receptacle, the rational basis test has become a real mess."[43]

The predictable result of this judicial abdication has been an avalanche of special interest legislation.[44] Evidently, no occupation is too innocent in the eyes of legislators to escape regulation. For instance, in Louisiana anyone who arranges flowers must be licensed, and to become licensed the arranger must pass a test. This proves to be no simple task, as the test is designed, administered, and evaluated by existing florists who have a direct incentive to limit competition. No wonder the test has a pass rate of 36 percent.[45]

Courts have become astonishingly cynical in their application of the rational basis test. For a particularly appalling example, consider this pronouncement from the U.S. Court of Appeals for the Tenth Circuit, upholding an Oklahoma law requiring anyone who sells caskets to become a licensed funeral director. The court brushed aside the blatantly protectionist motives for the law, observing that "while baseball may be the national pastime of the citizenry, dishing out special economic benefits to certain in-state industries remains the favored pastime of state and local governments."[46]

This rapid growth of special interest legislation and its attendant pathologies would not have surprised the Founders; they were well acquainted with the "mischiefs of faction," the latent causes of which "are sown in the nature of man."[47] When factions are given the opportunity to enrich themselves at the expense of others, "neither moral nor religious motives can be relied on as an adequate control."[48] James Madison recognized the danger, ignored by the Court in *Carolene Products*, of allowing the legislature unlimited discretion as to the means by which lawmakers seek the public good: "It is in vain to say that enlightened statesmen will be able to adjust these clashing interests and render them all subservient to the public good. Enlightened statesmen will not always be at the helm. Nor, in many cases, can such an adjustment be made at all without taking into view indirect and remote considerations, which will rarely prevail over the immediate interest which one party may find in disregarding the rights of another or the good of the whole."[49]

Despite such clear warning, the Court has taken precisely this approach with respect to economic liberties. With each restatement of the rational basis standard of review, the Court reminds the aggrieved grocer or manufacturer or optician who would rather not compete against industry newcomers that his proper place of redress is with supposedly enlightened statesmen in the legislature.[50] It is a refrain that is as hollow today as it was for Carolene Products in 1938. If grocers, manufacturers, and opticians had the political clout to repeal special interest legislation, they surely could have prevented its passage in the first place.

The fact that one in five occupations is now subject to licensure bears witness to the futility of legislative solutions.[51] The Court was the last and only place of redress, and it failed miserably. As a result, special interest legislation and protectionist laws stifle or prohibit outright the pursuit of productive livelihoods in a vast array of occupations ranging from African hair braiders to casket retailers to taxicab drivers.

Hector Ricketts and Melony Armstrong, with the help of the Institute for Justice, were able to use a combination of litigation, media exposure, and legislation to strike down the arbitrary laws that afflicted them. But accomplishing that was not easy, and it required resources beyond those of most fledgling entrepreneurs. Until the U.S. Supreme Court abandons its practice of treating economic liberty as a second-class provision of the Constitution, the American dream remains "a dream deferred, an opportunity denied."[52]

CHAPTER 12

Equal Protection and Racial Preferences

The Dirty Dozen List: *Grutter v. Bollinger* (2003)
Dishonorable Mention: *Regents of the University of California v. Bakke* (1978)

It is plainly true that in our society blacks have suffered discrimination immeasurably greater than any directed at other racial groups. But those who believe that racial preferences can help to "even the score" display, and reinforce, a manner of thinking by race that was the source of the injustice and that will, if it endures within our society, be the source of more injustice still. The relevant proposition is not that it was blacks, or Jews, or Irish who were discriminated against, but that it was individual men and women, "created equal," who were discriminated against. And the relevant resolve is that that should never happen again.
—*Richmond v. J.A. Croson Co.*, 488 U.S. 469, 527–28 (1989) (Scalia, J., concurring)

What Is the Constitutional Issue?

"[N]or shall any State . . . deny to any person within its jurisdiction the equal protection of the laws." —U.S. Constitution, Fourteenth Amendment, Section 1.

Our Constitution was a remarkable political innovation that radically altered the way citizens conceived of their relationship to government—as no other document had done before, and none since. Regrettably, that same document was also remarkable in its contradictions. While its preamble spoke of "We the People," it counted some as three-fifths of a person.[1] And the "blessings of liberty" it purported to secure did not extend to African slaves, whose continued importation was protected by the text of the Constitution until 1808.[2]

It would take more than seventy-five years and a bloody civil war before the Constitution would receive much-needed correction in the form of the Thirteenth, Fourteenth, and Fifteenth Amendments: abolishing slavery, ensuring equal protection of the law, and guaranteeing blacks the right to vote. But even in the wake of Reconstruction, Jim Crow laws, implemented brutally for nearly a century, would undermine the Constitution's new commitment to the equal rights of all citizens. Against this historical backdrop—and given the disparities in educational achievement and income between blacks and whites that exist to this day—it can be no surprise that issues of race and equality remain a sensitive topic in America. Nor is it surprising that there is vigorous debate about the extent to which the state may allocate benefits and burdens on the basis of race without violating the amended Constitution.

Grutter v. Bollinger dealt with the constitutionality of race preferences in university admissions.[3] The issue had last come before the Court twenty-five years earlier, in *Regents of the University of California v. Bakke*.[4] In *Bakke* the Court examined the admissions process at the University of California, Davis Medical School. The school, which admitted one hundred students annually, had set aside sixteen seats for minority applicants who were "economically and/or educationally disadvantaged." Rather than going through ordinary admissions channels, these applicants were referred to a special admissions committee, which would review their applications and make recommendations until all sixteen seats had been filled.

Allan Bakke was a white applicant who had been denied admission to Davis in 1973 and 1974. In both years, special applicants had been admitted with significantly lower scores than his. Bakke brought suit, alleging that the admissions process violated the Equal Protection Clause of the Fourteenth Amendment and Title VI of the Civil Rights Act of 1964.[5]

After considering the case, a fractured Supreme Court issued six opinions, none of which commanded a majority of the Court. Justices Harry A. Blackmun, William J. Brennan, Thurgood Marshall, and Byron R. White found the program constitutionally permissible, while Chief Justice Warren E. Burger, along with Justices William H. Rehnquist, John Paul Stevens, and Potter Stewart, would have struck down the program for violating Title VI. This left the deciding vote to Justice Lewis F. Powell.

Powell, arguing on different grounds, agreed with the Chief Justice and with Justices Rehnquist, Stevens, and Stewart that the program should be struck down and Bakke admitted to the medical school. Powell felt that the fatal defect in the special admissions program was that it operated as a "quota," totally excluding white students from a specific percentage of seats in the entering class, while allowing minority students the opportunity to compete for every seat.[6] At the same time Powell refused to uphold the lower court's order enjoining the medical school from *ever* considering race in admissions. Powell suggested that attaining "educational diversity" was a sufficiently compelling interest to merit the consideration of race in university admissions, provided that race or ethnicity was "simply one element—to be weighed fairly against other elements—in the selection process."[7] As an illustration, Powell cited the Harvard College admissions program, which he argued took race into account while evaluating students in a more holistic fashion, "treat[ing] each applicant as an individual in the admissions process."[8]

No other justice joined the portion of Powell's opinion endorsing the Harvard plan. Moreover, while it met with Powell's approval, the constitutionality of the Harvard plan was not an issue that the Court had to decide. Whether a program patterned on that plan was constitutional would remain an open question for the next twenty-five years, until finally addressed in *Grutter v. Bollinger.*

Although Powell had spoken only for himself in *Bakke*, many took his endorsement of the Harvard plan as a signal that such a plan would withstand judicial scrutiny. Subsequently, many colleges and universities, including the University of Michigan Law School, adopted similar admission plans. Lee Bollinger had been dean of the law school and was president of the university in 1997 when Barbara Grutter challenged the Michigan scheme. A victory for Grutter would have rendered these plans unconstitutional and required colleges and universities to adopt race-neutral admissions policies.

While the stakes for colleges and universities were high, the constitutional stakes were higher still. *Grutter* would test our commitment to the principle articulated in the Fourteenth Amendment that every individual is entitled to equal protection of the law, regardless of skin color. Because of the danger posed by racial distinctions, the Court had traditionally required government to overcome a high bar before it would uphold race-based policymaking. Indeed, if the Court were to hold that discriminatory admissions policies could be justified by the desire to achieve an arbitrary racial composition in higher education, that exception might swallow the general rule of nondiscrimination.

The real-world consequences of affirmative action are far more invidious than supporters admit. The sad reality is that African Americans admitted to elite universities through affirmative action perform at lower academic levels than their non–affirmative-action classmates. Not surprisingly, then, they drop out at a much higher rate.[9] As scholar and member of the U.S. Commission on Civil Rights Abigail Thernstrom and Harvard professor Stephan Thernstrom noted: "The combination of significantly higher dropout rates and underachievement surely perpetuates stigmatizing myths about black academic talent. When few Jews could get into Ivy League schools, and Jewish students had to be superqualified to gain admission, a Jewish stereotype was created: Jews are smart. Admitting black students by *lower* standards has precisely the opposite effect: It reinforces the pernicious notion that blacks are not academically talented."[10]

At the same time, there are real victims of affirmative action.

Individuals who are innocent of any wrongdoing are punished to advance group interests. Some minorities (such as Asians) and whites receive prejudicial treatment as a group. Resentments and racial polarization are fueled.

WHAT WERE THE FACTS?

The University of Michigan Law School is, by all measures, an elite institution. Among its alumni are former Supreme Court justice George Sutherland, famed defense attorney Clarence Darrow, and scores of current and former United States senators, representatives, and state supreme court justices. The University of Michigan is routinely ranked as one of the top law schools in the nation, and competition for admission is fierce.[11] The school receives "more than 3,500 applications each year for a class of around 350 students."[12]

The size of the law school's applicant pool would allow it to fill its ranks easily with only those students with the highest undergraduate grade point averages (GPAs) and Law School Admissions Test (LSAT) scores. In addition to wanting a high-scoring student body, however, the law school also wanted to enroll a "critical mass" of racially and ethnically diverse students. But these two goals were in tension because some minority groups had lower average scores using objective admissions criteria such as GPA and the LSAT. To compensate, the law school took applicants' race into consideration in deciding whether or not they should be admitted, giving preference to "underrepresented minority" students over similarly ranked white or Asian students.

In December 1996 one of the law school's many applicants was Barbara Grutter, who had little in common with the typical twenty-something law school applicant. Eighteen years out of college, Grutter was forty-three years old, married, a mother of two, and ran her own health care consulting business. Of course, like most of the law school's applicants, she had solid academic credentials; her undergraduate GPA was 3.8, and her LSAT score was 161 (placing her in the 86th percentile nationally).[13] In addition, like the majority of the other applicants, Barbara Grutter was white.

In April 1997, Grutter's application was wait-listed, and two months later she received a formal letter of rejection.[14] Aggrieved at her rejection, she filed suit, arguing, as Allan Bakke had, that the law school's consideration of race in admissions was a violation of the Fourteenth Amendment and Title VI of the Civil Rights Act of 1964. She was successful at trial, and the District Court issued an injunction prohibiting the law school's use of race in its admissions process.[15] On May 14, 2001, the U.S. Court of Appeals for the Sixth Circuit, sitting *en banc*, reversed the District Court by a 5-4 vote.[16] Grutter then appealed to the Supreme Court.

WHERE DID THE COURT GO WRONG?

The issue of racial preferences is as divisive in the Supreme Court as it is in the court of public opinion. *Grutter* generated six opinions—the same number, coincidentally, produced in *Bakke* twenty-five years previously.[17] Unlike *Bakke*, however, one of these opinions commanded a majority of the Court. In an opinion authored by Justice Sandra Day O'Connor, the Court upheld the law school's admissions program by a vote of 5–4.

O'Connor began her analysis by identifying the appropriate standard of review. While many state actions enjoy deferential "rational basis" review, O'Connor correctly noted, "All racial classifications imposed by government must be analyzed by a reviewing court under strict scrutiny."[18] Under this most stringent level of review, state actions will be upheld only if "narrowly tailored to further compelling governmental interests."[19] The difficulty of meeting both the "compelling interest" and "narrow tailoring" prongs of the test has led to the observation that strict scrutiny is "'strict' in theory and fatal in fact."[20] While this quip is hyperbolic—the Court had, in fact, expressly disavowed it eight years before *Grutter* was decided—it underscores the seriousness of this level of review.[21] Unfortunately, in upholding the law school's admissions program, Justice O'Connor's review not only failed to be "strict"; it was so lax that it barely qualified as "scrutiny."

While O'Connor had no trouble asserting that a "compelling governmental interest" existed, she was unclear as to what precisely that interest was. Initially, she identified the issue before the Court as "whether *diversity* is a compelling interest that can justify the narrowly tailored use of race in selecting applicants for admission to public universities."[22] She then quoted the law school's brief, identifying the interest as obtaining "the *educational benefits* that flow from a diverse student body."[23] O'Connor adopted the view that those benefits included livelier classroom discussions and better preparation for an increasingly diverse workplace and society. "In other words," she wrote, "the Law School asks us to recognize, in the context of higher education, a compelling state interest in *student body diversity.*"[24] Just how diversity based on race would achieve those goals was never explained; it was apparently self-evident.

By making educational benefits and student body diversity synonymous, O'Connor had the option of jumping back and forth, focusing on one of them as the *actual* compelling interest, then analyzing whether the program was "narrowly tailored" to achieve the other. Using this strategy, O'Connor focused her actual discussion of the "compelling interest" primarily on educational benefits—alleged to be the promotion of "cross-racial understanding" and "better prepar[ing] students for an increasingly diverse workforce and society"—and easily found them to be compelling.[25]

Yet, even if attaining these benefits were a compelling governmental interest, the law school's program should have failed the "narrow tailoring" requirement. Among other things, narrow tailoring demands that the same ends could not be attained without discriminating against nonminorities. In other words, the law school must have considered and rejected "the possibility of achieving the ends of [an] affirmative action program by race-neutral means."[26] Of course, the benefits the law school sought could have been achieved without granting race preferences, and there was no shortage of other organizations to serve as proof. As Justice Antonin Scalia noted in dissent, the lesson the law school seeks to impart to its students

> is a lesson of life rather than law—essentially the same
> lesson taught to (or rather learned by, for it cannot be

"taught" in the usual sense) people three feet shorter and twenty years younger than the full-grown adults at the University of Michigan Law School, in institutions ranging from Boy Scout troops to public-school kindergartens. If properly considered an "educational benefit" at all, it is surely not one that is either uniquely relevant to law school or uniquely "teachable" in a formal educational setting.[27]

In addition to admitting objectively qualified minorities to its rolls, the law school could, for example, invite speakers and host debates on issues of race in America or assign readings by minority legal scholars with diverse viewpoints. Or the school could mandate that all students perform pro bono work for minority clients. Any of these options would help produce the educational benefits that supposedly flow from diversity, yet none of them would take account of any student's race.

While the availability of race-neutral means for pursuing these educational benefits should have doomed the law school's program, O'Connor was undeterred. She had left herself the option of shifting between "compelling interests," so she started with "educational benefits" and then switched—defending the law school's program as narrowly tailored to achieve "diversity." Had O'Connor's opinion been subject to review by a yet higher court, diversity for the sake of diversity would not likely have qualified as a compelling interest; it seems indistinguishable from "outright racial balancing," which the Court admits is "patently unconstitutional."[28]

If one assumes that "diversity" is a compelling governmental interest—which is effectively what O'Connor allowed herself to do by shifting between interests—the narrow tailoring requirement is much easier to satisfy. After all, it is difficult to imagine how a school could achieve a diverse racial composition among its students without giving *some* consideration to the race of the students it admits.

Even though O'Connor's strategy opened up the option of using race in some fashion, the availability of race-neutral alternatives is only one test for narrow tailoring. Indeed, O'Connor cited *Bakke* for the proposition that "[t]o be narrowly tailored, a race-conscious admissions program cannot use a quota system."[29] Having identified the applicable law, however, O'Connor then proceeded to elevate semantics above substance by arguing that the law school hadn't established a "quota." It merely sought a "critical mass" of minority students. That distinction is pure sophistry, as clearly illustrated during oral arguments in an exchange between Justice Scalia and the law school's attorney, Maureen Mahoney:

Justice Scalia: Is two percent a critical mass, Ms. Mahoney?

Ms. Mahoney: I don't think so, Your Honor.

Justice Scalia: Okay. Four percent?

Ms. Mahoney: No, Your Honor, what—

Justice Scalia: You have to pick some number, don't you?

Ms. Mahoney: Well, actually what—

Justice Scalia: Like eight, is eight percent?

Ms. Mahoney: Now, Your Honor.

Justice Scalia: Now, does it stop being a quota because it's somewhere between 8 and 12, but it is a quota if it's 10? I don't understand that reasoning. Once you use the term critical mass and—you're—you're into quota land?

Ms. Mahoney: Your Honor, what a quota is under this Court's cases is a fixed number. And there is no fixed number here. The testimony was that it depends on the characteristics of the applicant pool.

Justice Scalia: As long as you say between 8 and 12, you're okay? Is that it? If you said 10 it's bad, but between 8 and 12 it's okay, because it's not a fixed number? Is that—that's what you think the Constitution is?[30]

Scalia's incredulous final question nicely captures the insincerity of the law school's argument. The law school had established the goal of enrolling a tightly constrained range of minority students, had given admission preferences to minority students in order to achieve that goal, and had managed to admit approximately the same number of minority students year after year. That sounds very much like a de facto quota. The school could not, by softening its tone and calling it "critical mass," satisfy the narrow tailoring requirement; a quota by any other name is just as unconstitutional.

Even if we were to accept O'Connor's argument that "critical mass" varies in some meaningful way from a "quota," the law school would still have to establish that its admissions policy is actually designed to admit a "critical mass" of minority students, whatever that may be. It is on this point that O'Connor's argument utterly collapses.

In a devastating dissent, Chief Justice Rehnquist, joined by Justices Anthony M. Kennedy, Scalia, and Clarence Thomas, attacked the law school's program, arguing that its so-called narrow tailoring bore "little or no relation to its asserted goal of achieving [a] 'critical mass'" of underrepresented minority students.[31]

Rehnquist noted that "[f]rom 1995 through 2000, the Law School admitted between 1,130 and 1,310 students" of which, in each year, "between 13 and 19 were Native American, between 91 and 108 were African-Americans, and between 47 and 56 were Hispanic."[32] If the law school were to be taken at its word—that it was focused on attaining "critical mass"—these different admissions rates lead to puzzling contradictions. Do thirteen to nineteen Native American students qualify as a "critical mass"? If they do, then there is no justification in providing preferences for more than a similar number of African American or Hispanic students. Do forty-seven to fifty-six Hispanic students qualify as a critical mass? In that case, African American students were likely granted too great a preference.

Moreover, Native American applicants—of whom there were fewer than thirty-six in an average year and never more than forty-five in a single year—would *never* be capable of achieving critical mass.[33] This suggests that Native American applicants should not be granted any preference whatsoever; if there are too few Native American students in the applicant pool to ever assemble a "critical mass," then no preference, large or small, could ever be said to serve that interest.

The law school's admissions practices become even more inexplicable if the number of admitted African American students is taken to represent the "critical mass":

> [I]n 2000, 12 Hispanics who scored between a 159–160 on the LSAT and earned a GPA of 3.00 or higher applied for admission and only 2 were admitted. Meanwhile, 12 African-Americans in the same range of qualifications applied for admission and all 12 were admitted. Likewise, that same year, 16 Hispanics who scored between a 151–153 on the LSAT and earned a 3.00 or higher applied for admission and only 1 of those applicants was admitted. Twenty-three similarly qualified African-Americans applied for admission and 14 were admitted.[34]

The only way these admissions practices could possibly be narrowly tailored to achieve a "critical mass" of minority students is to believe that "critical mass" varies by race. Not only must it vary by race, but it must do so dramatically. After examining law school admissions data over a five-year period, Rehnquist observed: "In order for this pattern of admission to be consistent with the Law School's explanation of 'critical mass,' one would have to believe that the objectives of 'critical mass' offered by respondents are achieved with only half the number of Hispanics and one-sixth the number of Native Americans as compared to African-Americans."[35]

This notion—that some minority races are "better" at contributing to a diverse student body than others—is so absurd and so offensive that it could not possibly have been the law school's true motivation. The much more likely explanation, and the one identified by Rehnquist, is that the law school's "alleged goal of 'critical mass' is simply a sham."[36]

Rehnquist offered further evidence that the "critical mass" goal was a sham by comparing the percentage of each minority group in the applicant pool to the percentage of each minority group admitted to the incoming class. In 1995, for example, African Americans, Hispanics, and Native Americans made up, respectively, 9.7 percent, 5.1 percent, and 1.1 percent of the applicant pool, and 9.4 percent, 5 percent, and 1.2 percent of the admitted students.[37] These striking correlations repeated themselves year after year, with the percentage of admitted minority students never more than one percentage point off the rate at which each racial group applied to the law school.[38] Rehnquist concluded the obvious: that the law school's admissions program operated as "a carefully managed program designed to ensure proportionate representation of applicants from selected minority groups."[39]

In the face of this overwhelming empirical attack on the program's "narrow tailoring," what was Justice O'Connor's response? It amounted to a single sentence: "But, as the Chief Justice concedes, the number of underrepresented minority students who ultimately *enroll* in the Law School differs substantially from their representation in the applicant pool and varies considerably for each group from year to year."[40]

In other words, the law school was perfectly free to *attempt* to enroll minority students in the precise percentages in which they apply—the very "outright racial balancing" that, in the Court's own words, is "patently unconstitutional"—as long as they were not entirely successful in doing so. This, the Court called "narrow tailoring."

As a parting gesture, O'Connor gave a nod to first principles, reminding us—for it could not be detected from the rest of her opinion—that "a core purpose of the 14th Amendment was to do away with all governmentally imposed discrimination based on race."[41] "Accordingly," she continued, "race-conscious admissions policies must be limited in time."[42] Finally, she concluded with the hope "that 25 years from now, the use of racial preferences will no longer be necessary to further the interest approved today."[43] As constitutional scholar Roger Pilon has noted, this goal is as empty as it is noble: "For if diversity is indeed such a compelling state interest, then discrimination to achieve it should be legitimate for as long as it is needed."[44] In any event, this arbitrary deadline, whether offered as an aspiration or in atonement,[45] is little comfort to those who believe, as Justice Thomas expressed in

dissent, "that the Law School's *current* use of race violates the Equal Protection Clause and that the Constitution means the same thing today as
it will in 300 months."[46]

WHAT ARE THE IMPLICATIONS?

Even while endorsing the Harvard plan, Justice Powell's opinion in
Bakke demonstrated that he was acutely aware of the dangers inherent
in such a scheme:

> *All* state-imposed classifications that rearrange burdens
> and benefits on the basis of race are likely to be viewed
> with deep resentment by the individuals burdened. The
> denial to innocent persons of equal rights and opportu-
> nities may outrage those so deprived and therefore may
> be perceived as invidious. These individuals are likely
> to find little comfort in the notion that the deprivation
> they are asked to endure is merely the price of member-
> ship in the dominant majority and that its imposition is
> inspired by the supposedly benign purpose of aiding
> others. One should not lightly dismiss the inherent un-
> fairness of, and the perception of mistreatment that ac-
> companies, a system of allocating benefits and privileges
> on the basis of skin color and ethnic origin.[47]

To whatever degree the decision in *Grutter* creates exactly this type
of interracial resentment, that is only the most immediate and visceral
of its effects. In order to fully grasp the implications of *Grutter*, it is important also to know a little bit about its companion case, *Gratz v. Bollinger*, which was decided on the same day.

While Barbara Grutter was challenging the law school, two undergraduate students, Jennifer Gratz and Patrick Hamacher, brought a
similar challenge against the admissions program at the University of
Michigan's College of Literature, Science, and the Arts. The undergraduate admissions process, due in part to the much larger number of

applications, considered race in a more mechanical way than the law school. Applicants received points based on personal characteristics including GPA, test scores, in-state residency, and race. Applicants earning 100 out of a possible 150 points were automatically admitted to the college. Applicants who happened to be members of "underrepresented minority groups" received an automatic 20 points, one-fifth of the points necessary for admission.

Gratz and Hamacher argued their case before the U.S. Court of Appeals for the Sixth Circuit on the same day as Barbara Grutter. The Sixth Circuit had not yet rendered a judgment on their case when Grutter appealed to the Supreme Court. Gratz and Hamacher petitioned the Court to hear their case as well so that the Court could address the constitutionality of race-based university admissions in a wider context. The Court agreed to do so and heard both *Grutter v. Bollinger* and *Gratz v. Bollinger* on April 1, 2003. Voting 6–3, with Justices O'Connor and Stephen G. Breyer providing the swing votes, the Court struck down the undergraduate admissions program, holding that its mechanically applied point system failed the narrow tailoring requirement.

Following the *Grutter-Gratz* split, race preferences in higher education remain constitutional, but an applicant's race must be considered part of a "highly individualized, holistic review" and not simply an automatic numerical bonus.[48] As Justice David H. Souter, a *proponent* of racial preferences, recognized in his dissent, this distinction is irrational: "The very nature of a college's permissible practice of awarding value to racial diversity means that race must be considered in a way that increases some applicants' chances for admission. . . . Justice Powell's plus factors necessarily are assigned some values. The college simply does by a numbered scale what the law school accomplishes in its 'holistic review'. . . ."[49]

This artificial distinction between point systems and "holistic review" is not merely irrational, it is dangerous. Prudence demands that race preferences, if they are to be permitted at all, be subject to meaningful judicial review. As Justice Souter put it, "Equal protection cannot become an exercise in which the winners are the ones who hide the ball."[50] Courts must be able to look at an admissions program and determine whether an applicant's race is a thumb on the scale or an anvil.[51] *Grutter* and *Gratz* frustrate this review by discouraging transparency; combined, they send the message that admissions programs that employ race preferences in a deliberately vague and unreviewable manner will be upheld, while those that do so forthrightly will be struck down.

Wholly apart from its effect on our Equal Protection jurisprudence, O'Connor's opinion may weaken constitutional protection for other rights. For whatever reason, the Court could not bring itself to say, "Henceforth, we will not apply strict scrutiny in reviewing racial preferences that are intended to benefit minorities."[52] Instead, the *Grutter* opinion disingenuously recites the language of strict scrutiny while actually applying a standard of review that is far less rigorous. That duplicity does more than undermine public confidence in the Court; it provides a dangerous precedent for a new definition of "strict scrutiny."

Strict scrutiny applies in numerous contexts beyond racial preferences; any government action that affects a "fundamental right" is subject to strict scrutiny review. What protection can we expect, say, freedom of speech to receive when a university determines that some purported educational benefit might be derived from its suppression?[53] Perhaps these concerns are overblown and the Court simply takes some fundamental rights more seriously than the right to equal protection of the law, but that conclusion cannot be derived from anything in the *Grutter* opinion.

Finally, the most heart-wrenching consequence of *Grutter* is that it allows states to continue to cover up their utter failure to close the racial gap in precollege education. Instead, states have attacked a mere symptom by artificially inflating minority enrollment in higher education. It is unconscionable that the incentive to address the real cause—disparity in K–12 education—should be delayed. Ending disparity will require a fundamental reassessment of the way public education is provided in America. Teacher performance and merit pay, infrastructure improvements, lower overhead and administration costs, curriculum reforms, and other major innovations will be parts of the solution. But a crucial ingredient for a constitutional, race-neutral solution will be school choice.

School choice can take many forms: vouchers, tax credits, charters, and so forth. The more choices, the more robust the competitive incentives for reform. When schools are required to compete for students through carefully crafted choice programs, they are accountable for the education they provide. Parents dissatisfied with a school's performance can place their child in another school. Public schools have the incentive to improve as they respond to the competitive pressures from choice. Minority students currently consigned disproportionately to woefully inadequate public schools will have a way out that offers the chance for an education that meets their needs. That chance can make the difference between success and failure in life. Furthermore, choice would benefit all minority students, not just those that go on to attend college or the tiny percentage that go on to attend a professional school.

In 2007 the Court had a chance to reconsider the diversity rationale in *Grutter* but left it largely intact. The Court examined race-based admissions programs at the K-12 grade level in Seattle, Washington, and Jefferson County, Kentucky.[54] Both school districts had adopted plans that allowed students a choice of public schools but tempered that choice with racial enrollment goals. Jefferson County required all public schools to seek a black enrollment of 15 to 50 percent. Seattle intended for its goals to foster "racial and cultural understanding" and instill the desire to "socialize with people of different races."[55] Whenever there were more applicants than slots at a specific school, Seattle evaluated the racial demographics of the school, and if there was a deviation of more than ten percentage points from the district's total mix, race would be used as a tiebreaker to award admissions.

Chief Justice John G. Roberts's opinion, joined in full by three other justices, found the plans unconstitutional because they were not necessary to remedy past segregation, and they relied on race as the sole factor for assignments rather than one of several factors designed to achieve diversity. Roberts stated that the programs were "directed only to racial balance, pure and simple."[56] In other words, the case was more like *Gratz* than *Grutter*. That prompted Justice Kennedy to write a concurring opinion restating that "Diversity, depending on its meaning, is a compelling educational goal a school district may pursue."[57]

Despite the fact that the Court left in place the holding of *Grutter*, Justice Breyer was apparently fearful that *Grutter's* diversity rationale might be at risk. He read a sharply worded dissent from the bench and prefaced it with the biting observation that "It is not often in the law that so few have so quickly changed so much."[58] That remains to be seen. The use of racial classifications has had a long, complicated, and often tragic history in American jurisprudence. The Court remains sharply divided on when and how racial classifications will be permitted, but it cannot avoid confronting the issue indefinitely.

Racial classifications are offensive when practiced by private individuals. When carried out by the state, they are intolerable. The surest protection against this injustice is nothing revolutionary; Justice John Marshall Harlan articulated the relevant principle more than a century ago: "Our constitution is color-blind, and neither knows nor tolerates classes among citizens. In respect of civil rights, all citizens are equal before the law. The humblest is the peer of the most powerful. The law regards man as man, and takes no account of his surroundings or of his color when his civil rights as guaranteed by the supreme law of the land are involved."[59]

When Harlan wrote these words, he spoke only for himself, the sole dissenter in *Plessy v. Ferguson*, one of the most reviled decisions in Supreme Court history. For all of our progress as a nation, including the dismantling of the state-sanctioned segregation upheld in *Plessy*, Harlan's words have never commanded a majority of the Court. How profoundly sad that in the wake of *Grutter*, it may be years before they are given their due regard.

AFTERWORD

Judicial Activism and Tomorrow's Supreme Court

Over the past seven decades the U.S. Supreme Court has rewritten major parts of our Constitution, including the General Welfare Clause, Commerce Clause, Contracts Clause, Non-Delegation Doctrine, and the First, Second, Fourth, Fifth, and Fourteenth Amendments. Typically, one or two votes have decided the outcome in highly charged cases involving federalism, civil rights, property rights, religion, campaign finance, and more. Without doubt the composition of the Court has been vital in determining the direction of the country.

According to Article II, section 2, of the Constitution, the president "by and with the Advice and Consent of the Senate, shall appoint . . . Judges of the supreme Court." Thus, President Bush and his successors will shape the Court's future. To make the most of that opportunity they must learn from their predecessors' mistakes—the kind of mistakes that produced the wrongheaded opinions cataloged in the past twelve chapters of this book. In that respect, *The Dirty Dozen* is a clarion call for the appointment of justices who are willing to take clear and consistent stands in favor of the framers' understanding of the Constitution.

Textualism Versus the Living Constitution

Ideally, the president will appoint "textualists," that is, justices who assign great importance to the words actually in the Constitution. Most textualists are also "originalists"; they interpret the Constitution in accordance with its meaning when the underlying provisions were ratified, not the meaning that would necessarily be derived from a modern reading of the text. As the term implies, originalists insist that the text be interpreted as it was originally understood by those who first wrote and read it.

(Original understanding is not synonymous, however, with "original intent," a related but distinct interpretive tool supposedly favored by conservatives that focuses on the values and objectives of the drafters and ratifiers when they enacted a particular provision.) The difficulty in applying original intent is that it begs several questions: Which drafters or ratifiers are authoritative? How do we know their intent? What if they changed their mind during the ratification process? How are differing views among the drafters and ratifiers to be resolved?

Original intent does, however, play a subordinate role for textualists. Basically, if the original meaning of the text is unambiguous, textualists adopt that meaning unless it would lead to absurd consequences. But if the meaning is unclear, textualists will consult the structure, purpose, and history of the Constitution.) Structure relates, first, to the internal relationship among the various provisions of the Constitution and, second, to the overall design or framework of government that the Constitution establishes. Purpose is discerned from the intent of the drafters and ratifiers. History involves the law or practices that preceded enactment as well as early post-enactment interpretations.[1]

Just as textualism is not the same as original intent, neither should it be equated with "strict constructionism." Justice Hugo L. Black, for example, was a First Amendment strict constructionist. He argued that the First Amendment's mandate—"Congress shall make no law" infringing on speech, religious exercise, and other protected freedoms—must be construed literally: On one hand, the term "no law" permitted no exceptions; on the other hand, the term "speech" did not extend to conduct such as flag burning. Neither view reflects the Supreme Court's current position.

Strict constructionism is often identified with more conservative legal scholars. Yet Justice Antonin Scalia has carefully distinguished it from his own preference for textualism: "Strict constructionism . . . is a degraded form of textualism that brings the whole philosophy into disrepute. I am not a strict constructionist, and no one ought to be. . . . A text should not be construed strictly, and it should not be construed leniently; it should be construed reasonably, to contain all that it fairly means."[2] Thus, to interpret the Constitution ratified in 1789, one might consult a contemporaneous dictionary, which would define words neither strictly nor loosely, but in accordance with their actual meaning and usage at the time.

The polar opposite of textualism is a theory preferred by many of today's liberals—the so-called living Constitution theory. Liberals want the Constitution to be interpreted in light of new circumstances—a malleable document that can be adapted to current societal demands. Justice Stephen G. Breyer described the living Constitution as one "designed to provide a framework for government across the centuries, a framework that is flexible enough to meet modern needs."[3] Our constitutional system, says Breyer, requires "structural flexibility sufficient to adapt substantive laws and institutions to rapidly changing social, economic and technological conditions."[4] Hence, the Eighth Amendment's prohibition on "cruel and unusual punishments" should be read in light of evolving standards of decency to exclude the death penalty, despite overwhelming evidence that the death penalty was not considered cruel and unusual at the time the Eighth Amendment was ratified.

Textualists respond that the framers provided an amendment process for "structural flexibility." If the Constitution needs to be updated, it should be accomplished by amendment, not by pretending that the written document doesn't mean what it says. Indeed, what is the purpose of a written document—whether a private contract or a Constitution—if we act as though it does not exist? Instead of following the steps carefully laid out in Article V to amend the Constitution, the Court's liberals have invoked their notion of a living document—treating the Constitution as if it empowered the federal government to regulate anything and everything while redistributing private resources from anyone to anyone else.

That cavalier attitude toward government powers can lead directly to the same attitude toward individual rights. "If powers can be expanded with impunity, so too can rights be contracted," observes constitutional scholar Roger Pilon. "In fact," he continues, "a 'living' constitution,' interpreted to maximize political discretion, can be worse than no constitution at all, because it preserves the patina of constitutional legitimacy while unleashing the political forces that a constitution is meant to restrain."[5]

THE RUBBER-STAMP JUDICIARY

Meanwhile, the Court's conservatives cannot escape their share of the blame. They selectively enforce textual constraints on federal power, but rarely when that power is used to enforce the criminal law, balance national security and civil liberties (see Chapter 7), or impose restrictions on private moral and social behavior. And some conservatives demand that courts indiscriminately defer to—perhaps "rubber-stamp" is more accurate—the decisions of Congress and state legislatures. Yet blanket judicial deference effectively removes the courts from the meticulously crafted system of checks and balances that was designed by the framers to prevent abuse of power. Consequently, government at all levels has grown in surprising and virtually unchecked ways at the expense of individual rights.

Two of those rights in particular—economic liberties (see Chapter 11) and property rights (see Chapters 9 and 10)—have been accorded second-class status because of the Court's abdication. In both areas, advocates of judicial restraint have won the battle over advocates of judicial engagement. As a result, two essential American rights—to earn an honest living and to own private property—have been stripped of vital constitutional protections, leaving entrepreneurs and small property owners especially vulnerable to backroom deals and majoritarian whims.

Thus, without realizing it, liberals and some conservatives have been working from opposite ends of the political spectrum, under opposing rationales, to reach the same end: expanded government power.[6] Here is how that development unfolded.

The framers envisioned a system in which individuals enjoyed rights equally, and the rights they enjoyed were treated with equal respect under the Constitution. But in 1938 the U.S. Supreme Court decided *United States v. Carolene Products* (see Chapter 11). That opinion, through its infamous footnote 4, created an artificial dichotomy of rights under the Constitution. Some rights, notably free speech, were elevated to a preferred tier and now rightly receive vigorous constitutional protection. Rights demoted to the second tier—specifically economic liberty and property rights—receive virtually no constitutional protection.

Indeed, the protection for economic liberty is so feeble that bureaucrats and judges may simply invent justifications for challenged laws, even if those justifications are purely hypothetical and even if it is quite clear they had nothing to do with the legislature's decision to pass the law. While property rights have received a somewhat greater degree of protection from the Court during the past twenty years, they remain under siege from government through eminent domain (see Chapter 9), zoning, and environmental regulations.

When the legislative or executive branch exceeds its legitimate enumerated powers, the courts have the authority, indeed the duty, to declare that exercise of power unconstitutional. Modern liberals, however, tend to reject the notion that the courts have a role in seriously protecting economic liberty or property rights. (Paradoxically, some liberals strongly advocate court protection for other rights—such as welfare or living wages—whose constitutional pedigree is nonexistent.) During recent decades, liberal judges, urged on by activist groups, have issued numerous opinions upholding the broad scope of economic and property regulation. Having achieved a judicially sanctioned regulatory state, liberals now favor letting the political process operate unimpeded by court oversight.

For their part, conservatives, who often support property rights and economic liberty on policy grounds, are nevertheless reluctant to have courts rein in legislatures. Reacting to the perceived excesses of the Warren Court and the ability of liberal interest groups to advance their agendas through the courts, many conservatives have come to view the judiciary with suspicion, at times bordering on outright animosity. Increasingly, their touchstone is judicial restraint—requiring deference to legislatures. That deference, coupled with an allegiance to precedent, means that conservatives are rarely willing to overrule prior cases, leaving entrenched the very foundations of the regulatory state they rail against. In practice, judicial restraint has mutated into judicial passivism, with a predictable result: more government power and fewer constitutionally protected individual rights.

Both liberals and conservatives take comfort in their often unfounded belief that legislatures will respond to the will of the public and make informed policy decisions that can be changed as public sentiment dictates. Although appealing in principle, that trust in the democratic process ignores the realities of governmental institutions. Through gerrymandering and other means, elected representatives are increasingly insulated from their constituents. Meanwhile, many policies are set and enforced by unelected, unaccountable agencies, boards, and commissions (see Chapter 4). What is more, politically powerful special interests often capture the regulatory process to keep out competition or gain control over property that doesn't belong to them. In the absence of judicially imposed limitations on the executive and legislative branches, protection of economic and property rights is ever more dependent on the self-restraint of government institutions—a commodity that is chronically in short supply.

In such a climate the Court's role in reviewing the constitutionality of laws becomes especially important. Without judicially recognized constitutional constraints, perverse incentives lead inexorably to expansion of federal power and contraction of personal freedoms. That dynamic is nowhere more evident than in the areas of property rights and economic liberty, where the current constitutional debate is whether there should be any real limits on governmental power.

A classic example is *Kelo v. New London* (see Chapter 9) in which the Supreme Court decided that the government, as part of an economic development project, can take well-maintained property from one owner and give it to another private party because the new owner might pay higher taxes. Under this standard, no home and no small business would be safe from tax-hungry governments and land-hungry developers. In upholding the taking of fifteen properties owned by seven families to make way for private office space and other unspecified projects, the Court deferred to the city council and an unelected private development corporation, which had been given the government's power of eminent domain.

The state of economic liberty jurisprudence is even more dire, as reflected in a 2005 decision by the U.S. Circuit Court of Appeals for the Tenth Circuit upholding Oklahoma's retail casket cartel. Oklahoma law requires anyone selling a casket to become a government-licensed funeral director—no small task considering the years of study and the requirement that an applicant embalm twenty-five bodies. All this despite the fact that casket retailers never handle dead bodies or perform funerals; they merely sell what amounts to a box. The Tenth Circuit explained, as noted in Chapter 11, that "dishing out special economic benefits to certain in-state industries remains the favored pastime of state and local governments" and upheld the law on the grounds "that intrastate economic protectionism . . . is a legitimate state interest."[7] In effect, we now have a federal appeals court giving a green light to the rankest form of cronyism and favoritism. Despite the starkness of the Tenth Circuit's ruling, the Supreme Court declined to review the case.

As long as courts show such extraordinary deference to legislatures and maintain a two-tier approach to constitutional rights, the ratchet operates in one direction: to increase government power. In important respects, judges have stopped judging. For all practical purposes, the Supreme Court has ceded nearly unbridled authority to government. Naturally, bureaucrats become adroit at maximizing their power. The result is a regulatory regime that too often leaves individuals at the mercy of the political branches, without judicial recourse.

If the lost liberties chronicled in this book are to be restored to their rightful place in the constitutional constellation, the courts must reinstitute constitutional protections. Judicial abdication has read those rights out of the Constitution; it is essential that consistent and principled judicial engagement rehabilitate them. Respect for precedent must not mean refusal to reexamine wrongly decided cases. Instead, the courts must fulfill their responsibility to recognize and implement constitutional constraints on government authority while at the same time making any adjustments as smooth as possible.

With judicially enforced constitutional constraints in place, liberals, conservatives, and others can compete to establish policies through the deliberations of their elected representatives. Wishes of the majority can prevail as long as the rights of the minority are respected. And entrepreneurs and small property owners, secure in their rights, can once again focus their energies on productive activities instead of trying to fend off arbitrary laws and regulations.

THE NEED FOR JUDICIAL ENGAGEMENT

Are we to conclude, therefore, that judicial activism—that is, the type of judicial intervention routinely condemned by liberals and conservatives alike—is actually a good thing? Yes, if activism means willing engagement in applying the law and the Constitution to scrutinize the acts (or omissions) of the executive and legislative branches. No, if activism means rendering legal judgments based on the judge's public policy preferences.

To illustrate: Judicial engagement can be appropriate even if, according to some Court critics, it means finding rights that are expressed nowhere in the Constitution. That is precisely what judges are instructed to do by the Ninth Amendment, which states that we "retain" rights beyond those that are enumerated. Federal courts are constitutionally authorized to remedy the violation of properly defined unenumerated rights—namely, those rights, such as privacy and travel, that we possessed even before our government was formed. That type of judicial "activism" is essential if the courts are to be our final bulwark against overreaching government.

Courts are not authorized, however, to create quasi-legislative entitlements such as welfare (see Chapter 1) or a minimum wage (see

Chapter 3), which are neither expressed in the Constitution nor traceable to our common law and natural rights heritage.

Judicial engagement can also be appropriate even in cases when an unelected judge overturns the enactment of an elected legislature. Judges have a responsibility to invalidate all laws that do not conform to the Constitution. Courts would be derelict if they endorsed unconstitutional acts merely because they were passed by our elected representatives. Ever since *Marbury v. Madison* (1803), the famous decision in which Chief Justice John Marshall first declared that an act of Congress was unconstitutional, federal judges have exercised a unique power—the power of judicial review—to determine the constitutionality of applicable laws. Marshall described judicial review in these terms: "The judicial power of the United States is extended to all cases arising under the constitution. Could it be the intention of those who gave this power, to say that, in using it, the constitution should not be looked into? That a case arising under the constitution should be decided without examining the instrument under which it arises? This is too extravagant to be maintained."[8]

Then again, judicial intervention would be inappropriate—and clearly distinguishable from judicial review—if a judge were to overturn a law simply because, as a policy matter, he disapproved of the legislative outcome. Rather than decide cases according to subjective value judgments, judges should be following objective standards for interpreting laws and constitutional provisions. Results-oriented jurisprudence, focused on reaching a particular outcome, may be proper for a legislator but not for a judge. His role is to apply the law, not impose his policy preferences.

Thus, whether judicial involvement is appropriate, argues law professor David Mayer, depends on the basis for the court's decision—not on the outcome. A court abuses its judicial review power when it decides questions of constitutionality on policy grounds, regardless of whether it ultimately finds the law in question constitutional. Mayer reminds us that some of the most egregious instances of improper activism are those cases where the courts have deferred to the legislature and upheld laws they should have found unconstitutional.[9]

The campaign finance reform cases, highlighted in Chapter 5, are a prime example. Applying a wholly fabricated standard—to prevent "the appearance of corruption"—the Supreme Court, by a razor-thin majority, decided that free political expression was expendable. In effect, the Court relegated the First Amendment to scrap paper because some justices agreed with some legislators on policy grounds—never mind the Constitution—that too much money was being spent on elections.

The trick, of course, is to distinguish proper from improper judicial actions to uphold or overturn democratically enacted legislation. That task is complicated by laws that are often unclear—either because the legislature has not done its job or has intentionally left gaps for the courts to fill; or because the meaning of the law depends on the meaning of the Constitution, which can also be unclear. Members of the Court must therefore have a theory of the Constitution—about separation of powers, federalism, limited government, and individual rights—and an allegiance to that theory.

The lesson of *The Dirty Dozen* is straightforward: Judicial engagement is essential to maintaining our liberties. Judges must honor our founding principles—expansive personal freedom coupled with tightly constrained legislative and executive powers—which have preserved and protected this nation for more than two centuries. That theory of constitutional jurisprudence charts the course to a free citizenry and a properly bounded government. As the saying goes, those who do not learn from the past are condemned to repeat it. This country, founded on liberty and justice, can do even better. Not only must we avoid repeating the mistakes of the past, but we must act affirmatively to ensure a Supreme Court with the vision to restore constitutional government.

POSTSCRIPT #1: *ROE V. WADE*

*R*oe v. *Wade* (1973) is not one of the Dirty Dozen—principally because it produced a result that many state legislatures might also
have produced—even though the legal reasoning in the opinion was
wrongheaded.[1] Jane Roe, whose real name was Norma L. McCorvey,
was a single woman who wished to terminate her pregnancy. Henry
Wade was the district attorney of Dallas County, Texas.

The central holding of the case, as modified by *Planned Parenthood of
Southeastern Pennsylvania v. Casey* (1992), was that states can regulate
pre-viability abortions but only if the restrictions do not impose an
"undue burden" on the mother.[2] That means state regulations cannot
have "the purpose or effect of placing a substantial obstacle in the path
of a woman seeking an abortion of a nonviable fetus."[3] Post-viability
abortions can be regulated and even prohibited unless necessary to preserve the woman's health.

The Court's two-part standard was an attempt to reconcile two
conflicting rights protected by the Constitution: the mother's liberty
right to control her own body and the unborn child's right to life.

The obvious problem is that the validity of the Court's holding depends on the definition of the beginning of human life—which determines, in turn, whether abortion is murder. That scientific-philosophical

quandary is a classic example of a policy question, which, under our system of separated powers, is resolved by legislatures, not courts. And the proper legislature, under our constitutional scheme of limited federal government, is at the state level. After all, state legislatures have each adopted criminal codes where murder is defined. Instead, acting on behalf of an entire nation but without constitutional authority, the Supreme Court in *Roe v. Wade* dictated when the mother's rights end and the fetus's rights begin.

Ironically, Justice Harry Blackmun, who wrote the majority opinion in *Roe*, seemed to agree that the Court should bow out. "We need not resolve the difficult question of when life begins," he stated. "When those trained in the respective disciplines of medicine, philosophy, and theology are unable to arrive at any conclusions, the judiciary, at this point in the development of man's knowledge, is not in a position to speculate as to the answer."[4] Having made that powerful point, Justice Blackmun then proceeded to do precisely what he said the Court should not do: He decided when life—and therefore the right to life—begins.

Blackmun's inconsistency was not unique. Conservatives and liberals can be equally unprincipled on the so-called social issues. That is especially evident when contrasting their positions on *Roe v. Wade* with the arguments they put forward in the sad case of Terri Schiavo. She was the young lady who died in Florida on March 31, 2005, thirteen days after the third removal of her feeding tube and more than fifteen years after she suffered brain damage that left her in a persistent vegetative state.

Despite repeated appeals to state and federal courts, Ms. Schiavo's parents were ultimately unable to override the wishes of her husband, who claimed that Ms. Schiavo would not have wanted to live on life-support equipment. While this distressing drama was unfolding, President Bush and the U.S. Congress intervened to enact a special bill directing the federal courts to resolve the Terri Schiavo dispute.

Thus, conservatives—usually strong proponents of states' rights, who vigorously argue that abortion rules should be decided state-by-state—pushed for federal preemption of state decisions in the Schiavo affair.

And liberals—who express outrage when state sovereignty arguments are advanced by pro-lifers in the abortion battles—invoked identical arguments to support Ms. Schiavo's right to die.

The Schiavo case—when does life end?—is the flip side of *Roe v. Wade*—when does life begin? Neither decision is the province of the federal judiciary. Judges have no special moral authority on such matters. The rules governing abortion and the right to die are best left to the political process—to be decided by voters through their state legislatures. If disputes arise, those rules can be applied to individual cases like *Roe* and Schiavo by state courts.

Of course, the job of judges is to judge, and we have argued (see, for example, Chapter 11) that judges have an obligation to determine the meaning of such abstract terms as "due process," "privileges or immunities of citizens," and "rights . . . retained by the people." Should not judges also define for legal purposes when life begins? No, they should not. Even if the definition were to be applied in a legal context, the subject matter—the beginning of life—is outside the scope of a judge's legal training and expertise. While judges are charged with interpreting express provisions in the Constitution, such as "due process," they are not assigned responsibility or specially equipped to assess the metaphysical and ethical implications of abortion.

That is the primary reason—judicial overreaching—that *Roe v. Wade* is a flawed decision, and that is why we are not surprised that some of our colleagues would include *Roe* in the Dirty Dozen. On the other hand, the outcome in *Roe* and *Casey*—different rules for pre-viability and post-viability abortions—might well be the middle ground that many states would adopt if it were left to them. Because of that result, we do not count *Roe* among our worst cases.

Nonetheless, by assuming a legislative role and intruding on state prerogatives, the Court violated two vital tenets of our constitutional structure: separation of powers among the executive, legislative, and judicial branches; and federalism, a system of dual sovereignty whereby state and federal governments divide authority to guard against abuse by either. As a legal matter, therefore, *Roe* was a dreadful case. But separation of powers and federalism are means, not ends, and the end result of *Roe* is a legal regime that many proponents of individual liberty consider a permissible compromise. That surely does not qualify *Roe* as good legal scholarship, but it disqualifies *Roe* from our list of the twelve worst cases since 1933.

POSTSCRIPT #2: *BUSH V. GORE*

Bush v. Gore (2000) was an easier call than *Roe v. Wade*—partly because none of our colleagues thought it was bad enough to include in the Dirty Dozen and partly because the Court's legal analysis was correct.[5]

Many liberals argue that Chief Justice William H. Rehnquist and Justices Antonin Scalia, Clarence Thomas, Sandra Day O'Connor, and Anthony M. Kennedy—the five more conservative justices—managed to look the other way when the federal government stepped in to tell the state of Florida how to run its presidential election. Let us see if that objection is valid or if the Supreme Court majority remained true to its supposed federalist principles.

The Court's opinion in *Bush v. Gore* mercifully ended the most contentious and turbulent election in modern American history.[6] Seven justices (excluding John Paul Stevens and Ruth Bader Ginsburg) ruled that the Florida vote recounts, conducted pursuant to subjective and contradictory standards, were incompatible with equal protection guarantees in the U.S. Constitution. "Having once granted the right to vote on equal terms, the state may not, by later arbitrary and disparate treatment, value one person's vote over that of another."[7]

Separately, a smaller, five-member majority (excluding Stevens, Ginsburg, David Souter, and Stephen Breyer) observed that Article II of the U.S. Constitution gives state legislatures comprehensive power to set the rules for presidential elections.[8] Exercising that power, the Florida legislature established an election scheme intended to secure a slate of electors immune from challenge by the U.S. Congress. To qualify for immunity, however, the electors had to be chosen by December 12, 2000—a date that could not possibly have been met if further recounts were to ensue. Thus, said the U.S. Supreme Court, to allow more recounts would have contravened the intent of the Florida legislature and therefore violated Article II of the U.S. Constitution.

In the abstract, recounts are neither right nor wrong. If recounts are done properly, votes erroneously discarded are appropriately included, and the result is a fairer representation of the popular will. But if recounts are done improperly, votes that should have been discarded are instead counted, thereby diminishing the weight of legitimate votes. The problem with Florida's manual recount was that political operatives were given unbridled discretion; there were no objective rules, no guidelines, no uniformity, and few checks against abuse. It seemed quite certain that the arbitrary, standardless procedures for recounts under the control of party loyalists would lead to less equitable results than the machine recount that had already been conducted.

That said, how could George W. Bush's lawyers exhort the U.S. Supreme Court to intervene in a matter that traditionally and constitutionally had been consigned to state jurisdiction? Didn't the request for Court intervention run counter to professed Republican regard for state sovereignty and federal forbearance? The answer is no, for two reasons.

First, the Florida controversy was, first and foremost, a bitter struggle between the legislative and judicial branches of state government. The Supreme Court was asked by the Republicans to umpire that struggle because it implicated both the U.S. Constitution and federal statutes. But regardless which branch of state government prevailed, final authority vested in a state, not federal, institution.

Second, federalism is not just about states' rights. Yes, the framers originally established a federal government of enumerated powers. And the Tenth Amendment provided that "the powers not delegated to the United States by the Constitution . . . are reserved to the States respectively, or to the people." But in 1868, when the Fourteenth Amendment was ratified, the relationship between federal and state governments was fundamentally restructured.

For the first time the Constitution provided for federal recourse when state governments "abridge the privileges or immunities of citizens" or "deprive any person of life, liberty, or property, without due process" or "deny to any person . . . the equal protection of the laws." In short, the legislative and judicial branches of federal government were empowered by the Fourteenth Amendment to remedy violations of constitutional rights. It is in that context that the U.S. Supreme Court was justified in preventing Florida state officials from denying equal protection to voters within and without the state. That was not mere activism. It was judicial responsibility, allegiance to the law and to the Constitution.

Moreover, there is another basis apart from the Court's equal protection rationale on which the Court could have intervened to stop the Florida recount. In his concurring opinion, Chief Justice Rehnquist, joined by Justices Scalia and Thomas, noted that the Florida Supreme Court had interpreted the state's election laws in a manner that "impermissibly distorted them beyond what a fair reading required."[9] That alone was sufficient to justify U.S. Supreme Court involvement because the Florida legislature, not its courts, has exclusive power under Article II of the U.S. Constitution to establish a regime for selecting presidential electors. As Rehnquist observed, "The general coherence of the legislative scheme may not be altered by judicial interpretation so as to wholly change the statutorily provided [plan]."[10]

Thus, when it comes to presidential elections, the Florida Supreme Court must be more deferential to the state's legislature than might otherwise be the case. And when the U.S. Supreme Court acts to enforce that mandate, that act does not reflect federal disrespect for state courts but, rather, a proper respect for the U.S. Constitution.

ACKNOWLEDGMENTS

To David Boaz and Gene Healy at the Cato Institute, we are indebted for their helpful comments on preliminary drafts of *The Dirty Dozen*. Likewise, we are grateful to Scott Bullock, Clark Neily, and Steve Simpson at the Institute for Justice for insightful suggestions on the final draft. And to Paul Sherman, also at the Institute for Justice, our appreciation for valuable assistance during early stages of the book.

In addition, many thanks to Bernadette Serton, our first-rate editor at Sentinel; to Eric Lupfer, our unrelenting agent at William Morris; and to our expert marketing and media advisors, Robert Garber at Cato and Will Weisser at Sentinel. Finally, our special gratitude goes to John Kramer at the Institute for Justice, who was instrumental in fine-tuning and launching *The Dirty Dozen*.

Of course, we are personally responsible for any errors, omissions, and misstatements.

THE CONSTITUTION OF THE
UNITED STATES OF AMERICA

We the People of the United States, in Order to form a more perfect Union, establish Justice, insure domestic Tranquility, provide for the common defence, promote the general Welfare, and secure the Blessings of Liberty to ourselves and our Posterity, do ordain and establish this Constitution for the United States of America.

Article. I.

Section. 1. All legislative Powers herein granted shall be vested in a Congress of the United States, which shall consist of a Senate and House of Representatives.

Section. 2. The House of Representatives shall be composed of Members chosen every second Year by the People of the several States, and the Electors in each State shall have the Qualifications requisite for Electors of the most numerous Branch of the State Legislature.

No Person shall be a Representative who shall not have attained to the Age of twenty five Years, and been seven Years a Citizen of the United States, and who shall not, when elected, be an Inhabitant of that State in which he shall be chosen.

[Representatives and direct Taxes shall be apportioned among the several States which may be included within this Union, according to their respective Numbers, which shall be determined by adding to the whole Number of free Persons, including those bound to Service for a Term of Years, and excluding

Indians not taxed, three fifths of all other Persons.][1] The actual Enumeration shall be made within three Years after the first Meeting of the Congress of the United States, and within every subsequent Term of ten Years, in such Manner as they shall by Law direct. The number of Representatives shall not exceed one for every thirty Thousand, but each State shall have at Least one Representative; and until such enumeration shall be made, the State of New Hampshire shall be entitled to chuse three, Massachusetts eight, Rhode-Island and Providence Plantations one, Connecticut five, New-York six, New Jersey four, Pennsylvania eight, Delaware one, Maryland six, Virginia ten, North Carolina five, South Carolina five, and Georgia three.

When vacancies happen in the Representation from any State, the Executive Authority thereof shall issue Writs of Election to fill such Vacancies.

The House of Representatives shall chuse their Speaker and other Officers; and shall have the sole Power of Impeachment.

Section. 3. The Senate of the United States shall be composed of two Senators from each State, [chosen by the Legislature thereof,][2] for six Years; and each Senator shall have one Vote.

Immediately after they shall be assembled in Consequence of the first Election, they shall be divided as equally as may be into three Classes. The Seats of the Senators of the first Class shall be vacated at the Expiration of the second Year, of the second Class at the Expiration of the fourth Year, and of the third Class at the Expiration of the sixth Year, so that one third may be chosen every second Year; [and if Vacancies happen by Resignation, or otherwise, during the Recess of the Legislature of any State, the Executive thereof may make temporary Appointments until the next Meeting of the Legislature, which shall then fill such Vacancies.][3]

No Person shall be a Senator who shall not have attained to the Age of thirty Years, and been nine Years a Citizen of the United States, and who shall not, when elected, be an Inhabitant of that State for which he shall be chosen.

The Vice President of the United States shall be President of the Senate, but shall have no Vote, unless they be equally divided.

The Senate shall chuse their other Officers, and also a President pro tempore, in the Absence of the Vice President, or when he shall exercise the Office of President of the United States.

The Senate shall have the sole Power to try all Impeachments. When sitting for that Purpose, they shall be on Oath or Affirmation. When the President of the United States is tried, the Chief Justice shall preside: And no Person shall be convicted without the Concurrence of two thirds of the Members present.

Judgment in Cases of Impeachment shall not extend further than to

[1]Changed by section 2 of the Fourteenth Amendment.
[2]Changed by the Seventeenth Amendment.
[3]Changed by the Seventeenth Amendment.

removal from Office, and disqualification to hold and enjoy any Office of honor, Trust or Profit under the United States: but the Party convicted shall nevertheless be liable and subject to Indictment, Trial, Judgment and Punishment, according to Law.

Section. 4. The Times, Places and Manner of holding Elections for Senators and Representatives, shall be prescribed in each State by the Legislature thereof; but the Congress may at any time by Law make or alter such Regulations, except as to the Places of chusing Senators.

The Congress shall assemble at least once in every Year, and such Meeting shall be [on the first Monday in December,]⁴ unless they shall by Law appoint a different Day.

Section. 5. Each House shall be the Judge of the Elections, Returns and Qualifications of its own Members, and a Majority of each shall constitute a Quorum to do Business; but a smaller Number may adjourn from day to day, and may be authorized to compel the Attendance of absent Members, in such Manner, and under such Penalties as each House may provide.

Each House may determine the Rules of its Proceedings, punish its Members for disorderly Behaviour, and, with the Concurrence of two thirds, expel a Member.

Each House shall keep a Journal of its Proceedings, and from time to time publish the same, excepting such Parts as may in their Judgment require Secrecy; and the Yeas and Nays of the Members of either House on any question shall, at the Desire of one fifth of those Present, be entered on the Journal.

Neither House, during the Session of Congress, shall, without the Consent of the other, adjourn for more than three days, nor to any other Place than that in which the two Houses shall be sitting.

Section. 6. The Senators and Representatives shall receive a Compensation for their Services, to be ascertained by Law, and paid out of the Treasury of the United States. They shall in all Cases, except Treason, Felony and Breach of the Peace, be privileged from Arrest during their Attendance at the Session of their respective Houses, and in going to and returning from the same; and for any Speech or Debate in either House, they shall not be questioned in any other Place.

No Senator or Representative shall, during the Time for which he was elected, be appointed to any civil Office under the Authority of the United States, which shall have been created, or the Emoluments whereof shall have been encreased during such time; and no Person holding any Office under the United States, shall be a Member of either House during his Continuance in Office.

Section. 7. All Bills for raising Revenue shall originate in the House of Representatives; but the Senate may propose or concur with Amendments as on other Bills.

⁴Changed by section 2 of the Twentieth Amendment.

Every Bill which shall have passed the House of Representatives and the Senate, shall, before it becomes a Law, be presented to the President of the United States; If he approve he shall sign it, but if not he shall return it, with his Objections to that House in which it shall have originated, who shall enter the Objections at large on their Journal, and proceed to reconsider it. If after such Reconsideration two thirds of that House shall agree to pass the Bill, it shall be sent, together with the Objections, to the other House, by which it shall likewise be reconsidered, and if approved by two thirds of that House, it shall become a Law. But in all such Cases the Votes of both Houses shall be determined by yeas and Nays, and the Names of the Persons voting for and against the Bill shall be entered on the Journal of each House respectively. If any Bill shall not be returned by the President within ten Days (Sundays excepted) after it shall have been presented to him, the Same shall be a Law, in like Manner as if he had signed it, unless the Congress by their Adjournment prevent its Return, in which Case it shall not be a Law.

Every Order, Resolution, or Vote to which the Concurrence of the Senate and House of Representatives may be necessary (except on a question of Adjournment) shall be presented to the President of the United States; and before the Same shall take Effect, shall be approved by him, or being disapproved by him, shall be repassed by two thirds of the Senate and House of Representatives, according to the Rules and Limitations prescribed in the Case of a Bill.

Section. 8. The Congress shall have Power To lay and collect Taxes, Duties, Imposts and Excises, to pay the Debts and provide for the common Defence and general Welfare of the United States; but all Duties, Imposts and Excises shall be uniform throughout the United States;

To borrow Money on the credit of the United States;

To regulate Commerce with foreign Nations, and among the several States, and with the Indian tribes;

To establish an uniform Rule of Naturalization, and uniform Laws on the subject of Bankruptcies throughout the United States;

To coin Money, regulate the Value thereof, and of foreign Coin, and the Standard of Weights and Measures;

To provide for the Punishment of counterfeiting the Securities and current Coin of the United States;

To establish Post Offices and post Roads;

To promote the Progress of Science and useful Arts, by securing for limited Times to Authors and Inventors the exclusive Right to their respective Writings and Discoveries;

To constitute Tribunals inferior to the supreme Court;

To define and punish Piracies and Felonies committed on the high Seas, and Offenses against the Law of Nations;

To declare War, grant Letters of Marque and Reprisal, and make Rules concerning Captures on Land and Water;

To raise and support Armies, but no Appropriation of Money to that Use shall be for a longer Term than two Years;

To provide and maintain a Navy;

To make Rules for the Government and Regulation of the land and naval Forces;

To provide for calling forth the Militia to execute the Laws of the Union, suppress Insurrections and repel Invasions;

To provide for organizing, arming, and disciplining, the Militia, and for governing such Part of them as may be employed in the Service of the United States, reserving to the States respectively, the Appointment of the Officers, and the Authority of training the Militia according to the discipline prescribed by Congress;

To exercise exclusive Legislation in all Cases whatsoever, over such District (not exceeding ten Miles square) as may, by Cession of particular States, and the Acceptance of Congress, become the Seat of the Government of the United States, and to exercise like Authority over all Places purchased by the Consent of the Legislature of the State in which the Same shall be, for the Erection of Forts, Magazines, Arsenals, dock-Yards and other needful Buildings;—And

To make all Laws which shall be necessary and proper for carrying into Execution the foregoing Powers, and all other Powers vested by this Constitution in the Government of the United States, or in any Department or Officer thereof.

Section. 9. The Migration or Importation of such Persons as any of the States now existing shall think proper to admit, shall not be prohibited by the Congress prior to the Year one thousand eight hundred and eight, but a Tax or duty may be imposed on such Importation, not exceeding ten dollars for each Person.

The Privilege of the Writ of Habeas Corpus shall not be suspended, unless when in Cases of Rebellion or Invasion the public Safety may require it.

No Bill of Attainder or ex post facto Law shall be passed.

No Capitation, or other direct, Tax shall be laid, unless in Proportion to the Census or Enumeration herein before directed to be taken.[5]

No Tax or Duty shall be laid on Articles exported from any State.

No Preference shall be given by any Regulation of Commerce or Revenue to the Ports of one State over those of another: nor shall Vessels bound to, or from, one State, be obliged to enter, clear, or pay Duties in another.

No Money shall be drawn from the Treasury, but in Consequence of Appropriations made by Law; and a regular Statement and Account of the Receipts and Expenditures of all public Money shall be published from time to time.

No Title of Nobility shall be granted by the United States: And no Person

---

[5]See the Sixteenth Amendment.

holding any Office of Profit or Trust under them, shall, without the Consent of the Congress, accept of any present, Emolument, Office, or Title, of any kind whatever, from any King, Prince, or foreign State.

Section. 10. No State shall enter into any Treaty, Alliance, or Confederation; grant Letters of Marque and Reprisal; coin Money; emit Bills of Credit; make any Thing but gold and silver Coin a Tender in Payment of Debts; pass any Bill of Attainder, ex post facto Law, or Law impairing the Obligation of Contracts, or grant any Title of Nobility.

No State shall, without the Consent of the Congress, lay any Imposts or Duties on Imports or Exports, except what may be absolutely necessary for executing its inspection Laws: and the net Produce of all Duties and Imposts, by any State on Imports or Exports, shall be for the Use of the Treasury of the United States; and all such Laws shall be subject to the Revision and Controul of the Congress.

No State shall, without the Consent of Congress, lay any Duty of Tonnage, keep Troops, or Ships of War in time of Peace, enter into any Agreement or Compact with another State, or with a foreign Power, or engage in War, unless actually invaded, or in such imminent Danger as will not admit of delay.

Article. II.

Section. 1. The executive Power shall be vested in a President of the United States of America. He shall hold his Office during the Term of four Years, and, together with the Vice President, chosen for the same Term, be elected, as follows

Each State shall appoint, in such Manner as the Legislature thereof may direct, a Number of Electors, equal to the whole Number of Senators and Representatives to which the State may be entitled in the Congress: but no Senator or Representative, or Person holding an Office of Trust or Profit under the United States, shall be appointed an Elector.

[The Electors shall meet in their respective States, and vote by Ballot for two Persons, of whom one at least shall not be an Inhabitant of the same State with themselves. And they shall make a List of all the Persons voted for, and of the Number of Votes for each; which List they shall sign and certify, and transmit sealed to the Seat of the Government of the United States, directed to the President of the Senate. The President of the Senate shall, in the Presence of the Senate and House of Representatives, open all the Certificates, and the Votes shall then be counted. The Person having the greatest Number of Votes shall be the President, if such Number be a Majority of the whole Number of Electors appointed; and if there be more than one who have such Majority, and have an equal Number of Votes, then the House of Representatives shall immediately chuse by Ballot one of them for President; and if no Person have a Majority, then from the five highest on the List the said House shall in like Manner chuse the President. But in chusing the President, the Votes shall be taken by States, the Representation from each State having one Vote; A quorum for this Purpose shall consist of a Member or Members from two thirds of the States, and a Majority of all the States shall be necessary to a Choice. In every Case, after the Choice of the President, the Person having the greatest Number of Votes of the Electors shall be the Vice President. But if there should remain two or more who have equal Votes, the Senate shall chuse from them by Ballot the Vice President.][6]

The Congress may determine the Time of chusing the Electors, and the Day on which they shall give their Votes; which Day shall be the same throughout the United States.

No Person except a natural born Citizen, or a Citizen of the United States, at the time of the Adoption of this Constitution, shall be eligible to the Office of President; neither shall any person be eligible to that Office who shall not have attained to the Age of thirty five Years, and been fourteen Years a Resident within the United States.

[In Case of the Removal of the President from Office, or of his Death, Resignation, or Inability to discharge the Powers and Duties of the said Office, the Same shall devolve on the Vice President, and the Congress may by Law provide for the Case of Removal, Death, Resignation or Inability, both of the President and Vice President, declaring what Officer shall then act as President, and such Officer shall act accordingly, until the Disability be removed, or a President shall be elected.][7]

The President shall, at stated Times, receive for his Services, a Compensation, which shall neither be increased nor diminished during the Period for which he shall have been elected, and he shall not receive within that Period any other Emolument from the United States, or any of them.

Before he enter on the Execution of his Office, he shall take the following Oath or Affirmation:—"I do solemnly swear (or affirm) that I will faithfully execute the Office of President of the United States, and will to the best of my Ability, preserve, protect and defend the Constitution of the United States."

Section. 2. The President shall be Commander in Chief of the Army and Navy of the United States, and of the Militia of the several States, when called into the actual Service of the United States; he may require the Opinion, in writing, of the principal Officer in each of the executive Departments, upon any Subject relating to the Duties of their respective Offices, and he shall have Power to grant Reprieves and Pardons for Offenses against the United States, except in Cases of Impeachment.

He shall have Power, by and with the Advice and Consent of the Senate, to

[6]Changed by the Twelfth Amendment.
[7]Changed by the Twenty-Fifth Amendment.

make Treaties, provided two thirds of the Senators present concur; and he shall nominate, and by and with the Advice and Consent of the Senate, shall appoint Ambassadors, other public Ministers and Consuls, Judges of the supreme Court, and all other Officers of the United States, whose Appointments are not herein otherwise provided for, and which shall be established by Law: but the Congress may by Law vest the Appointment of such inferior Officers, as they think proper, in the President alone, in the Courts of Law, or in the Heads of Departments.

The President shall have Power to fill up all Vacancies that may happen during the Recess of the Senate, by granting Commissions which shall expire at the End of their next Session.

Section. 3. He shall from time to time give to the Congress Information of the State of the Union, and recommend to their Consideration such Measures as he shall judge necessary and expedient; he may, on extraordinary Occasions, convene both Houses, or either of them, and in Case of Disagreement between them, with Respect to the Time of Adjournment, he may adjourn them to such Time as he shall think proper; he shall receive Ambassadors and other public Ministers; he shall take Care that the Laws be executed, and shall Commission all the Officers of the United States.

Section. 4. The President, Vice President and all civil Officers of the United States, shall be removed from Office on Impeachment for, and Conviction of, Treason, Bribery, or other high Crimes and Misdemeanors.

Article. III.

Section. 1. The judicial Power of the United States, shall be vested in one supreme Court, and in such inferior Courts as the Congress may from time to time ordain and establish. The Judges, both of the supreme and inferior Courts, shall hold their Offices during good Behaviour, and shall, at stated Times, receive for their Services, a Compensation, which shall not be diminished during their Continuance in Office.

Section. 2. The judicial Power shall extend to all Cases, in Law and Equity, arising under this Constitution, the Laws of the United States, and Treaties made, or which shall be made, under their Authority;—to all Cases affecting Ambassadors, other public Ministers and Consuls;—to all Cases of admiralty and maritime Jurisdiction;—to Controversies to which the United States shall be a Party;—to Controversies between two or more States;—[between a State and Citizens of another State;—][8] between Citizens of different States,—between Citizens of the same State claiming Lands under Grants of different States, [and between a State, or the Citizens thereof, and foreign States, Citizens or Subjects.][9]

In all Cases affecting Ambassadors, other public Ministers and Consuls,

[8]Changed by the Eleventh Amendment.
[9]Changed by the Eleventh Amendment.

and those in which a State shall be Party, the supreme Court shall have original Jurisdiction. In all the other Cases before mentioned, the supreme Court shall have appellate Jurisdiction, both as to Law and Fact, with such Exceptions, and under such Regulations as the Congress shall make.

The Trial of all Crimes, except in Cases of Impeachment; shall be by Jury; and such Trial shall be held in the State where the said Crimes shall have been committed; but when not committed within any State, the Trial shall be at such Place or Places as the Congress may by Law have directed.

Section. 3. Treason against the United States, shall consist only in levying War against them, or in adhering to their Enemies, giving them Aid and Comfort. No Person shall be convicted of Treason unless on the Testimony of two Witnesses to the same overt Act, or on Confession in open Court.

The Congress shall have Power to declare the Punishment of Treason, but no Attainder of Treason shall work Corruption of Blood, or Forfeiture except during the Life of the Person attainted.

Article. IV.

Section. 1. Full Faith and Credit shall be given in each State to the public Acts, Records, and judicial Proceedings of every other State; And the Congress may by general Laws prescribe the Manner in which such Acts, Records and Proceedings shall be proved, and the Effect thereof.

Section. 2. The Citizens of each State shall be entitled to all Privileges and Immunities of Citizens in the several States.

A Person charged in any State with Treason, Felony, or other Crime, who shall flee from Justice, and be found in another State, shall on Demand of the executive Authority of the State from which he fled, be delivered up, to be removed to the State having Jurisdiction of the Crime.

[No Person held to Service or Labour in one State, under the Laws thereof, escaping into another, shall, in Consequence of any Law or Regulation therein, be discharged from such Service or Labour; but shall be delivered up on Claim of the Party to whom such Service or Labour may be due.][10]

Section. 3. New States may be admitted by the Congress into this Union; but no new State shall be formed or erected within the Jurisdiction of any other State; nor any State be formed by the Junction of two or more States, or Parts of States, without the Consent of the Legislatures of the States concerned as well as of the Congress.

The Congress shall have Power to dispose of and make all needful Rules and Regulations respecting the Territory or other Property belonging to the United States; and nothing in this Constitution shall be so construed as to Prejudice any Claims of the United States, or of any particular State.

[10]Changed by the Thirteenth Amendment.

Section. 4. The United States shall guarantee to every State in this Union a Republican Form of Government, and shall protect each of them against Invasion; and on Application of the Legislature, or of the Executive (when the Legislature cannot be convened) against domestic Violence.

Article. V.

The Congress, whenever two thirds of both Houses shall deem it necessary, shall propose Amendments to this Constitution, or, on the Application of the Legislatures of two thirds of the several States, shall call a Convention for proposing Amendments, which, in either Case, shall be valid to all Intents and Purposes, as Part of this Constitution, when ratified by the Legislatures of three fourths of the several States, or by Conventions in three fourths thereof, as the one or the other Mode of Ratification may be proposed by the Congress; Provided that no Amendment which may be made prior to the Year One thousand eight hundred and eight shall in any Manner affect the first and fourth Clauses in the Ninth Section of the first Article; and that no State, without its Consent, shall be deprived of its equal Suffrage in the Senate.

Article. VI.

All Debts contracted and Engagements entered into, before the Adoption of this Constitution, shall be as valid against the United States under this Constitution, as under the Confederation.

This Constitution, and the Laws of the United States which shall be made in Pursuance thereof; and all Treaties made, or which shall be made, under the Authority of the United States, shall be the supreme Law of the Land; and the Judges in every State shall be bound thereby, any Thing in the Constitution or Laws of any State to the Contrary notwithstanding.

The Senators and Representatives before mentioned, and the Members of the several State Legislatures, and all executive and judicial Officers, both of the United States and of the several States, shall be bound by Oath or Affirmation, to support this Constitution; but no religious Test shall ever be required as a Qualification to any Office or public Trust under the United States.

Article. VII.

The Ratification of the Conventions of nine States, shall be sufficient for the Establishment of this Constitution between the States so ratifying the Same.

done in Convention by the Unanimous Consent of the States present the Seventeenth Day of September in the Year of our Lord one thousand seven hundred and Eighty seven and of the Independence of the United States of America the Twelfth. . . .

AMENDMENTS TO THE CONSTITUTION OF THE UNITED STATES OF AMERICA[11]

Amendment I.

Congress shall make no law respecting an establishment of religion, or prohibiting the free exercise thereof; or abridging the freedom of speech, or of the press, or the right of the people peaceably to assemble, and to petition the Government for a redress of grievances.

Amendment II.

A well regulated Militia, being necessary to the security of a free State, the right of the people to keep and bear Arms, shall not be infringed.

Amendment III.

No Soldier shall, in time of peace be quartered in any house, without the consent of the Owner, nor in time of war, but in a manner to be prescribed by law.

Amendment IV.

The right of the people to be secure in their persons, houses, papers, and effects, against unreasonable searches and seizures, shall not be violated, and no Warrants shall issue, but upon probable cause, supported by Oath or affirmation, and

[11]The first ten Amendments (the Bill of Rights) were ratified effective December 15, 1791.

particularly describing the place to be searched, and the persons or things to be seized.

Amendment V.

No person shall be held to answer for a capital, or otherwise infamous crime, unless on a presentment or indictment of a Grand Jury, except in cases arising in the land or naval forces, or in the Militia, when in actual service in time of War or public danger; nor shall any person be subject for the same offence to be twice put in jeopardy of life or limb, nor shall be compelled in any criminal case to be a witness against himself, nor be deprived of life, liberty, or property, without due process of law; nor shall private property be taken for public use without just compensation.

Amendment VI.

In all criminal prosecutions, the accused shall enjoy the right to a speedy and public trial, by an impartial jury of the State and district wherein the crime shall have been committed; which district shall have been previously ascertained by law, and to be informed of the nature and cause of the accusation; to be confronted with the witnesses against him; to have compulsory process for obtaining witnesses in his favor, and to have the assistance of counsel for his defence.

Amendment VII.

In Suits at common law, where the value in controversy shall exceed twenty dollars, the right of trial by jury shall be preserved, and no fact tried by a jury shall be otherwise re-examined in any Court of the United States, than according to the rules of the common law.

Amendment VIII.

Excessive bail shall not be required, nor excessive fines imposed, nor cruel and unusual punishments inflicted.

Amendment IX.

The enumeration in the Constitution of certain rights shall not be construed to deny or disparage others retained by the people.

Amendment X.

The powers not delegated to the United States by the Constitution, nor prohibited by it to the States, are reserved to the States respectively, or to the people.

Amendment XI.[12]

The Judicial power of the United States shall not be construed to extend to any suit in law or equity, commenced or prosecuted against one of the United States by Citizens of another State, or by Citizens or Subjects of any Foreign State.

Amendment XII.[13]

The Electors shall meet in their respective states, and vote by ballot for President and Vice President, one of whom, at least, shall not be an inhabitant of the same state with themselves; they shall name in their ballots the person voted for as President, and in distinct ballots the person voted for as Vice-President, and they shall make distinct lists of all persons voted for as President, and of all persons voted for as Vice-President, and of the number of votes for each, which lists they shall sign and certify, and transmit sealed to the seat of the government of the United States, directed to the President of the Senate;—The President of the Senate shall, in the presence of the Senate and House of Representatives, open all the certificates and the votes shall then be counted;—The person having the greatest number of votes for President, shall be the President, if such number be a majority of the whole number of Electors appointed; and if no person have such majority, then from the persons having the highest numbers not exceeding three on the list of those voted for as President, the House of Representatives shall choose immediately, by ballot, the President. But in choosing the President, the votes shall be taken by states, the representation from each state having one vote; a quorum for this purpose shall consist of a member or members from two-thirds of the states, and a majority of all the states shall be necessary to a choice. [And if the House of Representatives shall not choose a President whenever the right of choice shall devolve upon them, before the fourth day of March next following, then the Vice-President shall act as President, as in the case of the death or other constitutional disability of the President–][14] The person having the greatest number of votes as Vice-President, shall be the Vice-President, if such number be a majority of the whole number of Electors appointed, and if no person have a majority, then from the two highest numbers on the list, the Senate shall choose the Vice-President; a quorum for the purpose shall consist of two-thirds of the whole number of Senators, and a majority of the whole number shall be necessary to a choice. But no person constitutionally ineligible to the office of President shall be eligible to that of Vice-President of the United States.

[12]The Eleventh Amendment was ratified February 7, 1795.
[13]The Twelfth Amendment was ratified June 15, 1804.
[14]Superseded by section 3 of the Twentieth Amendment.

Amendment XIII.[15]

Section 1. Neither slavery nor involuntary servitude, except as a punishment for crime whereof the party shall have been duly convicted, shall exist within the United States, or any place subject to their jurisdiction.

Section 2. Congress shall have power to enforce this article by appropriate legislation.

Amendment XIV[16]

Section 1. All persons born or naturalized in the United States and subject to the jurisdiction thereof, are citizens of the United States and of the State wherein they reside. No State shall make or enforce any law which shall abridge the privileges or immunities of citizens of the United States; nor shall any State deprive any person of life, liberty, or property, without due process of law; nor deny to any person within its jurisdiction the equal protection of the laws.

Section 2. Representatives shall be apportioned among the several States according to their respective numbers, counting the whole number of persons in each State, excluding Indians not taxed. But when the right to vote at any election for the choice of electors for President and Vice President of the United States, Representatives in Congress, the Executive and Judicial officers of a State, or the members of the Legislature thereof, is denied to any of the male inhabitants of such State, being twenty-one years of age, and citizens of the United States, or in any way abridged, except for participation in rebellion, or other crime, the basis of representation therein shall be reduced in the proportion which the number of such male citizens shall bear to the whole number of male citizens twenty-one years of age in such State.

Section 3. No person shall be a Senator or Representative in Congress, or elector of President and Vice President, or hold any office, civil or military, under the United States, or under any State, who, having previously taken an oath, as a member of Congress, or as an officer of the United States, or as a member of any State legislature, or as an executive or judicial officer of any State, to support the Constitution of the United States, shall have engaged in insurrection or rebellion against the same, or given aid or comfort to the enemies thereof. But Congress may by a vote of two-thirds of each House, remove such disability.

Section 4. The validity of the public debt of the United States, authorized by law, including debts incurred for payment of pensions and bounties for services in suppressing insurrection or rebellion, shall not be questioned. But neither the United States nor any State shall assume or pay any debt or obligation incurred in aid of insurrection or rebellion against the United

---

[15]The Thirteenth Amendment was ratified December 6, 1865.
[16]The Fourteenth Amendment was ratified July 9, 1868.

States, or any claim for the loss or emancipation of any slave; but all such debts, obligations and claims shall be held illegal and void.

Section 5. The Congress shall have power to enforce, by appropriate legislation, the provisions of this article.

Amendment XV.[17]

Section 1. The right of citizens of the United States to vote shall not be denied or abridged by the United States or by any State on account of race, color, or previous condition of servitude.

Section 2. The Congress shall have power to enforce this article by appropriate legislation.

Amendment XVI.[18]

The Congress shall have power to lay and collect taxes on incomes, from whatever source derived, without apportionment among the several States, and without regard to any census or enumeration.

Amendment XVII.[19]

The Senate of the United States shall be composed of two Senators from each State, elected by the people thereof, for six years; and each Senator shall have one vote. The electors in each State shall have the qualifications requisite for electors of the most numerous branch of the State legislatures.

When vacancies happen in the representation of any State in the Senate, the executive authority of such State shall issue writs of election to fill such vacancies: *Provided*, That the legislature of any State may empower the executive thereof to make temporary appointments until the people fill the vacancies by election as the legislature may direct.

This amendment shall not be so construed as to affect the election or term of any Senator chosen before it becomes valid as part of the Constitution.

Amendment XVIII.[20]

[**Section 1.** After one year from the ratification of this article the manufacture, sale, or transportation of intoxicating liquors within, the importation

---

[17]The Fifteenth Amendment was ratified February 3, 1870.
[18]The Sixteenth Amendment was ratified February 3, 1913.
[19]The Seventeenth Amendment was ratified April 8, 1913.
[20]The Eighteenth Amendment was ratified January 16, 1919. It was repealed by the Twenty-First Amendment, December 5, 1933.

thereof into, or the exportation thereof from the United States and all territory subject to the jurisdiction thereof for beverage purposes is hereby prohibited.

Section 2. The Congress and the several States shall have concurrent power to enforce this article by appropriate legislation.

Section 3. This article shall be inoperative unless it shall have been ratified as an amendment to the Constitution by the legislatures of the several States, as provided in the Constitution, within seven years from the date of the submission hereof to the States by the Congress.]

Amendment XIX.[21]

The right of citizens of the United States to vote shall not be denied or abridged by the United States or by any State on account of sex.

Congress shall have power to enforce this article by appropriate legislation.

Amendment XX.[22]

Section 1. The terms of the President and Vice President shall end at noon on the 20th day of January, and the terms of Senators and Representatives at noon on the 3d day of January, of the years in which such terms would have ended if this article had not been ratified; and the terms of their successors shall then begin.

Section 2. The Congress shall assemble at least once in every year, and such meeting shall begin at noon on the 3d day of January, unless they shall by law appoint a different day.

Section 3. If, at the time fixed for the beginning of the term of the President, the President elect shall have died, the Vice President elect shall become President. If a President shall not have been chosen before the time fixed for the beginning of his term, or if the President elect shall have failed to qualify, then the Vice President elect shall act as President until a President shall have qualified; and the Congress may by law provide for the case wherein neither a President elect nor a Vice President elect shall have qualified, declaring who shall then act as President, or the manner in which one who is to act shall be selected, and such person shall act accordingly until a President or Vice President shall have qualified.

Section 4. The Congress may by law provide for the case of the death of any of the persons from whom the House of Representatives may choose a President whenever the right of choice shall have devolved upon them, and for the case of the death of any of the persons from whom the Senate may choose a Vice President whenever the right of choice shall have devolved upon them.

[21]The Nineteenth Amendment was ratified August 18, 1920.
[22]The Twentieth Amendment was ratified January 23, 1933.

Section 5. Sections 1 and 2 shall take effect on the 15th day of October following the ratification of this article.

Section 6. This article shall be inoperative unless it shall have been ratified as an amendment to the Constitution by the legislatures of three-fourths of the several States within seven years from the date of its submission.

Amendment XXI.[23]

Section 1. The eighteenth article of amendment to the Constitution of the United States is hereby repealed.

Section 2. The transportation or importation into any State, Territory, or possession of the United States for delivery or use therein of intoxicating liquors, in violation of the laws thereof, is hereby prohibited.

Section 3. This article shall be inoperative unless it shall have been ratified as an amendment to the Constitution by conventions in the several States, as provided in the Constitution, within seven years from the date of the submission hereof to the States by the Congress.

Amendment XXII.[24]

Section 1. No person shall be elected to the office of the President more than twice, and no person who has held the office of President, or acted as President, for more than two years of a term to which some other person was elected President shall be elected to the office of the President more than once. But this Article shall not apply to any person holding the office of President when this Article was proposed by the Congress, and shall not prevent any person who may be holding the office of President, or acting as President, during the term within which this Article becomes operative from holding the office of President or acting as President during the remainder of such term.

Section 2. This article shall be inoperative unless it shall have been ratified as an amendment to the Constitution by the legislatures of three-fourths of the several States within seven years from the date of its submission to the States by the Congress.

Amendment XXIII.[25]

Section 1. The District constituting the seat of Government of the United States shall appoint in such manner as the Congress may direct:

A number of electors of President and Vice President equal to the whole

---

[23]The Twenty-First Amendment was ratified December 5, 1933.
[24]The Twenty-Second Amendment was ratified February 27, 1951.
[25]The Twenty-Third Amendment was ratified March 29, 1961.

number of Senators and Representatives in Congress to which the District would be entitled if it were a State, but in no event more than the least populous State; they shall be in addition to those appointed by the States, but they shall be considered, for the purposes of the election of President and Vice President, to be electors appointed by a State; and they shall meet in the District and perform such duties as provided by the twelfth article of amendment.

Section 2. The Congress shall have power to enforce this article by appropriate legislation.

Amendment XXIV.[26]

Section 1. The right of citizens of the United States to vote in any primary or other election for President or Vice President, for electors for President or Vice President, or for Senator or Representative in Congress, shall not be denied or abridged by the United States or any State by reason of failure to pay any poll tax or other tax.

Section 2. The Congress shall have power to enforce this article by appropriate legislation.

Amendment XXV.[27]

Section 1. In case of the removal of the President from office or of his death or resignation, the Vice President shall become President.

Section 2. Whenever there is a vacancy in the office of the Vice President, the President shall nominate a Vice President who shall take office upon confirmation by a majority vote of both Houses of Congress.

Section 3. Whenever the President transmits to the President pro tempore of the Senate and the Speaker of the House of Representatives his written declaration that he is unable to discharge the powers and duties of his office, and until he transmits to them a written declaration to the contrary, such powers and duties shall be discharged by the Vice President as Acting President.

Section 4. Whenever the Vice President and a majority of either the principal officers of the executive departments or of such other body as Congress may by law provide, transmit to the President pro tempore of the Senate and the Speaker of the House of Representatives their written declaration that the President is unable to discharge the powers and duties of his office, the Vice President shall immediately assume the powers and duties of the office as Acting President.

Thereafter, when the President transmits to the President pro tempore of the Senate and the Speaker of the House of Representatives his written

---

[26]The Twenty-Fourth Amendment was ratified January 23, 1964.
[27]The Twenty-Fifth Amendment was ratified February 10, 1967.

declaration that no inability exists, he shall resume the powers and duties of his office unless the Vice President and a majority of either the principal officers of the executive department or of such other body as Congress may by law provide, transmit within four days to the President pro tempore of the Senate and the Speaker of the House of Representatives their written declaration that the President is unable to discharge the powers and duties of his office. Thereupon Congress shall decide the issue, assembling within forty-eight hours for that purpose if not in session. If the Congress, within twenty-one days after receipt of the latter written declaration, or, if Congress is not in session, within twenty-one days after Congress is required to assemble, determines by two-thirds vote of both Houses that the President is unable to discharge the powers and duties of his office, the Vice President shall continue to discharge the same as Acting President; otherwise, the President shall resume the powers and duties of his office.

Amendment XXVI.[28]

Section 1. The right of citizens of the United States, who are eighteen years of age or older, to vote shall not be denied or abridged by the United States or by any State on account of age.

Section 2. The Congress shall have power to enforce this article by appropriate legislation.

Amendment XXVII.[29]

No law, varying the compensation for the services of the Senators and Representatives, shall take effect, until an election of Representatives shall have intervened.

[28]The Twenty-Sixth Amendment was ratified July 1, 1971.
[29]Congress submitted the text of the Twenty-Seventh Amendment to the States as part of the proposed Bill of Rights on September 25, 1789. The Amendment was not ratified together with the first ten Amendments, which became effective on December 15, 1791. The Twenty-Seventh Amendment was ratified on May 7, 1992, by vote of Michigan.

TABLE OF CASES

NOTES

Introduction

1. *Table of Federal Register Issue Pages and Dates* (Washington, D.C.: U.S. Government Printing Office, May 17, 2006), frwebgate.access.gpo.gov/cgi-bin/getdoc.cgi?dbname=2006_mar_lsa&docid=06marlsa-53.pdf.
2. The amendment concerning congressional pay was ultimately ratified on May 7, 1992. It became the Twenty-seventh (and most recent) Amendment to the U.S. Constitution.
3. Article V also permits "Legislatures of two thirds of the several States [to] call a Convention for proposing Amendments." Although attempted twice, that alternative has never succeeded.
4. Randy E. Barnett, "Restoring the Lost Constitution," Cato Policy Report, January/February 2004, p. 15 (emphasis in original).
5. Our discussion of contrasting constitutional perspectives is drawn in part from Robert A. Levy, "The Rorschach Test of Limited Government," *Liberty*, June 2003, p. 31.

PART ONE: EXPANDING GOVERNMENT

Chapter 1: Promoting the General Welfare

1. In *Flemming v. Nestor*, 363 U.S. 603 (1960), the Supreme Court ruled that workers have no legally binding contractual or property right to their Social Security benefits.
2. *Helvering v. Davis*, 301 U.S. 619 (1937).
3. "We the People of the United States, in Order to . . . promote the general

Welfare, . . . do ordain and establish this Constitution for the United States of America." U.S. Const. preamble.

4. Alexander Hamilton, "Report on the Subject of Manufactures," in *Industrial and Commercial Correspondence of Alexander Hamilton*, ed. Arthur Harrison Cole (New York: Augustus M. Kelley, 1968), pp. 245, 247.

5. 4 Annals of Cong. 170 (1794).

6. 6 Annals of Cong. 1724 (1796).

7. 4 Reg. Deb. 1632–34 (1828).

8. 18 Cong. Rec. 1875 (1887).

9. See, e.g., *A.L.A. Schechter Poultry Corp. v. United States,* 295 U.S. 495 (1935).

10. *United States v. Butler,* 297 U.S. 1 (1936).

11. *Butler,* 297 U.S. at 66.

12. *Butler,* 297 U.S. at 68. The Tenth Amendment provides that "The powers not delegated to the United States by the Constitution, nor prohibited by it to the States, are reserved to the States respectively, or to the people."

13. See, e.g., *National Labor Relations Board v. Jones & Laughlin Steel Corp.,* 301 U.S. 1 (1937); *United States v. Darby Lumber Co.,* 312 U.S. 100 (1941); *Wickard v. Filburn,* 317 U.S. 111 (1942).

14. *Butler,* 297 U.S. at 87.

15. *Helvering,* 301 U.S. at 641.

16. *Helvering,* 301 U.S. at 640.

17. *Helvering,* 301 U.S. at 644.

18. Roger Pilon, vice president for legal affairs, Cato Institute, testimony on "Guns and Butter: Setting Priorities in Federal Spending in the Context of Natural Disasters, Deficits, and War," before the Committee on Homeland Security and Government Affairs, Subcommittee on Federal Financial Management, Government Information, and International Security, U.S. Senate, October 25, 2005, www.cato.org/testimony/ct-rp102005.html.

19. Letter from Franklin D. Roosevelt to Rep. Samuel B. Hill (July 6, 1935), in 4 *The Public Papers and Addresses of Franklin D. Roosevelt,* ed. Samuel I. Rosenman (New York: Random House, 1938), pp. 91–92 (emphasis added).

20. Rexford G. Tugwell, "A Center Report: Rewriting the Constitution," *Center Magazine,* March 1968, p. 20.

21. U.S. Const. art. I, sec. 8, cl. 7 & cl. 1.

22. U.S. Const. art. I, sec. 8, cl. 2.

23. U.S. Const. art. IV, sec. 3.

24. For an elaboration on this point, see Gary Lawson, "Making a Federal Case Out of It: *Sabri v. United States* and the Constitution of Leviathan," *2003–2004 Cato Supreme Court Review* 119 (2004): 134–38.

25. Jeffrey T. Renz, "What Spending Clause? (or the President's Paramour):

An Examination of the Views of Hamilton, Madison, and Story on Article I, Section 8, Clause 1 of the United States Constitution," *John Marshall Law Review* 33 (1999): 83.

26. *Butler*, 297 U.S. at 85 (Stone, J., dissenting).

27. *Butler*, 297 U.S. at 85–86 (Stone, J., dissenting) (internal citations omitted).

28. *South Dakota v. Dole*, 483 U.S. 203 (1987).

29. *Butler*, 297 U.S. at 86 (Stone, J., dissenting).

30. *Dole*, 483 U.S. at 207–08.

31. *Dole*, 483 U.S. at 217 (O'Connor, J., dissenting) (internal quotations and citation omitted).

32. Cited in Daniel Griswold, Stephen Slivinski, and Christopher Preble, "Ripe for Reform: Six Good Reasons to Reduce U.S. Farm Subsidies and Trade Barriers," Cato Trade Policy Analysis No. 30, September 14, 2005, pp. 3–4, www.freetrade.org/pubs/pas/tpa-030.pdf.

33. Organization for Economic Cooperation and Development, "Agricultural Policies in OECD Countries: Monitoring and Evaluation 2005," June 2005, p. 9.

34. U.S. General Accounting Office, "Sugar Program: Supporting Sugar Prices Has Increased Users' Costs While Benefiting Producers," GAO/RCED00–126, June 2000, pp. 6–7.

35. Office of Management and Budget, *Budget of the United States Government: Fiscal Year 2006, Historical Tables* (Washington, D.C.: U.S. Government Printing Office), table 3.2, p. 58.

36. Chris Edwards, "Ten Reasons to Cut Farm Subsidies," Cato Institute, June 28, 2007, www.freetrade.org/node/697.

37. Ibid.

38. Roger Pilon, vice president for legal affairs, Cato Institute, Testimony on "Guns and Butter: Setting Priorities in Federal Spending in the Context of Natural Disasters, Deficits, and War," before the Committee on Homeland Security and Government Affairs, Subcommittee on Federal Financial Management, Government Information, and International Security, U.S. Senate, October 25, 2005, www.cato.org/testimony/ct-rp102005.html.

39. Ibid.

Chapter 2: Regulating Interstate Commerce

1. *Gibbons v. Ogden*, 22 U.S. (9 Wheat.) 1, 231 (1824) (Johnson, J., concurring).

2. See, e.g., *Robbins v. Shelby County Taxing Dist.*, 120 U.S. 489, 497 (1887); *Walling v. Michigan*, 116 U.S. 446, 461 (1886); *Case of State Freight Tax*, 82 U.S. 232, 279–80 (1873).

3. President Roosevelt had asked Congress for additional Supreme Court

positions in an effort to pack the Court with New Deal supporters. The court-packing plan became unnecessary when Justice Roberts switched positions to side with the more liberal justices. See, e.g., Stephen M. Feldman, "Unenumerated Rights in Different Democratic Regimes," *University of Pennsylvania Journal of Constitutional Law* 9 (2006): 63–72.

4. *Nat'l Labor Relations Bd. v. Jones & Laughlin Steel Corp.*, 301 U.S. 1 (1937).
5. *Wickard v. Filburn*, 317 U.S. 111 (1942).
6. *Federalist No. 45* (James Madison).
7. *Wickard*, 317 U.S. at 115.
8. *Wickard*, 317 U.S. at 114.
9. Ibid.
10. *Wickard*, 317 U.S. at 115.
11. See, e.g., Randy Barnett, "The Original Meaning of the Commerce Clause," *University of Chicago Law Review* 68 (2001): 101–47; Randy Barnett, "New Evidence of the Original Meaning of the Commerce Clause," *Arkansas Law Review* 55 (2003): 847–99.
12. *United States v. Darby Lumber Co.*, 312 U.S. 100 (1941).
13. *Wickard*, 317 U.S. at 119–20 (emphasis added).
14. *Wickard*, 317 U.S. at 120.
15. For a discussion of "writtenness" and its centrality to constitutional interpretation, see Randy E. Barnett, "An Originalism for Nonoriginalists," *Loyola Law Review* 45 (1999): 629.
16. *Gibbons*, 22 U.S. (9 Wheat.) 1.
17. *Wickard*, 317 U.S. at 120.
18. "No way," stated University of Chicago law professor Richard A. Epstein, in dismissing Jackson's characterization of Marshall's position in *Gibbons*. Richard A. Epstein, "The Proper Scope of the Commerce Power," *Virginia Law Review* 73 (1987): 1408.
19. Coasting trade refers to trade carried on by water between neighboring ports within one country.
20. *Gibbons*, 22 U.S. (9 Wheat.) at 193.
21. *Gibbons*, 22 U.S. (9 Wheat.) at 189–90.
22. *Gibbons*, 22 U.S. (9 Wheat.) at 196.
23. *Gibbons*, 22 U.S. (9 Wheat.) at 197.
24. *Wickard*, 317 U.S. at 122.
25. *Wickard*, 317 U.S. at 125.
26. *Wickard*, 317 U.S. at 128–29 (emphasis added).
27. Memorandum for Mr. Costelloe, Re. *Wickard* Case (July 10, 1942) (Robert Jackson MSS, Box 125, on file with the Manuscript Division, Library of Congress), quoted in Barry Cushman, "Formalism and Realism in Commerce Clause Jurisprudence," *University of Chicago Law Review* 67 (2000): 1144.
28. John S. Baker, Jr., "Measuring the Explosive Growth of Federal Crime Legislation," *The Federalist Society,* April 2004, p. 3.

29. "Whoever, [except as authorized], knowingly and for profit manufactures, reproduces, or uses the character 'Smokey Bear' . . . or the name 'Smokey Bear' shall be fined under this title *or imprisoned not more than six months*, or both." 18 U.S.C. § 711 (2006) (emphasis added).

30. Baker, "Measuring the Explosive Growth of Federal Crime Legislation," p. 6.

31. Such dual punishment does not technically violate the Fifth Amendment's Double Jeopardy Clause because the state and federal governments are separate sovereigns. *United States v. Lanza*, 260 U.S. 377, 382 (1922).

32. See Stephen F. Smith, "Proportionality and Federalization," *Virginia Law Review* 91 (2005): 879–952.

33. *United States v. Lopez*, 514 U.S. 549 (1995).

34. *Lopez*, 514 U.S. at 567.

35. *United States v. Morrison*, 529 U.S. 598 (2000).

36. *Morrison*, 529 U.S. at 615–617.

37. *Gonzales v. Raich*, 545 U.S. 1 (2005).

38. *Raich*, 545 U.S. at 19.

39. *Raich*, 545 U.S. at 43 (O'Connor, J., dissenting).

40. *Raich*, 545 U.S. at 47 (O'Connor, J., dissenting).

41. Craig M. Bradley, "Whatever Happened to Federalism?" *Trial Magazine*, August 1, 2005, p. 52.

42. *Raich*, 545 U.S. at 57–58 (Thomas, J., dissenting).

43. *Raich*, 545 U.S. at 69 (Thomas, J., dissenting).

44. *Federalist No. 51* (James Madison).

45. *United States v. E.C. Knight Co.*, 156 U.S. 1, 12 (1895).

Chapter 3: Rescinding Private Contracts

1. *Norman v. Baltimore & Ohio Railroad Co.*, 294 U.S. 240 (1935); *Nortz v. United States*, 294 U.S. 317 (1935); and *Perry v. United States*, 294 U.S. 330 (1935).

2. Quoted in Thomas E. Baker, *The Most Wonderful Work: Our Constitution Interpreted* (St. Paul, Minn.: West Publishing Co., 1996), 397.

3. *Perry*, 294 U.S. at 375 (McReynolds, J., dissenting).

4. Retroactive *criminal* laws are precluded by the "ex post facto" provision of article I, section 10, of the Constitution. According to the Supreme Court, however, that provision does not apply to *civil* matters. See *Calder v. Bull*, 3 U.S. 386 (1798). Nonetheless, *Black's Law Dictionary* defines "ex post facto" to include any law "which, assuming to regulate civil rights and remedies only, in effect imposes a penalty or the deprivation of a right [for engaging in conduct] which, when done, was lawful." By that definition, Roosevelt's abrogation of gold clauses surely qualifies as ex post facto.

5. To be precise, the Contracts Clause does not apply to the federal

government: "No *State* shall . . . pass any . . . Law impairing the Obligation of Contracts. . . ." But retroactive federal legislation, because it can upset vested rights and deprive parties of fair notice, may violate the Due Process Clause of the Fifth Amendment. Moreover, the Tenth Amendment provides that "The powers not delegated to the United States by the Constitution, nor prohibited by it to the States, are reserved to the States respectively, or to the people." Thus, the Constitution is first and foremost a limitation on federal power. If a power is not enumerated and delegated to the federal government, then the power does not exist. And because the Constitution does not authorize the federal government to impair the obligation of contracts, the federal government, like the states, may not do so.

6. See Note, "Rediscovering the Contract Clause," *Harvard Law Review* 97 (1984): 1414, 1423–30.

7. For a short-lived attempt to revive the Contracts Clause, see *United States Trust Co. of New York v. New Jersey*, 431 U.S. 1 (1977) and *Allied Structural Steel Co. v. Spannaus*, 438 U.S. 234 (1978). Several years later those two cases were sharply limited in *Energy Reserves Group, Inc. v. Kansas Power & Light Co.*, 459 U.S. 400 (1983) and *Exxon Corp. v. Eagerton*, 462 U.S. 176 (1983).

8. *Home Building & Loan Association v. Blaisdell*, 290 U.S. 398 (1934).

9. Cicero, *De Officiis* [*On Obligations*] (Cambridge, Mass.: Harvard University Press, Loeb edition, 1975), 261 (quoted in Hadley Arkes, "On the Novelties of an Old Constitution: Settled Principles and Unsettling Surprises," *American Journal of Jurisprudence* 44 (1999): 15, 17).

10. See *Blaisdell*, 290 U.S. at 454 (Sutherland, J., dissenting).

11. *Ogden v. Saunders*, 25 U.S. (12 Wheat.) 213, 354–55 (1827).

12. For a brief history of Supreme Court pronouncements on the Contracts Clause, see Jethro K. Lieberman, *A Practical Companion to the Constitution* (Berkeley: University of California Press, 1999), pp. 326–27.

13. *Fletcher v. Peck*, 10 U.S. (6 Cranch) 87 (1810).

14. *New Jersey v. Wilson*, 11 U.S. (7 Cranch) 164 (1812).

15. *Dartmouth College v. Woodward*, 17 U.S. (4 Wheat.) 518 (1819).

16. See, e.g., *Ogden v. Saunders*, 25 U.S. (12 Wheat.) 213 (1827). For a contrary view, arguing against *Ogden*'s refusal to give the Contracts Clause any prospective effect, see Richard A. Epstein, "Toward the Revitalization of the Contracts Clause," *University of Chicago Law Review* 51 (1984): 723–30.

17. But see Chapter 11, "Earning an Honest Living," for a broader discussion of freedom to contract.

18. *Atlantic Coast Line Railroad Co. v. City of Goldsboro*, 232 U.S. 548, 558 (1914).

19. See *Stone v. Mississippi*, 101 U.S. 814 (1879).

20. Richard A. Epstein, "Obligation of Contract," in *The Heritage Guide to the*

Constitution, eds. David F. Forte and Matthew Spalding (Washington, D.C.: Regnery Publishing, 2005), 171–75 at 174.

21. *Blaisdell*, 290 U.S. at 445–46.

22. *Blaisdell*, 290 U.S. at 448 (Sutherland, J., dissenting).

23. *Blaisdell*, 290 U.S. at 426.

24. *Blaisdell*, 290 U.S. at 472–73 (Sutherland, J., dissenting).

25. *Ex parte Milligan*, 71 U.S. (4 Wall.) 2, 120–21 (1866).

26. *Blaisdell*, 290 U.S. at 451 (Sutherland, J., dissenting).

27. *Blaisdell*, 290 U.S. at 452–53 (Sutherland, J., dissenting).

28. *Blaisdell*, 290 U.S. at 448–49 (Sutherland, J., dissenting).

29. *Blaisdell*, 290 U.S. at 434–35.

30. *Blaisdell*, 290 U.S. at 442.

31. *Blaisdell*, 290 U.S. at 436.

32. *Blaisdell*, 290 U.S. at 475 (Sutherland, J., dissenting).

33. *Blaisdell*, 290 U.S. at 478 (Sutherland, J., dissenting).

34. Ibid.

35. *Blaisdell*, 290 U.S. at 438.

36. *Blaisdell*, 290 U.S. at 445.

37. *Blaisdell*, 290 U.S. at 482 (Sutherland, J., dissenting) (emphasis in original).

38. *Blaisdell*, 290 U.S. at 474 (Sutherland, J., dissenting).

39. *Blaisdell*, 290 U.S. at 482 (Sutherland, J., dissenting) (emphasis in original).

40. *Blaisdell*, 290 U.S. at 481 (Sutherland, J., dissenting).

41. *Blaisdell*, 290 U.S. at 483.

42. *Energy Reserves Group*, 459 U.S. at 411–13.

43. See Jonathan Brennan Butler, "Insurers under Fire: Assessing the Constitutionality of Florida's Residential Property Insurance Moratorium after Hurricane Andrew," *Florida State University Law Review* 22 (1995): 731, 732–35.

44. *Vesta Fire Insurance Corp. v. State of Florida*, 141 F.3d 1427, 1434 (11th Cir. 1998).

45. See, e.g., Reuters, "Insured Losses from Katrina Seen at up to $60 Billion," September 9, 2005, today.reuters.com/news/articlebusiness.aspx?type=bankingFinancial&storyID=nN09541490&from=business.

46. *State of Louisiana v. All Property and Casualty Insurance Carriers Authorized and Licensed to Do Business in the State of Louisiana*, 937 So. 2d 313, 327 (La. 2006).

47. Lino Graglia, "Our Constitution Faces Death by 'Due Process,'" *Wall Street Journal*, May 24, 2005.

48. Lino Graglia, "Judicial Activism of the Right: A Mistaken and Futile Hope," in *Liberty, Property, and the Future of Constitutional Government*, eds. Ellen Frankel Paul and Howard Dickman (Buffalo, N.Y.: SUNY Press, 1990), 67.

Chapter 4: Lawmaking by Administrative Agencies

1. *Table of Federal Register Issue Pages and Dates* (Washington, D.C.: U.S. Government Printing Office, May 17, 2006), frwebgate.access.gpo.gov/cgi-bin/getdoc.cgi?dbname=2006_mar_lsa&docid=06marlsa-53.pdf.

2. *U.S. Government Manual*, Appendix C: Agencies Appearing in the Code of Federal Regulations (Washington, D.C.: U.S. Government Printing Office, 2005–06), p. 655.

3. David Schoenbrod, *Saving Our Environment from Washington* (New Haven, Conn.: Yale University Press, 2005), p. 214.

4. W. Mark Crain and Thomas D. Hopkins, *Small Business Research Summary: The Impact of Regulatory Costs on Small Firms* (Washington, D.C.: Small Business Administration, Office of Advocacy, October 2001), p. 3.

5. David Schoenbrod, Testimony on "Monitoring Administrative Rulemaking" before the Subcommittee on Commercial and Administrative Law, Judiciary Committee, U.S. House of Representatives, September 12, 1996, www.cato.org/testimony/ct-ds091296.html pp. 1–3.

6. *Whitman v. American Trucking Associations, Inc.*, 531 U.S. 457 (2001).

7. Quoted in brief of the Institute for Justice and the Cato Institute for Respondent, *American Trucking*, 531 U.S. 457 (No. 99–1257), p. 7, www.cato.org/pubs/legalbriefs/brownervtrucking.pdf.

8. This brief history of the nondelegation doctrine is drawn from William Consovoy, et al., *Can Bush Supreme Court Appointments Lead to a Rollback of the New Deal?* (Washington, D.C.: Federalist Society), pp. 14–15, www.fed-soc.org/doclib/20070403_newdeal.pdf.

9. *Wayman v. Southard*, 23 U.S. 1, 42 (1825).

10. *Wayman*, 23 U.S. at 43.

11. *J.W. Hampton Jr. Co. v. United States*, 276 U.S. 394, 409 (1928) (emphasis added).

12. *Panama Refining Co. v. Ryan*, 293 U.S. 388, 430 (1935).

13. *Panama Refining*, 293 U.S. at 430.

14. Ibid.

15. *A.L.A. Schechter Poultry Corp. v. United States*, 295 U.S. 495, 539, 537 (1935).

16. *Schechter Poultry*, 295 U.S. at 542.

17. *Schechter Poultry*, 295 U.S. at 553 (Cardozo, J., concurring).

18. Kermit L. Hall, ed., *The Oxford Guide to United States Supreme Court Decisions* (New York: Oxford University Press, 1999), p. 232.

19. *NBC Co. v. United States*, 319 U.S. 190, 215 (1943).

20. *Yakus v. United States*, 321 U.S. 414, 420 (1944).

21. Jethro K. Lieberman, *A Practical Companion to the Constitution* (Berkeley: University of California Press, 1999), p. 140 (citations omitted).

22. *Solid Waste Agency of Northern Cook County v. Army Corps of Engineers*, 531 U.S. 159 (2001).

23. *Rapanos v. United States*, No. 04–1034, 2006 U.S. Lexis 4887, at 73 (June 19, 2006) (Kennedy, J., concurring in the judgment).

24. *Chevron U.S.A., Inc. v. Natural Resources Defense Council*, 467 U.S. 837 (1984).

25. *Chevron*, 467 U.S. at 843.

26. 42 U.S.C. § 7409(b)(1).

27. *American Trucking Associations, Inc. v. Environmental Protection Agency*, 175 F.3d 1027, 1034 (D.C. Cir. 1999).

28. See brief of the Institute for Justice and the Cato Institute for Respondent, *American Trucking*, 531 U.S. 457 (No. 99–1257), pp. 2–4, www.cato.org/pubs/legalbriefs/brownervtrucking.pdf.

29. See Legislative History of the Clean Air Amendments of 1977, vol. 4, pp. 2577, 2594.

30. *American Trucking*, 531 U.S. at 472.

31. *American Trucking*, 531 U.S. at 475 (citation omitted).

32. *American Trucking*, 531 U.S. at 474.

33. *American Trucking*, 531 U.S. at 475 (citation omitted).

34. Ibid.

35. *American Trucking*, 531 U.S. at 488 (Stevens, J., concurring in part and concurring in the judgment).

36. *American Trucking*, 531 U.S. at 489 (Stevens, J., concurring in part and concurring in the judgment).

37. Ibid. (internal citations omitted).

38. *American Trucking*, 531 U.S. at 486–87 (Thomas, J., concurring).

39. *American Trucking*, 531 U.S. at 487 (Thomas, J., concurring).

40. Ibid.

41. Gary Lawson, "Delegation and the Constitution," *Regulation,* vol. 22, no. 1 (1999), www.cato.org/pubs/regulation/regv22n2/delegation.pdf, pp. 27–29.

42. Joel Schwartz, "Getting Real on Air Pollution and Health," *Washington Post,* June 14, 2006, www.washingtonpost.com/wp-dyn/content/article/2006/06/13/AR2006061301759.html.

43. Ibid.

44. 21 U.S.C. § 355(d).

45. Ronald L. Trowbridge and Steven Walker, "The FDA's Deadly Track Record," *Wall Street Journal*, August 14, 2007.

46. Ibid.

47. *Metropolitan Washington Airports Authority v. Citizens for the Abatement of Aircraft Noise*, 501 U.S. 252, 272 (1991).

48. David Schoenbrod and Jerry Taylor, "The Delegation of Legislative Powers," in *Cato Handbook on Policy,* 6th ed. (Washington, D.C.: Cato Institute, 2005), p. 155, www.cato.org/pubs/handbook/hb109/hb_109–14.pdf.

49. Ibid.

50. Ibid., p. 156.

51. Stephen G. Breyer, "The Legislative Veto after Chadha," *Georgetown Law Journal* 72 (1984): 785–99.

52. Schoenbrod and Taylor, "The Delegation of Legislative Powers," p. 155.

PART TWO: ERODING FREEDOM

Chapter 5: Campaign Finance Reform and Free Speech

1. *McConnell v. Federal Election Commission*, 540 U.S. 93 (2003).

2. Many of the constitutional arguments cited in this chapter were adapted from the brief of *Amicus Curiae* the Cato Institute and the Institute for Justice in support of Appellants, *McConnell v. Federal Election Commission* (Nos. 02–1674 and Consolidated Cases).

3. For a brief history of campaign finance reform, see Jethro K. Lieberman, *A Practical Companion to the Constitution* (Berkeley: University of California Press, 1999), pp. 78–79.

4. *Buckley v. Valeo*, 424 U.S. 1, 26 (1976).

5. *Buckley*, 424 U.S. at 48–49.

6. George W. Bush, "President Signs Campaign Finance Reform Act," White House press release, March 27, 2002, www.whitehouse.gov/news/releases/2002/03/20020327.html.

7. *Register of Debate*, 22–1:76 App. (July 10, 1832).

8. *McConnell*, 540 U.S. at 224.

9. *McConnell*, 540 U.S. at 268–69 (Thomas, J., dissenting). Indeed, in the post-BCRA environment, politicians have already discovered a new "abuse" to curb. Congressional Republicans want to "reform" campaign finance once again—this time by eliminating so-called 527 groups, which are allied with political parties but not run by them. Contributions to such groups are not limited by federal law. Financier George Soros, for example, reportedly gave over $20 million to 527 groups in an abortive effort to elect John Kerry in 2004. Overall, Democrats took in four times what Republicans raised through such groups. See John Samples, "Playing the Irony Card: Restricting 527s Betrays Republican Principles," *Washington Times*, May 5, 2005.

10. *McConnell*, 540 U.S. at 248 (Scalia, J., dissenting).

11. *McConnell*, 540 U.S. at 126.

12. Ibid.

13. *McConnell*, 540 U.S. at 207.

14. *McConnell*, 540 U.S. at 208.

15. *McConnell*, 540 U.S. at 124–25.

16. *McConnell*, 540 U.S. at 297 (Kennedy, J., dissenting).

17. See Paul Burstein, "Is Congress Really for Sale?" *Contexts*, vol. 2, no. 3, summer 2003, www.contextsmagazine.org/content_sample_v2–3.php.

18. See Richard A. Epstein, "McConnell v. Federal Election Commission: A Deadly Dose of Double Deference," *Election Law Journal*, vol. 3, spring 2004, p. 231.

19. *McConnell*, 540 U.S. at 259 (Scalia, J., dissenting).

20. See Erik S. Jaffe and Robert A. Levy, "Real Campaign Reform," *Regulation*, vol. 25, no. 3, fall 2002, pp. 8–9, from which we draw the remainder of this chapter.

21. *Buckley*, 424 U.S. at 21.

22. Arguably, FECA's disclosure requirements inhibit persons from making contributions for fear that publicizing their associations might result in adverse consequences. As the Supreme Court has written: "Anonymity is a shield from the tyranny of the majority. . . . It thus exemplifies the purpose behind the Bill of Rights and of the First Amendment in particular: to protect unpopular individuals from retaliation." *McIntyre v. Ohio Elections Comm'n*, 514 U.S. 334, 357 (1995). To be sure, the right to anonymity is not absolute, but the disclosures required by FECA may go too far for the purpose of curbing corruption. In order to preserve privacy, anonymous disclosure, without identifying the donor, would be preferable. A candidate accepting large amounts of anonymous donations may well be suspect, but the public can judge that for itself and vote accordingly. Any candidate who wants to win will be responsive to voters, and if voters object to un-named contributors, the candidate will decline sizable contributions from donors who insist on anonymity. Practical politics rather than constitutionally suspect laws can discipline the system. At some point more detailed disclosure—by name—might be justified, but only if there is evidence that corruption remains a serious problem.

23. *Federal Election Commission v. Wisconsin Right to Life*, No. 06–969, 2007 U.S. Lexis 8515 (June 25, 2007).

24. *Wisconsin Right to Life*, 2007 U.S. Lexis 8515, at *39.

Chapter 6: Gun Owners' Rights

1. Timothy Wheeler, "Life and Death in the City: Two Restaurants, Two Robberies, Two Outcomes," *San Diego Union-Tribune*, May 31, 2000.

2. J. Neil Schulman, "Perspective on Gun Control: A Massacre We Didn't Hear About," *Los Angeles Times,* January 1, 1992.

3. Wheeler, "Life and Death in the City."

4. Anahad O'Connor and Sarah Garland, "Woman in Wheelchair Has .357 Surprise for Mugger in Harlem, Police Say," *New York Times*, September 9, 2006.

5. John R. Lott Jr., "NY Gun Laws & the Granny," *New York Post*, September 14, 2006.

6. Jill Gardiner, "Bloomberg Criticizes as 'Soft' Politicians Who Stand in Way of Gun Crackdown," *New York Sun*, September 8, 2006.
7. Schulman, "Perspective on Gun Control."
8. Suzanna M. Gratia, "If I Had My Gun . . . ," *Washington Post*, February 27, 1993.
9. Paul Craig Roberts, "Without Guns to Go to a Victim's Defense," *Washington Times*, July 24, 1994.
10. Ibid.
11. Editorial, "No Self-Defense Allowed," *Washington Times*, November 5, 1995.
12. Greg Esposito, "Gun Bill Gets Shot Down by Panel," *Roanoke Times*, January 31, 2006.
13. *United States v. Miller*, 307 U.S. 174 (1939).
14. In this section ("What Were the Facts?") and the following section ("Where Did the Court Go Wrong?"), we have drawn from an unpublished paper by Roy Lucas, "Miller Revisited & the Individual Right to Bear Arms" (copy on file with the authors). See also Roy Lucas, "From *Patsone & Miller* to *Silveira v. Lockyer*: To Keep and Bear Arms," *Thomas Jefferson Law Review* 26 (2004): 257–331.
15. *United States v. Miller*, 26 F. Supp. 1002 (W.D. Ark. 1939).
16. The Criminal Appeals Act of 1907, since repealed, allowed direct appeals to the Supreme Court whenever a trial court held a federal statute unconstitutional.
17. Portions of this material have appeared in the authors' previously published articles.
18. Nelson Lund, "A Primer on the Constitutional Right to Bear Arms," Virginia Institute for Public Policy Report No. 7, June 2002, p. 5 (citing Ronald S. Resnick, "Private Arms as the Palladium of Liberty: The Meaning of the Second Amendment," *U. Det. Mercy L. Rev.* 77 (1999): 1, 4). We have also relied on Professor Lund's paper for other arguments advanced, passim, in this chapter.
19. *Silveira v. Lockyer*, 328 F.3d 567, 569–70 (9th Cir. 2003) (Kozinski, J., dissenting from denial of rehearing en banc).
20. *Miller*, 307 U.S. at 178.
21. Ibid.
22. Ibid. (citation omitted).
23. *Miller*, 307 U.S. at 179.
24. *Miller*, 307 U.S. at 179–80 (citation omitted).
25. *Nunn v. Georgia*, 1 Ga. 243, 251 (1846).
26. *Miller*, 307 U.S. at 178.
27. *Thomas v. City Council of Portland*, 730 F.2d 41, 42 (1st Cir. 1984) (citation omitted).
28. *Cases v. United States*, 131 F.2d 916, 922 (1st Cir. 1942).

29. *United States v. Toner*, 728 F.2d 115, 128 (2d Cir. 1984).

30. *United States v. Graves*, 554 F.2d 65, 66 n.2 (3d Cir. 1977).

31. *Love v. Pepersack*, 47 F.3d 120, 124 (4th Cir.), *cert. denied*, 516 U.S. 813 (1995).

32. *United States v. Warin*, 530 F.2d 103, 106 (6th Cir.), *cert. denied*, 426 U.S. 948 (1976).

33. *Gillespie v. City of Indianapolis*, 185 F.3d 693, 710 (7th Cir. 1999), *cert. denied*, 528 U.S. 1116 (2000).

34. *United States v. Lippman*, 369 F.3d 1039, 1044 (8th Cir. 2004) (citation omitted), *cert. denied*, 543 U.S. 1080 (2005).

35. *Hickman v. Block*, 81 F.3d 98, 101 (9th Cir. 1996).

36. *United States v. Parker*, 362 F.3d 1279, 1282 (10th Cir.), *cert. denied*, 543 U.S. 874 (2004).

37. *United States v. Wright*, 117 F.3d 1265, 1273 (11th Cir.), *cert. denied*, 522 U.S. 1007 (1997).

38. *United States v. Emerson*, 270 F.3d 203 (5th Cir. 2001).

39. *Emerson*, 270 F.3d at 260.

40. Letter from John Ashcroft, then–U.S. attorney general, to James Jay Baker, executive director, National Rifle Association, May 17, 2001, www.nraila .org/images/Ashcroft.pdf.

41. Letter from Bill Pryor, then–Alabama attorney general, to John Ashcroft, then–U.S. attorney general, July 8, 2002, www.nraila.org/media/misc/ pryorlet.pdf.

42. The "collective rights" model of the Second Amendment comes in two alternative versions: (1) The Second Amendment secures a right of states to arm the members of their militias. (2) Individuals have a right to bear arms provided by themselves, but only when participating in a militia, and then only if the state and federal governments haven't provided the necessary weapons.

43. U.S. Department of Justice, "Whether the Second Amendment Secures an Individual Right," August 24, 2004, www.usdoj.gov/olc/secondamend-ment2.htm.

44. Quoted in Dan Gifford, "The Conceptual Foundations of Anglo-American Jurisprudence in Religion and Reason," *Tenn. L. Rev.* 62 (1995): 759, 789.

45. Laurence H. Tribe and Akhil Reed Amar, "Well-Regulated Militias, and More," *New York Times*, October 28, 1999, p. A31.

46. *Parker v. District of Columbia*, 478 F.3d 370 (D.C. Cir. 2007). One of this book's authors (Levy) is co-counsel in the *Parker* case.

47. U.S. Const., art. I, sec. 8.

48. *Parker*, 478 F.3d at 395.

49. Ibid.

50. Ibid.

51. Linda Gorman and David B. Kopel, "Self-defense: The Equalizer," *Forum for Applied Research and Public Policy* 15 (2000): 92.

52. Don B. Kates, "The Laws That Misfire," *Legal Times*, August 7, 2006, p. 61.

53. Ibid., p. 60.

54. See Brandeis brief for appellant filed on behalf of *amici* professors, Second Amendment Foundation, Citizens Committee for the Right to Keep and Bear Arms, and the Madison Society, *Parker v. District of Columbia*, 478 F.3d 370 (D.C. Cir. 2007) (No. 04-7041), pp. 6–8, 10. The data cited covers varying years from 1998 to 2004.

55. Ibid., pp. 24–25.

56. Kates, "The Laws That Misfire."

57. Charles F. Wellford, John V. Pepper, and Carol V. Petrie, eds., *Firearms and Violence: A Critical Review* (Washington, D.C.: National Academy of Sciences, 2004).

58. Robert A. Hahn et al., "First Reports Evaluating the Effectiveness of Strategies for Preventing Violence: Firearms Laws," Centers for Disease Control and Prevention, October 3, 2003, www.cdc.gov/mmwr/preview/mmwrhtml/rr5214a2.htm.

Chapter 7: Civil Liberties Versus National Security

1. In 1954, Chief Justice Earl Warren, writing for a unanimous Court in *Bolling v. Sharpe*, 347 U.S. 497 (1954), held that the Due Process Clause of the Fifth Amendment implicitly barred most racial discrimination by the federal government, just as the Equal Protection Clause of the Fourteenth Amendment barred such discrimination by the states. (The issue in the 1954 case was the enforcement of school desegregation orders against the District of Columbia, which is not a state.)

2. *Korematsu v. United States*, 323 U.S. 214 (1944).

3. *Korematsu*, 323 U.S. at 243 (Jackson, J., dissenting).

4. *Korematsu*, 323 U.S. at 246 (Jackson, J., dissenting).

5. Glick to Eisenhower, April 15, 1942, Document 6–0076, cited in Peter Irons, *Justice at War* (Berkeley: University of California Press, 1993), p. 126.

6. John W. Dean, "How Does President Bush Compare with Other Wartime Presidents with Respect to Free Speech Issues?" *FindLaw Legal News and Commentary*, May 19, 2006, http://writ.news.findlaw.com/dean/20060519.html, citing Roosevelt's biographer Conrad Black, *Franklin Delano Roosevelt: Champion of Freedom* (New York: Public Affairs, 2005).

7. Ibid.

8. Irons, *Justice at War*, p. 68.

9. Gerald T. Dunne, *Hugo Black and the Judicial Revolution* (New York: Simon and Schuster, 1977), p. 213, cited in Irons, *Justice at War*, p. 356.

10. Quoted in Irons, *Justice at War*, p. 239.

11. Irons, *Justice at War*, p. 228.
12. Ibid., p. 277.
13. *Korematsu* trial record, pp. 24–25, cited in Irons, *Justice at War*, pp. 94, 153.
14. Ibid.
15. *Korematsu,* 323 U.S. at 227–31 (Roberts, J., dissenting).
16. *Korematsu v. United States,* 140 F.2d 289 (9th Cir. 1943).
17. *Korematsu,* 323 U.S. at 230.
18. Ringle to Chief of Naval Operations, "Report on Japanese Question," January 26, 1942, File ASW 014.311, cited in Irons, *Justice at War*, p. 203 (emphasis in original).
19. Biddle to Roosevelt, December 30, 1943, OF 4849, cited in Irons, *Justice at War*, p. 271.
20. Irons, *Justice at War*, p. 271.
21. Hoover to Biddle, February 7, 1944, Box 37, Folder 3, Fahy Papers, cited in Irons, *Justice at War*, p. 281.
22. Fly to Biddle, April 4, 1944, Box 37, Folder 3, Fahy Papers, cited in Irons, *Justice at War*, p. 284.
23. Burling to Fahy, April 13, 1944, Box 37, Folder 3, Fahy Papers, cited in Irons, *Justice at War*, p. 285.
24. *Korematsu,* Records and Briefs of the Supreme Court, Brief for the United States, p. 11.
25. Irons, *Justice at War*, p. 320.
26. *Korematsu,* 323 U.S. at 216.
27. *Hirayabashi v. United States,* 320 U.S. 81 (1943).
28. *Hirayabashi,* 320 U.S. at 102.
29. *Hirayabashi,* 320 U.S. at 99.
30. *Korematsu,* 323 U.S. at 217–18.
31. *Korematsu,* 323 U.S. at 223.
32. *Korematsu,* 323 U.S. at 219.
33. Irons, *Justice at War*, p. 337.
34. *Korematsu,* 323 U.S. at 221.
35. Irons, *Justice at War*, p. 329.
36. *Korematsu,* Records and Briefs of the Supreme Court, Brief for the United States, p. 28.
37. *Ex parte Endo,* 323 U.S. 283 (1944).
38. *Korematsu,* 323 U.S. at 232 (Roberts, J., dissenting).
39. Ibid.
40. *Korematsu,* 323 U.S. at 233 (Roberts, J., dissenting).
41. *Korematsu,* 323 U.S. at 225–26 (Roberts, J., dissenting).
42. *Hirayabashi,* 320 U.S. at 110–11 (Murphy, J., concurring).
43. *Korematsu,* 323 U.S. at 233 (Murphy, J., dissenting).
44. *Korematsu,* 323 U.S. at 236 (Murphy, J., dissenting).

45. *Korematsu*, 323 U.S. at 239 (Murphy, J., dissenting).

46. *Korematsu*, 323 U.S. at 240 (Murphy, J., dissenting).

47. *Korematsu*, 323 U.S. at 235 (Murphy, J., dissenting).

48. Commission on Wartime Relocation, *Personal Justice Denied*, p. 239, cited in Irons, *Justice at War*, p. 362.

49. William Fisher, "Famed Fighter Against Japanese Internment Dies at 86," *Inter Press Service News Agency*, April 1, 2005, www.ipsnews.net/print.asp ?idnews=28128.

50. *Korematsu*, 323 U.S. at 243 (Jackson, J., dissenting).

51. On congressional approval, see *United States v. Hicks*, Prosecution Response to Defense Motion to Dismiss, p. 3, October 18, 2004, www. pentagon.mil/news/Oct2004/d20041022lack.pdf. On CIA prisons, see Memorandum for Alberto R. Gonzales, Counsel to the President, "Re: Permissibility of Relocating Certain 'Protected Persons' from Occupied Iraq," March 19, 2004, www.humanrightsfirst.com/us_law/etn/gonzales/ memos_dir/memo_20040319_Golds_Gonz.pdf. On enemy combatants, see Memorandum from President Bush, "The Humane Treatment of al-Qaeda and Taliban Detainees," February 7, 2002, www.humanrights first.com/us_law/etn/gonzales/memos_dir/dir_20020207_Bush_Det.pdf. On interrogation techniques, see President's Statement on Signing of H.R. 2863, the "Department of Defense, Emergency Supplemental Appropriations to Address Hurricanes in the Gulf of Mexico, and Pandemic Influenza Act, 2006," December 30, 2005, www.whitehouse.gov/news/ releases/2005/12/20051230–8.html.

52. *Personal Justice Denied: The Report of the Commission on Wartime Relocation and Internment of Civilians, Part 1 of 2* (Washington, D.C.: U.S. Government Printing Office, 1982), www.digitalhistory.uh.edu/learning_history/japa nese_internment/personal_justice_denied.cfm.

53. *Ex parte Milligan*, 71 U.S. (4 Wall.) 2, 120–21 (1866).

Chapter 8: Asset Forfeiture Without Due Process

1. *Marbury v. Madison*, 5 U.S. (1 Cranch) 137 (1803); *Brown v. Board of Education*, 347 U.S. 483 (1954); *United States v. One 1970 Pontiac GTO*, 529 F.2d 65 (9th Cir. 1976).

2. See, e.g., *United States v. Four Million, Two Hundred Fifty-five Thousand Dollars*, 762 F.2d 895 (11th Cir. 1985); *United States v. One 1978 Chevrolet Impala*, 614 F.2d 983 (5th Cir. 1980); *United States v. One 1976 Chris-Craft 27 Foot Fiber Glass Boat*, 423 F.2d 1293 (5th Cir. 1970).

3. One early example can be found in Exodus 21:28: "If an ox gore a man or a woman, that they die: then the ox shall be surely stoned, and his flesh shall not be eaten; but the owner of the ox shall be [acquitted]."

4. Tamara R. Piety, "Scorched Earth: How the Expansion of Civil Forfeiture

Doctrine Has Laid Waste to Due Process," *Univ. of Miami Law Review* 45 (1991): 911, 935–42.

5. Unlike a criminal action, which requires proof beyond a reasonable doubt, "guilt" in the civil forfeiture context need only be demonstrated by a preponderance of the evidence.

6. Act of July 17, 1862, 12 Stat. 589; Act of August 6, 1861, 12 Stat. 319.

7. *Miller v. United States*, 78 U.S. (11 Wall.) 268 (1871); James Maxeiner, "Bane of American Forfeiture Law—Banished at Last?" *Cornell Law Review* 62 (1977): 768, 787.

8. *Bennis v. Michigan*, 516 U.S. 442, 459 (1996) (quoting *One 1958 Plymouth Sedan v. Pennsylvania*, 380 U.S. 693, 699 (1965)).

9. For example, one court upheld the forfeiture of the defendant's house when an ounce of heroin was found in the car parked in the driveway. The court reasoned that "even if the drugs were only kept in the car in the driveway rather than in the home itself, the property facilitated [the defendant's] drug activities." *United States v. Juluke*, 426 F.3d 323, 326 (5th Cir. 2005).

10. *Calero-Toledo v. Pearson Yacht Leasing Co.,* 416 U.S. 663, 689 (1974).

11. According to the supreme court of Michigan, "flagging" is "the manner in which prostitutes solicit business from potential customers in passing vehicles." *Michigan v. Bennis*, 447 N.W.2d 483, 486 (Mich. 1994).

12. *Foucha v. Louisiana*, 504 U.S. 71 (1992); *Austin v. United States*, 509 U.S. 602 (1993).

13. *Bennis*, 516 U.S. at 451.

14. Ibid. (quoting *Austin*, 509 U.S. at 618) (emphasis added).

15. *Bennis*, 516 U.S. at 452 (citing Mich. Comp. Laws § 257.401 (1979)).

16. *Smith v. Jones*, 382 Mich. 176 (1969). See also 22 Am. Jur. 2d *Damages* § 572 (2004) ("Punitive damages may also be awarded in a case involving the *negligent* entrustment of a vehicle to another *if* it constitutes a *willful* or *wanton* misconduct or *reckless* disregard for the safety of others") (emphasis added).

17. *Bennis*, 516 U.S. at 452.

18. *Bennis*, 516 U.S. at 453 (quoting *J. W. Goldsmith, Jr.-Grant Co. v. United States*, 254 U.S. 505, 511 (1921)).

19. *Bennis*, 516 U.S. at 458.

20. *Bennis*, 516 U.S. at 461.

21. *Bennis*, 516 U.S. at 462 (quoting *Phile v. Ship Anna*, 1 (1 Dall.) U.S. 197, 206 (1787)).

22. Rehnquist's rather unconvincing response to this point amounts to "we'll cross that bridge when we come to it." *Bennis*, 516 U.S. at 450–51. He fails, however, to provide any principled method by which that hypothetical case might be distinguished from that of Ms. Bennis.

23. See, for example, *Carroll v. United States*, 267 U.S. 132 (1925) and *Calero-Toledo*, 416 U.S. at 663.

24. "Excessive bail shall not be required, *nor excessive fines imposed*, nor cruel and unusual punishments inflicted." U.S. Const., amend. VIII (emphasis added).

25. *Bennis*, 516 U.S. at 471 ("For an individual who merely let her husband use her car to commute to work, even a modest penalty is out of all proportion to her blameworthiness").

26. *Bennis*, 516 U.S. at 472.

27. *Bennis*, 516 U.S. at 473.

28. Pub. L. 106–185, 114 Stat. 202 (2000).

29. Donald J. Boudreaux & A. C. Pritchard, "Civil Forfeiture and the War on Drugs: Lessons from Economics and History," *San Diego Law Review* 33 (1996): 79, 89.

30. Henry Hyde, *Forfeiting Our Property Rights* (Washington, D.C.: Cato Institute, 1995), pp. 38–39.

31. Scott Ehlers, "Asset Forfeiture," Drug Policy Foundation Policy Briefing, 1999, p. 9, www.drugpolicy.org/docUploads/Asset_Forfeiture_Briefing.pdf.

32. *Bennis*, 516 U.S. at 458.

33. *Bennis*, 516 U.S. at 454.

34. Oliver Wendell Holmes Jr., "The Path of the Law," *Harvard Law Review* 10 (1897): 457, 469.

35. *Calder v. Bull*, 3 U.S. 386, 388 (1798) (emphasis in original).

Chapter 9: Eminent Domain for Private Use

1. *VanHorne's Lessee v. Dorrance*, 2 U.S. 304, 311 (1795).

2. U.S. Const., amend. V; Conn. Const., art. I, sec. 11.

3. We discuss the "just compensation" component of the Takings Clause in Chapter 10.

4. See, e.g., *Pfeifer v. City of Little Rock*, 57 S.W.3d 714, 720 (Ark. 2001) ("[N]o more property of a private individual, and no greater interest therein, can be condemned and set apart for public use than is absolutely necessary") (citation omitted); *Miocene Ditch Co. v. Lyng*, 138 F. 544, 545 (9th Cir. 1905) ("The right of eminent domain can only be exercised in behalf of a public use authorized by law, and in the taking of property necessary to such public use the complaint or petition in such proceedings must show plainly and affirmatively the existence of the statutory authority for the public use, and the necessity of the property for such use") (citation omitted); *Fork Ridge Baptist Cemetery Ass'n v. Redd*, 10 S.E. 405, 406 (W. Va. 1889) ("Ownership and enjoyment of private property are sacred in the eye of the law. The owner's right yields only to public necessity. The great power of eminent domain does overcome this right of private prop-

erty, but never but for public use, under our constitution") (citation omitted).

5. *Berman v. Parker*, 348 U.S. 26 (1954).

6. *Berman*, 348 U.S. at 36.

7. District of Columbia Redevelopment Act of 1945, 79 Pub. L. No. 592, § 5(a), 60 Stat. 790 (1945).

8. *Berman*, 348 U.S. at 30 ("Surveys revealed that in Area B, 64.3% of the dwellings were beyond repair, 18.4% needed major repairs, only 17.3% were satisfactory; 57.8% of the dwellings had outside toilets, 60.3% had no baths, 29.3% lacked electricity, 82.2% had no wash basins or laundry tubs, 83.8% lacked central heating").

9. See, e.g., *City of Norwood v. Horney*, 853 N.E.2d 1115, 1144 (Ohio 2006) ("diversity of ownership . . . is not defined" and impermissibly vague).

10. *Poletown Neighborhood Council v. City of Detroit*, 304 N.W.2d 455 (Mich. 1981).

11. *Poletown*, 304 N.W. 2d at 462 n.9 (Fitzgerald, J., dissenting) ("The city did not proceed under the urban renewal statutes that were the basis for the earlier decisions, and it has never sought to justify the taking of the land for this project on the ground that the area is a 'slum' or 'blighted' area").

12. *Poletown*, 304 N.W. 2d at 459–60.

13. James Risen, "Poletown Becomes Just a Memory," *Los Angeles Times*, September 18, 1985, part 4, p. 1.

14. *County of Wayne v. Hathcock*, 684 N.W.2d 765, 786 (Mich. 2004).

15. *Hathcock*, 684 N.W.2d at 787.

16. Ibid.

17. In the intervening years, the U.S. Supreme Court further undercut the original definition of public use when it allowed Hawaii to break up highly concentrated land ownership patterns that predated statehood by engaging in a wholesale transfer of the land from owners to renters. See *Hawaii Housing Auth. v. Midkiff*, 467 U.S. 229 (1984).

18. Dana Berliner, "Public Power, Private Gain: A Five-Year State-by-State Report Examining the Abuse of Eminent Domain," Institute for Justice, 2003, p. 8, www.castlecoalition.org/publications/report/index.html. See also Dana Berliner, "Opening the Floodgates: Eminent Domain Abuse in a Post-*Kelo* World," Institute for Justice, 2006, p. 2, www.castlecoalition.org/publications/floodgates/index.html.

19. *Kelo v. City of New London*, 545 U.S. 469 (2005).

20. *Kelo v. City of New London*, 843 A.2d 500, 537 (Conn. 2004) ("With respect to Pfizer, the plaintiffs point out that it is, in the words of James Hicks, the executive vice president of RKG Associates, the firm that assisted the development corporation in the preparation of the development

plan, the '10,000-pound gorilla' and 'a big driving point' behind the development project").

21. *VanHorne's Lessee*, 2 U.S. 304 (1795).

22. *Kelo*, 545 U.S. at 478 n.6.

23. *Kelo*, 545 U.S. at 480.

24. Ibid.

25. *Berman*, 348 U.S. at 33.

26. *Midkiff*, 467 U.S. at 244.

27. *Kelo*, 545 U.S. at 484.

28. *Kelo*, 545 U.S. at 482.

29. *Kelo*, 545 U.S. at 476 n.4 (citation omitted).

30. *Kelo*, 545 U.S. at 488–89.

31. *Kelo*, 843 A.2d at 559.

32. *Kelo*, 545 U.S. at 490–93 (Kennedy, J., concurring).

33. See, generally, Berliner, "Opening the Floodgates."

34. *Nat'l R.R. Passenger Corp. v. Boston and Maine Corp.*, 503 U.S. 407 (1992) (railroad track transferred to another common carrier); *Midkiff*, 467 U.S. 229 (1984) (land ownership transferred to lessees as part of program to break up remnants of feudal land system dating from Hawaii's pre-state monarchy); *Ruckelshaus v. Monsanto Co.*, 467 U.S. 986 (1984) (pesticide research results available to later pesticide producers; obviously related to public health); *Berman*, 348 U.S. 26 (1954) (single unblighted building in severely blighted area taken as part of large project to clear slum and redevelop); *Strickley v. Highland Bay Mining Co.*, 200 U.S. 527 (1906) (aerial bucket line for mining ore, available to any user); *Fallbrook Irrigation Dist. v. Bradley*, 164 U.S. 112 (1905) (condemnation for construction of irrigation ditch as part of statewide irrigation infrastructure program); *Head v. Amoskeag*, 113 U.S. 9 (1985) (riparian rights for private mill; Court explicitly refused to hold that economic benefits justified condemnation).

35. *Kelo*, 545 U.S. at 497–98 (O'Connor, J., dissenting).

36. *Kelo*, 545 U.S. at 498 (O'Connor, J., dissenting).

37. See, for example, *Thompson v. Western States Med. Ctr.*, 535 U.S. 357 (2002) (Food and Drug Administration Modernization Act of 1997 banning advertising of compounded drugs unconstitutionally restricts pharmacies' commercial speech); *Reno v. American Civil Liberties Union*, 521 U.S. 844 (1997) (Communications Decency Act of 1996 violates First Amendment because restrictions are overbroad); *Schacht v. United States*, 398 U.S. 58 (1970) (statute prohibiting actor in theatrical production from discrediting government while wearing military uniforms is unconstitutional restriction of free speech); *Village of Skokie v. Nat'l Socialist Party of America*, 373 N.E.2d 21 (Ill. 1978) (Nazi party and members cannot be enjoined from

displaying swastika during public demonstration because demonstration is protected under First Amendment).

38. *Kelo*, 545 U.S. at 477 ("the City would no doubt be forbidden from taking petitioners' land for the purpose of conferring a private benefit on a particular private party") (citation omitted).

39. *Kelo*, 545 U.S. at 503 (O'Connor, J., dissenting).

40. *Kelo*, 545 U.S. at 505 (O'Connor, J., dissenting).

41. Berliner, "Opening the Floodgates," p. 1.

42. Ibid., p. 2.

43. Ibid., p. 5 (noting that, at the time of publication, at least ten cases in eight jurisdictions had relied on *Kelo*, including courts in the District of Columbia, Florida, Georgia, Minnesota, Missouri, New Jersey, New York, and Ohio).

44. "Legislative Action Since *Kelo*," Castle Coalition, January 16, 2007, p. 1, castlecoalition.org/pdf/publications/State-Summary-Publication.pdf.

45. *Kelo*, 545 U.S. at 489 ("We emphasize that nothing in our opinion precludes any State from placing further restrictions on its exercise of the takings power").

46. For a comprehensive list of polls and their results, see www.castlecoalition.org/resources/kelo_polls.html.

47. Ibid.

48. "Legislative Action Since *Kelo*."

49. The percentages of voters favoring constitutional amendments to limit eminent domain abuse by addressing "public use" were Arizona 65.2, Florida 69.1, Georgia 82.7, Louisiana 55, Michigan 80.1, New Hampshire 86, North Dakota 67.5, Oregon 67, and South Carolina 86.1. See http://www.castlecoalition.org/legislation/ballot-measures/index.html. In four other states initiatives coupled eminent domain abuse with a sweeping reform of regulatory takings. Only one of these, Arizona, passed.

50. *Norwood*, 853 N.E.2d 1115 (2006). Oklahoma's Supreme Court had previously rejected *Kelo* but without extensive analysis. *Board of County Commissioners of Muskogee County v. Lowery,* 136 P.3d 639 (Okla. 2006).

51. *Norwood*, 853 N.E.2d at 1139–40.

52. *Norwood*, 853 N.E.2d at 1153.

Chapter 10: Taking Property by Regulation

1. *Penn. Coal Co. v. Mahon*, 260 U.S. 393, 413 (1922).

2. *Pumpelly v. Green Bay Co.*, 81 U.S. (13 Wall.) 166, 177–78 (1872).

3. *Mahon*, 260 U.S. at 415.

4. *Penn Central Transportation Co. v. New York*, 438 U.S. 104 (1978).

5. This is not to say that all limitations on the use of property should require compensation from society at large. Regulations that prevent property from being used in a noxious or harmful way impose a cost, but that cost *should* be borne entirely by the property owner. While a property owner may desire to use his property for profit or pleasure in a way that harms his neighbor, he has no right to do so, and other property owners have a right to the use and enjoyment of their property without such disturbance.

6. N.Y.C. Admin. Code, ch. 8-A, § 205–1.0 *et seq.* (1976).

7. *Penn Central*, 438 U.S. at 138–39.

8. *Penn Central*, 438 U.S. at 117–18

9. *Penn Central*, 438 U.S. at 123–24 (internal citations omitted).

10. *Penn Central*, 438 U.S. at 124.

11. *Penn Central*, 438 U.S. at 130–31.

12. *Penn Central*, 438 U.S. at 136.

13. *Penn Central*, 438 U.S. at 143.

14. *Penn Central*, 438 U.S. at 139.

15. *Penn Central*, 438 U.S. at 140.

16. *Penn Central*, 438 U.S. at 150.

17. *Mahon*, 260 U.S. at 415.

18. See, generally, Joseph R. Daughen and Peter Bizen, *The Wreck of the Penn Central*, 2d ed. (Frederick, Md.: Beard Books, 1999), detailing the creation, struggle, and eventual demise of Penn Central.

19. *Tahoe-Sierra Preservation Council, Inc. v. Tahoe Regional Planning Agency*, 535 U.S. 302 (2002).

20. Lake Tahoe's clarity has been described as "not merely transparent, but dazzlingly, brilliantly so." *Tahoe-Sierra*, 535 U.S. at 307 (quoting Mark Twain, *Roughing It* (New York: Oxford University Press, 1872), pp. 174–75).

21. *Lucas v. South Carolina Coastal Council*, 505 U.S. 1003 (1992).

22. *First English Evangelical Lutheran Church of Glendale v. County of Los Angeles*, 482 U.S. 304, 318 (1987).

23. *Tahoe-Sierra*, 535 U.S. at 332.

24. *Tahoe-Sierra*, 535 U.S. at 356 (quoting John Maynard Keynes, *Monetary Reform* [London: Macmillan, 1924], p. 88); emphasis in original.

25. Richard A. Epstein, "The Ebbs and Flows in Takings Law: Reflections on the *Lake Tahoe* Case," *Cato Supreme Court Review* 2001–2002 (2002): 5, 8.

26. Ibid., p. 15 (noting that the *Penn Central* decision creates "a perverse incentive to rush to build to perfect one's development rights").

27. *Penn Central*, 438 U.S. at 146.

28. *Penn Central*, 438 U.S. at 114.

29. "It has been said that 'Europe has its cathedrals and we have Grand Central

Station.'" Steven J. Eagle, *Regulatory Takings*, 3d ed. (Charlottesville, Va.: Michie, 2005), p. 294 (quoting Philip Johnson) (citation omitted).

30. Eagle, *Regulatory Takings*, p. 132.

31. As the late Chief Justice Rehnquist observed in *First English Evangelical Lutheran Church of Glendale v. County of Los Angeles*: "[M]any of the provisions of the Constitution are designed to limit the flexibility and freedom of governmental authorities, and the Just Compensation Clause of the Fifth Amendment is one of them. As Justice Holmes aptly noted more than 50 years ago, 'a strong public desire to improve the public condition is not enough to warrant achieving the desire by a shorter cut than the constitutional way of paying for the change.'" 482 U.S. at 321–22 (internal citations omitted).

Chapter 11: Earning an Honest Living

1. To obtain a cosmetology license, Armstrong needed 1,200 class hours. She also needed a minimum of 2,000 hours to teach cosmetology. The Mississippi Code apparently requires 2,750 hours for teachers who have not been practicing cosmetologists for two years. Miss. Code Ann. § 73-7-15 (2007). But Mississippi regulations state that an applicant with less than two years' active experience needs to complete only a 2,000-hour course. CMSR [Code of Mississippi Rules] 50-009-001(V).

2. See CMSR 12-000-002 § 7.2 ("Minimum hours required for EMT Basic are 110 didactic, 12 hours of hospital emergency clinical lab, and 5 documented emergency runs aboard an ambulance"). See CMSR 12-000-002 § 8.2 ("Minimum hours required for EMT Paramedic are 800 didactic/lab, 200 clinical, 200 field"). In addition, one prerequisite for licensure is a valid EMT license requiring 122 additional classroom hours. CMSR 12-000-002 § 41-60-13(IV). See CMSR 12-000-002 § 6.2 ("Minimum hours required for EMS Driver are 4 didactic, and lab instruction sufficient to ensure operator competency, minimum four hours"). See Mississippi Department of Public Safety, www.dps.state.ms.us/dps/dps.nsf/trainingcalendar/0AB81E9B9C4411C886256CAA0050D296?OpenDocument. Estimating forty hours per week, basic law enforcement officer training would take four hundred hours. See Mississippi Department of Insurance, www.doi.state.ms.us/fireacad/fa_faqs.htm. Estimating forty hours per week, basic firefighter training would take 240 hours. See Miss. Code Ann. § 73-34-17 (2007) (real estate appraiser). See Mississippi's Hunter Education Program, www.mdwfp.com/level2/Education/Huntered.asp (the initial hunter education class takes ten hours). According to the Department of Wildlife, Fisheries and Parks, another eight-to-ten-hour course is required to teach the basic hunter education course.

3. Miss. Code Ann. § 73-7-7; Miss. Code Ann. § 73-7-1.

4. Miss. Code Ann. § 73-7-7. The board receives recommendations for regulation from the Mississippi Cosmetology Council, whose membership consists of five cosmetologists on the board plus five delegates each from the Mississippi Hairdressers and Cosmetologists Association, the Mississippi Cosmetology School Association, the Mississippi Independent Beauticians Association, and the School Owners and Teachers Association.

5. See S. David Young, *The Rule of Experts: Occupational Licensing in America* (Washington, D.C.: Cato Institute, 1987), pp. 4–5.

6. Morris M. Kleiner, National Bureau of Economic Research, "Occupational Licensing and the Internet: Issues for Policy Makers," for the Federal Trade Commission Hearings on Possible Anticompetitive Efforts to Restrict Competition on the Internet, October 1, 2002, www.ftc.gov/opp/ ecommerce/anticompetitive/panel/kleiner.pdf ("30 percent of the U.S. labor force works in a regulated occupation" and "[m]ore than 18 percent of the workforce requires a license in order to legally do certain types of work"). See also Morris M. Kleiner, "Occupational Licensing," *Journal of Economic Perspectives* 14 (Fall 2000): 189, 190.

7. Quoted in Jonathan Elliot, *Debates on the Adoption of the Federal Constitution*, vol. 3 (Philadelphia: J. B. Lippincott, 1859), p. 167 (cited by Randy E. Barnett, *Restoring the Lost Constitution* [Princeton, N.J.: Princeton University Press, 2005], p. 53).

8. *Federalist No. 84* (Alexander Hamilton).

9. Quoted in Philip A. Hamburger, "Trivial Rights," *Notre Dame Law Review* 70 (1994): 13 (citation omitted).

10. "The Citizens of each State shall be entitled to all Privileges and Immunities of Citizens in the several States." U.S. Const., art. IV, sec. 2. "[N]or shall any person . . . be deprived of life, liberty, or property, without due process of law." U.S. Const., amend. V.

11. *Corfield v. Coryell*, 6 F. Cas. 546 (E.D. Pa. 1823); *Travis v. Yale & Towne Mfg. Co.*, 252 U.S. 60 (1920).

12. "No State shall . . . abridge the privileges or immunities of citizens of the United States; nor shall any State deprive any person of life, liberty, or property, without due process of law; nor deny to any person within its jurisdiction the equal protection of the laws." U.S. Const., amend. XIV, sec. 1.

13. *Slaughter-House Cases*, 83 U.S. 36 (1873).

14. *Slaughter-House Cases*, 83 U.S. at 76.

15. The Fifth Amendment protects against federal deprivations of due process, while the Fourteenth Amendment addresses state violations.

16. *Lochner v. New York*, 198 U.S. 45 (1905).

17. *Lochner*, 198 U.S. at 53–54, 56.

18. *Nebbia v. New York*, 291 U.S. 502 (1934).

19. *Nebbia*, 291 U.S. at 543–44 (McReynolds, J., dissenting).

20. *Nebbia*, 291 U.S. at 537.

21. Timothy Sandefur, "The Right to Earn a Living," *Chapman Law Review* 6 (2003): 207.

22. Ibid., 215 (quoting *Case of Tailors of Ipswich*, 77 Eng. Rep. 1218, 1219 [K.B. 1615]).

23. *Barsky v. Board of Regents*, 347 U.S. 442 (1954).

24. *United States v. Carolene Products Co.*, 304 U.S. 144 (1938).

25. Geoffrey P. Miller, "The True Story of *Carolene Products*," *Supreme Court Review* (1987): 402.

26. 21 U.S.C. § 62.

27. "The Congress shall have Power . . . To regulate Commerce . . . among the several States." U.S. Const., art. I, sec. 8.

28. Miller, "The True Story of *Carolene Products*," 411.

29. *People v. Carolene Products Co.*, 177 N.E. 698 (Ill. 1931).

30. *United States v. Carolene Products Co.*, 7 F. Supp. 500, 507 (S.D. Ill. 1934).

31. *Carolene Products*, 7 F. Supp. at 507.

32. Justices Benjamin Cardozo and Stanley Reed did not participate in the decision.

33. Miller, "The True Story," p. 399.

34. *Carolene Products*, 304 U.S. at 152 (emphasis added).

35. Ibid., n.4 (citations omitted).

36. *Williamson v. Lee Optical of Oklahoma, Inc.*, 348 U.S. 483 (1955).

37. Okla. Stat. Ann. tit. 59, §§ 941–47 (1951).

38. *Lee Optical*, 348 U.S. at 487.

39. *Lee Optical*, 348 U.S. at 488 (emphasis added).

40. *Federal Communications Commission v. Beach Communications, Inc.*, 508 U.S. 307 (1993).

41. *Beach Communications*, 508 U.S. at 314–15 (emphasis added) (citations and quotation marks omitted).

42. *Beach Communications*, 508 U.S. at 323 n.3 (Stevens, J., concurring) (emphasis in original).

43. Clark Neily, "One Test, Two Standards: The On-Off Role of 'Plausibility' in Rational Basis Review," *Georgetown Journal of Law and Public Policy* 4 (2006): 199.

44. See Steven M. Simpson, "Judicial Abdication and the Rise of Special Interest," *Chapman Law Review* 6 (2003): 273.

45. "The historical pass rate on the florist exam is 36%—about half that of the Louisiana bar examination." Appellant's Brief at 4, *Meadows v. Odom*, 198 Fed. Appx. 348 (5th Cir. 2006) (No. 03–960-B-M2) (noting that out of 3,001 florist exams given from April 1995 through May 2004, only 1,087 applicants passed). For comparison, see Matthew Sanders, "LSU Graduates

Struggle on the 2004 Exam," *The Reveille*, October 5, 2004, p. 1 (the July 2004 bar examination pass rate in Louisiana was 65 percent).

46. *Powers v. Harris*, 379 F.3d 1208, 1221 (10th Cir. 2004).

47. *Federalist No. 10* (James Madison).

48. Ibid.

49. Ibid.

50. Neily, "One Test, Two Standards."

51. Morris M. Kleiner, "Our Guild-Ridden Economy," *Wall Street Journal*, Oct. 15, 2005, p. A7 (noting more than 20 percent of the U.S. workforce is covered by state licensing laws, in addition to federal, county, and city regulations).

52. Bob Faw, "Three Challenge Denver in Federal Court; Claim Excessive Regulations Are Unconstitutional Burden on Taxi Entrepreneurs," *CBS Evening News*, July 2, 1993.

Chapter 12: Equal Protection and Racial Preferences

1. U.S. Const., art. I, sec. 2, cl. 3.

2. U.S. Const., art. I, sec. 9, cl. 1.

3. *Grutter v. Bollinger*, 539 U.S. 306 (2003).

4. *Regents of the University of California v. Bakke*, 438 U.S. 265 (1978).

5. "No State shall . . . deny to any person within its jurisdiction the equal protection of the laws." U.S. Const., amend. XIV. "No person in the United States shall, on the ground of race, color, or national origin, be excluded from participation in, be denied the benefits of, or be subjected to discrimination under any program or activity receiving Federal financial assistance." 42 U.S.C. § 2000d (2000).

6. See *Bakke*, 438 U.S. at 289.

7. *Bakke*, 438 U.S. at 318.

8. Ibid.

9. "Since 1971, the white college drop-out rate (as a percentage of those who attend) has decreased from about 50 percent to about 47 percent in 2003 . . . [b]ut the black drop-out rate has risen some going from about 63 percent in 1971 to about 64 percent in 1980, and then to about 67 percent in 2003." Douglas J. Besharov, "The Economic Stagnation of the Black Middle Class (Relative to Whites)," American Enterprise Institute, testimony before the U.S. Commission on Civil Rights, July 15, 2005, www.aei.org/publications/filter.all,pubID.22851/pub_detail.asp. See also, "U.S. College Drop-out Rate Sparks Concern," Associated Press, September 27, 2006, www.diverseeducation.com/artman/publish/article_6422.shtml ("A 2004 Education Trust report found a quarter of schools have graduation gaps between Whites and Blacks of 20 points or more").

10. Abigail Thernstrom and Stephan Thernstrom, "Reflections on the Shape of the River," *UCLA Law Review* 46 (1999): 1608.

11. In the most recent *U.S. News & World Report* law school rankings, the University of Michigan tied for eighth place with the University of California, Berkeley. "Special Report: America's Best Graduate Schools—Schools of Law," *U.S. News & World Report*, April 9, 2007, p. 92, www.usnews.com/usnews/edu/grad/rankings/law/brief/lawrank_brief.php.

12. *Grutter,* 539 U.S. at 312–13.

13. Brief for the Petitioner at 2, *Grutter v. Bollinger*, 539 U.S. 306 (2003) (No. 02–241), www.cir-usa.org/legal_docs/grutter_v_bollinger_SupCt_brief.pdf.

14. Ibid.

15. *Grutter v. Bollinger*, 137 F. Supp. 2d 821 (E.D. Mich. 2001).

16. Federal courts of appeals generally hear cases before a panel of three judges. In rare circumstances, however, such as a matter of exceptional public importance, an *en banc* hearing by all members of a court may be ordered. *Grutter v. Bollinger*, 288 F.3d 732 (6th Cir. 2002).

17. In addition, *Grutter*'s companion case, *Gratz v. Bollinger*, 539 U.S. 244 (2003), discussed below, produced seven opinions.

18. *Grutter,* 539 U.S. at 326 (citing *Adarand Constructors, Inc. v. Peña,* 515 U.S. 200, 227 [1995]) (quotation marks omitted). Rational basis review is examined at length in Chapter 11, "Earning an Honest Living."

19. *Grutter,* 539 U.S. at 326.

20. Gerald Gunther, "The Supreme Court, 1971 Term—Foreword: In Search of Evolving Doctrine on a Changing Court: A Model for a Newer Equal Protection," *Harvard Law Review* 86 (1972): 8.

21. *Adarand*, 515 U.S. at 237.

22. *Grutter,* 539 U.S. at 322 (emphasis added).

23. *Grutter,* 539 U.S. at 328 (emphasis added).

24. Ibid. (emphasis added).

25. *Grutter,* 539 U.S. at 330.

26. Ian Ayres and Sydney Foster, "Don't Tell, Don't Ask: Narrow Tailoring after *Grutter* and *Gratz*," Yale Law School, John M. Olin Center for Studies in Law, Economics, and Public Policy, Working Paper no. 287, September 1, 2005, lsr.nellco.org/yale/lepp/papers/287.

27. *Grutter,* 539 U.S. at 347.

28. *Grutter,* 539 U.S. at 330.

29. *Grutter,* 539 U.S. at 334.

30. Transcript of Oral Argument, *Grutter,* 539 U.S. 306, www.vpcomm.umich.edu/admissions/legal/ussc-transcripts/ls-res-argument2.html.

31. *Grutter,* 539 U.S. at 381.

32. Ibid.

33. *Grutter*, 539 U.S. at 384.

34. *Grutter*, 539 U.S. at 382.

35. *Grutter*, 539 U.S. at 381.

36. *Grutter*, 539 U.S. at 383.

37. *Grutter*, 539 U.S. at 384.

38. Ibid.

39. *Grutter*, 539 U.S. at 386.

40. *Grutter*, 539 U.S. at 336 (emphasis added).

41. *Grutter*, 539 U.S. at 341 (quotation marks omitted).

42. *Grutter*, 539 U.S. at 342.

43. *Grutter*, 539 U.S. at 343.

44. Roger Pilon, "Principle and Policy in Public University Admissions: *Grutter v. Bollinger* and *Gratz v. Bollinger*," *Cato Supreme Court Review* 2002–2003 (2003): 61.

45. Ibid. ("One imagines that the Court broached this issue of duration because it senses, deep down, that there is something fundamentally wrong in its opinion, something wrong in denigrating principle for mere policy").

46. *Grutter,* 539 U.S. at 351 (emphasis added) (citations omitted).

47. *Bakke*, 438 U.S. at 294 n.34.

48. *Grutter*, 539 U.S. at 337.

49. *Gratz*, 539 U.S. at 295 (Souter, J., dissenting).

50. *Gratz*, 539 U.S. at 298 (Souter, J., dissenting).

51. Indeed, some researchers have concluded that the unquantified preferences in *Grutter* were actually larger than the quantified preferences in *Gratz*. See Ayres and Foster, "Don't Tell, Don't Ask."

52. The Court may have restrained itself from making this declaration partly because it had expressly repudiated that same notion only eight years earlier. See *Adarand*, 515 U.S. 200 (1995).

53. See, e.g., Paul Horwitz, "*Grutter*'s First Amendment," University of San Diego School of Law, Public Law and Legal Theory Research Paper Series, September 2004, law.bepress.com/cgi/viewcontent.cgi?article=1022 &context=sandiegolwps (discussing, among other things, *Grutter*'s implications for campus speech codes).

54. *Parents Involved in Community Schools v. Seattle School District No. 1*, 127 S. Ct. 2738 (2007).

55. *Parents Involved in Community Schools v. Seattle School District No. 1,* 137 F. Supp. 2d 1224, 1232 (W.D. Wash. 2001).

56. *Seattle*, 127 S. Ct. at 2755.

57. *Seattle*, 127 S. Ct. at 2789 (Kennedy, J., concurring).

58. *Parents Involved in Community Schools v. Seattle School District No. 1,* Nos.

05–908 and 05–915, dissenting hand-down statement at 11 (U.S. June 28, 2007) (Breyer, J., dissenting).

59. *Plessy v. Ferguson*, 163 U.S. 537, 559 (1896) (Harlan, J., dissenting).

Afterword

1. See Michael B. Rappaport, "Reconciling Textualism and Federalism: The Proper Textual Basis of the Supreme Court's Tenth and Eleventh Amendment Decisions," *Northwestern U.L. Rev.* 93 (1999): 819, 822–23.

2. Antonin Scalia, "Common-Law Courts in a Civil-Law System: The Role of United States Federal Courts in Interpreting the Constitution and Laws," Tanner Lecture on Human Values, Princeton University, March 8–9, 1995, www.tannerlectures.utah.edu/lectures/scalia97.pdf.

3. *Federal Maritime Commission v. South Carolina State Ports Authority*, 122 S. Ct. 1864, 1885 (2002) (Breyer, J., dissenting).

4. *Federal Maritime Commission*, 122 S. Ct. at 1889 (Breyer, J., dissenting).

5. Roger Pilon, vice president for legal affairs, Cato Institute, "Guns and Butter: Setting Priorities in Federal Spending in the Context of Natural Disasters, Deficits, and War," statement before the Subcommittee on Federal Financial Management, Government Information, and International Security of the Senate Committee on Homeland Security, 109th Cong. (October 25, 2005), p. 9.

6. Material in this section has been drawn in part from William H. Mellor, "Second-Class Protections: When It Comes to Property Rights and Economic Liberty, Judicial Activism and Judicial Abdication Have Made an Unholy Alliance," *The American Lawyer*, May 2005, www.law.com/jsp/tal/PubArticleTAL.jsp?id=1115037322681.

7. *Powers v. Harris*, 379 F.3d 1208, 1221 (2004).

8. *Marbury v. Madison*, 5 U.S. (1 Cranch) 137, 178–79 (1803).

9. David N. Mayer, "Judicial Activism, Real and Imagined," users.law.capital.edu/dmayer/Blog/blogIndex.asp?entry=20050404.asp.

Postscripts #1 and #2

1. *Roe v. Wade*, 410 U.S. 113 (1973).

2. *Planned Parenthood of Southeastern Pennsylvania v. Casey*, 505 U.S. 833 (1992).

3. *Planned Parenthood*, 505 U.S. at 877.

4. *Roe*, 410 U.S. at 159.

5. *Bush v. Gore*, 531 U.S. 98, 104–05 (2000).

6. Extracted in part from Robert A. Levy, "Constitution Wins: Judicial Responsibility—Not Activism—from the U.S. Supremes," *National Review Online*, December 18, 2000, www.nationalreview.com/comment/comment

121800e.shtml. Reprinted December 20, 2000: "A Matter of Judgment: How the Supreme Court Reached Its Verdict," *Boston Globe*, p. A25.

7. *Bush*, 531 U.S. at 104–05.

8. "Each State shall appoint, in such Manner as the *Legislature* thereof may direct, a Number of [presidential] Electors. . . ." U.S. Const., art. II, sec. 1, cl. 2 (emphasis added).

9. *Bush*, 531 U.S. at 115 (Rehnquist, C.J., concurring).

10. *Bush*, 531 U.S. at 114 (Rehnquist, C.J., concurring).

INDEX

ABOUT THE AUTHORS

Robert A. Levy is chairman of the board of directors at the Cato Institute, a free-market think tank in Washington, D.C. He joined Cato as senior fellow in constitutional studies in 1997 after twenty-five years in business. Bob also sits on boards of the Institute for Justice, the Federalist Society, and the George Mason law school. He received his PhD in business from the American University in 1966 and then founded CDA Investment Technologies, a major provider of investment information and software. After leaving CDA in 1991, Bob went to George Mason, where he was chief articles editor of the law review. He received his JD degree in 1994. The next two years he clerked for Judge Royce Lamberth on the U.S. District Court and Judge Douglas Ginsburg on the U.S. Court of Appeals, both in Washington, D.C.

For many years Bob was an adjunct professor of law at Georgetown University. His writing has appeared in the *New York Times*, *Wall Street Journal*, *USA Today*, *Washington Post*, *National Review*, and many other publications. His previous book, published in November 2004, is *Shakedown: How Corporations, Government, and Trial Lawyers Abuse the Judicial Process*. Bob has also discussed public policy on national radio and TV programs, including ABC's *Nightline*, Fox's *The O'Reilly Factor*, MSNBC's *Hardball*, NBC's *Today Show*, and PBS's *Newshour*. He served as co-counsel in *District of Columbia v. Heller*, the successful Second Amendment challenge to D.C.'s gun ban.

William H. (Chip) Mellor is president and general counsel of the Institute for Justice, which he cofounded in 1991. Chip litigates cutting-edge constitutional cases nationwide, protecting economic liberty, property rights, school choice, and the First Amendment. Under his leadership the institute has won two U.S. Supreme Court victories, one upholding Cleveland's school voucher program and the other striking down New York's prohibition on interstate wine sales. Chip is also responsible for drawing national attention to eminent domain abuse through the Institute for Justice's U.S. Supreme Court case *Kelo v. City of New London,* breaking Denver's fifty-year taxi monopoly, opening the commuter van market in New York, defending New Jersey's welfare reform, and launching the Institute for Justice Clinic on Entrepreneurship at the University of Chicago.

Chip has appeared in the *Wall Street Journal, Washington Post, New York Times, USA Today, Forbes, National Review,* and other prominent newspapers and magazines. He has also appeared on ABC, NBC, CBS, and CNN, among many radio and television shows. From 1986 until 1991, Mellor served as president of the Pacific Research Institute, a nationally recognized think tank located in San Francisco. Under his leadership PRI commissioned and published path-breaking books on economic liberty, property rights, and the First Amendment that laid the foundation for the Institute for Justice's long-term, strategic litigation. Chip also served in the Reagan administration as deputy general counsel for legislation and regulations in the Department of Energy.

Cato Institute

Founded in 1977, the Cato Institute is a public policy research foundation dedicated to broadening the parameters of policy debate to allow consideration of more options that are consistent with the traditional American principles of limited government, individual liberty, and peace. To that end, the Institute strives to achieve greater involvement of the intelligent, concerned lay public in questions of policy and the proper role of government.

The Institute is named for *Cato's Letters*, libertarian pamphlets that were widely read in the American Colonies in the early 18th century and played a major role in laying the philosophical foundation for the American Revolution.

Despite the achievement of the nation's Founders, today virtually no aspect of life is free from government encroachment. A pervasive intolerance for individual rights is shown by government's arbitrary intrusions into private economic transactions and its disregard for civil liberties.

To counter that trend, the Cato Institute undertakes an extensive publications program that addresses the complete spectrum of policy issues. Books, monographs, and shorter studies are commissioned to examine the federal budget, Social Security, regulation, military spending, international trade, and myriad other issues. Major policy conferences are held throughout the year, from which papers are published thrice yearly in the *Cato Journal*. The Institute also publishes the quarterly magazine *Regulation*.

In order to maintain its independence, the Cato Institute accepts no government funding. Contributions are received from foundations, corporations, and individuals, and other revenue is generated from the sale of publications. The Institute is a nonprofit, tax-exempt, educational foundation under Section 501(c)3 of the Internal Revenue Code.

CATO INSTITUTE
1000 Massachusetts Ave., N.W.
Washington, D.C. 20001
www.cato.org